Assessment of LightSquared Terrestrial Broadband System Effects on GPS Receivers and GPS-dependent Applications

Prepared By:

National Space-Based Positioning, Navigation, and Timing

Systems Engineering Forum (NPEF)

Approved by:	
Steve Steiner, Col, USAF Chief Engineer GPS Directorate NPEF Co-Chair	Deane Bunce GNSS SBAS Ground Segment Lead FAA NPEF Co-Chair
Signature: *//SIGNED//*	Signature: *//SIGNED//*
Date: 1 June 2011	Date: 1 June 2011

The views expressed in this paper are those of the authors and do not reflect the official policy or position of the United States Air Force, Department of Defense, or the U.S. Government.

DISTRIBUTION STATEMENT A: Approved for public release; distribution unlimited

UNITED STATES DEPARTMENT OF COMMERCE
The Assistant Secretary for Communications and Information
Washington, D.C. 20230

JUL 6 2011

The Honorable Julius Genachowski
Chairman
Federal Communications Commission
445 12th Street, SW
Washington, DC 20554

RE: LightSquared Subsidiary LLC; Request for Modification of its Authority
for an Ancillary Terrestrial Component, SAT-MOD-20101118-00239; Call Sign: S2358

Dear Chairman Genachowski:

For your consideration in the above-referenced matter, the National Telecommunications and Information Administration (NTIA) submits the attached report entitled, *Assessment of LightSquared Terrestrial Broadband System Effects on GPS Receivers and GPS-dependent Applications* (June 1, 2011), prepared by the National Space-Based Positioning, Navigation, and Timing Systems Engineering Forum (NPEF) on behalf of the National Executive Committee for Space-Based Positioning, Navigation, and Timing (EXCOM).[1] The results of these measurements clearly demonstrate that implementing the LightSquared Subsidiary LLC (LightSquared) planned deployment for terrestrial operations poses a significant potential for harmful interference to Global Positioning System (GPS) services. Thus, the concerns stated in my letter to you dated January 12, 2011, remain unresolved.

The NPEF based its test plan on LightSquared's planned deployment, and thus, its tests were limited in scope and did not consider or test other configurations of the LightSquared system. I note that LightSquared has now proposed a modification to its planned deployment. NTIA will work with the Federal Communications Commission (FCC) and the federal agencies to determine the impact of LightSquared's modification. Therefore, NTIA supports the EXCOM's recommendation that additional tests be performed and recommends that the FCC continue to withhold authorization for LightSquared to commence commercial operations until all the available test data can be analyzed and all valid concerns have been resolved.

NTIA recognizes that the FCC's Order established a Technical Working Group (TWG) co-chaired by LightSquared and the United States GPS Industry Council to address the GPS interference issues.[2] NTIA is reviewing the report recently filed by the TWG and will consider

---

[1] NTIA will provide additional classified results under separate cover.

[2] LightSquared Subsidiary LLC; Request for Modification of its Authority for an Ancillary Terrestrial Component, SAT-MOD-20101118-00239; Call Sign: S2358, Order and Authorization (Order), 26 F.C.C. Rcd. 566, 588 (2011).

the output of any other organizations that provide test results. The Order further provided that the FCC would consult with NTIA before making a final decision.[3] NTIA looks forward to consulting with the FCC when it has received all of the test results.

I look forward to working with you as the FCC continues to evaluate LightSquared's request. If you have any questions regarding this letter, please feel free to contact me.

Sincerely,

Lawrence E. Strickling

Enclosure

---

[3] *Id.* at 586-587.

June 14, 2011

MEMORANDUM FOR: ADMINISTRATOR, NTIA

FROM: National Space-Based PNT Executive Steering Group

SUBJECT: Assessment of LightSquared Terrestrial Broadband System Effects on GPS Receivers and GPS-dependent Applications

1. On behalf of the National Executive Committee (EXCOM) for Space-Based Positioning, Navigation and Timing (PNT), the National Space-Based PNT Systems Engineering Forum (NPEF) conducted an independent assessment of the effects of LightSquared's planned deployment of a terrestrial broadband network to Global Positioning System (GPS) receivers and GPS-dependent systems and networks.

2. Based on the NPEF's testing and analysis, the National Spaced-Based PNT Executive Steering Group (ESG) recommends that the Federal Communication Commission (FCC) rule that LightSquared cannot commence commercial services per its planned deployment for terrestrial operations in the 1525 - 1559 MHz Mobile-Satellite Service (MSS) Band due to harmful interference to GPS operations.

3. Through the EXCOM and the ESG, the participating agencies are committed to coordinate with the NTIA and the FCC to test and evaluate the feasibility of alternative signal configurations, and to discuss how the recent tests of representative Ancillary Terrestrial Component (ATC) equipment might inform current FCC ATC MSS L-band authorizations.

4. The classified and redacted versions of the NPEF Report are provided for submission to the Federal Communications Commission. If you have any questions or concerns, please contact Mr. Anthony Russo, Director, National Space-Based PNT Coordination Office (NCO) at Anthony.Russo@pnt.gov or (202) 482-5809.

TERI M. TAKAI
ESG Co-Chair
Department of Defense

JOEL M. SZABAT
ESG Co-Chair
Department of Transportation

2 Attachments:
1. Classified NPEF Report
2. Redacted NPEF Report (for public release)

Executive Summary

The Executive Steering Group (ESG) of the National Executive Committee (EXCOM) for Space-Based Positioning, Navigation, and Timing (PNT) directed the National Space-Based PNT Systems Engineering Forum (NPEF) to conduct an assessment of the effects of LightSquared's planned deployment of a terrestrial broadband network to Global Positioning System (GPS) receivers and GPS-dependent systems and networks. The NPEF was tasked to engage with the LightSquared Working Group established at the direction of the Federal Communications Commission (FCC), and the GPS manufacturing and applications communities through relevant industry bodies (e.g., the U.S. GPS Industry Council and RTCA, Inc.). The NPEF investigated and determined effects due to interference to a selected set of GPS receivers in operationally relevant scenarios from LightSquared's planned deployment for Ancillary Terrestrial Component (ATC) transmitters to utilize the mobile-satellite service (MSS) bands as follows: i) 1550.2 – 1555.2 MHz for Phase 0; ii) 1526.3 – 1531.3/1550.2 – 1555.2 MHz for Phase 1; and iii) 1526 – 1536/1545.2 – 1555.2 MHz for Phase 2. While the NPEF tasks were conducted in coordination with all involved entities to the extent possible, the NPEF report is considered to be an independent assessment. The contents of this Report consist of a compilation of findings from nine subtasks along with appendices that include summaries of all of the detailed test data and results collected over the last four months via a series of laboratory and field environment testing of GPS receivers. This Report is a technical summary of the work conducted during this effort and includes specific recommendations and responses to questions as requested by the EXCOM.

Based on analysis described in the main body of this Report, the NPEF has developed the following recommendations for ESG consideration.

Recommendation 1: *LightSquared should not commence commercial services per its planned deployment for terrestrial operations in the 1525 – 1559 MHz Mobile-Satellite Service (MSS) Band due to harmful interference to GPS operations.*

Test results of the LightSquared Phase 0, Phase 1, and Phase 2 deployments of ATC transmitters utilizing the MSS band (1550.2 – 1555.2 MHz for Phase 0, 1526.3 – 1531.3/1550.2 – 1555.2 MHz for Phase 1, and 1526 – 1536/1545.2 – 1555.2 MHz for Phase 2) have demonstrated there are significant detrimental impacts to all GPS applications assessed as part of this NPEF effort. These impacts encompassed both US Government and commercial GPS applications. The potential degradation of GPS operation due to LightSquared emissions was further characterized via simulation that showed that completion of the network of high-powered base stations envisioned by LightSquared would result in degradation or loss of GPS function (ranging, position) at standoff distances of a few kilometers extending to space operations. Possible mitigations for GPS applications were identified and evaluated but were deemed impractical as they would require significant modification or complete redesign and replacement of currently fielded GPS equipment. The timeline to field new GPS receivers for some applications, from initial concept development through production, can take 10-15 years. Finally, there remain certain applications (e.g., high precision) that, even with modification, may not be able to perform their current mission in the presence of LightSquared's network transmitting in the 1525 – 1559 MHz band.

Recommendation 2: *The U.S. Government should conduct more thorough studies on the operational, economic and safety impacts of operating the LightSquared Network, to include compatibility of ATC architectures in the MSS L Band with GPS-dependent applications, signal configurations not currently in LightSquared planned spectrum phases, effects on timing receivers, and transmissions from LightSquared handsets.*

Initial test results demonstrated that some applications (e.g. aviation) were able to operate with little to no degradation when only a 5 or 10 MHz channel (1526.3 – 1531.3 MHz or 1526 – 1536 MHz) in the lower portion of the MSS spectrum was utilized for the LightSquared broadcast. However, for other applications, GPS loss of function still occurs at unacceptable distances to LightSquared towers. Use of only the lower portion of the L-band MSS spectrum is *not* one of the planned Phases for the LightSquared Network evolution so only limited testing has been conducted under this scenario. Additionally, no tests on LightSquared handset (or user terminal) transmissions were conducted as part of this NPEF study, due to non-availability of hardware.

LightSquared handsets will transmit in the band 1626.5 – 1660.5 MHz and the potential for interference to GPS receivers given the very close proximity to an arbitrary number of LightSquared users remains to be evaluated. Evaluation of the LightSquared emissions effects on timing receivers was not thoroughly addressed during the course of this NPEF investigation. An additional evaluation period of at least six months would enable completion of a thorough assessment of the LightSquared Network and should be conducted to allow the EXCOM to make informed decisions on impacts, mitigations, and the way forward for all GPS users.

At the conclusion of this NPEF effort, significant technical concerns remain that operation of an ATC service can successfully coexist with GPS. Rigorous analysis of potential interference had been impossible prior to now due to non-availability of relevant commercial ATC equipment. This recommendation suggests there is a need for additional analysis to determine if ATC architectures can be accommodated in the MSS L-band without impacting GPS.

Table of Contents

Table of Figures

List of Tables

Background

U.S. Space-Based Positioning, Navigation, and Timing Policy states that a "fundamental goal of this policy is to ensure that the United States maintains space-based positioning, navigation, and timing services, augmentation, back-up, and service denial capabilities that: (1) provide uninterrupted availability of positioning, navigation, and timing services; (2) meet growing national, homeland, economic security, and civil requirements, and scientific and commercial demands; (3) remain the pre-eminent military space-based positioning, navigation, and timing services; (4) continue to provide civil services that exceed or are competitive with foreign civil space-based positioning, navigation, and timing services."

GPS modernization includes new signals and capabilities required to be compatible with the use of existing GPS receivers designed in compliance with specifications and standards in existence at the time of the receiver design. Compatibility with federal augmentation system (Wide Area Augmentation System [WAAS], Local Area Augmentation System [LAAS], Nationwide Differential GPS [NDGPS], and Maritime DGPS [MDGPS]) receivers in accordance with the specifications of these systems is also required.

Further, in 2004, the U.S. signed an agreement with the European Union establishing cooperation between GPS and the European Galileo system. The Agreement specifically states "The Parties shall work together to promote adequate frequency allocations for satellite-based navigation and timing signals, to ensure radio frequency compatibility in spectrum use between each other's signals, to make all practicable efforts to protect each other's signals from interference by the radio frequency emissions of other systems, and to promote harmonized use of spectrum on a global basis, notably at the ITU."

In 2007, the U.S. Federal Aviation Administration (FAA) submitted a letter to the International Civil Aviation Organization (ICAO), in lieu of an agreement, which "reaffirms the United States Government's commitment to provide the Global Positioning System (GPS) Standard Positioning Service (SPS) for aviation throughout the world. Further, the United States commits to provide the Wide-Area Augmentation System (WAAS) service within its prescribed service volume." The letter goes on to state that "The U.S. Government plans to take all necessary measures for the foreseeable future to maintain the integrity, reliability and availability of the GPS SPS and WAAS service and expects to provide at least six years' notice prior to any termination of such operations or elimination of such services."

On 9 Feb 2011, the Executive Steering Group (ESG), via the National Coordination Office (NCO) of the National Executive Committee (EXCOM) for Space-Based Positioning, Navigation, and Timing (PNT), directed the National Space-Based PNT Systems Engineering Forum (NPEF) to conduct an assessment of the effects of LightSquared's planned deployment of terrestrial broadband systems to GPS receivers and GPS-dependent systems and networks (see Appendix A).

This Report is a summary of the work conducted on this Task (see Appendix B) and includes specific Recommendations as requested by the EXCOM. Department of Defense (DoD) findings for the Task are captured separately given their security classification.

Summary of Task Findings

The following material is a summary of the various subtasks performed in response to the EXCOM NPEF request. Detailed reports for each of the subtasks performed by the NPEF are included in Appendix B and contain additional data and information.

Task 1: Signal Specifications & Characteristics

The relevant technical information on LightSquared specifications and GPS applications were investigated and documented. Details of the LightSquared signal include intended LightSquared channel configurations, antenna characteristics, out of band emissions, tower density and handset technical parameters. Figure 1 depicts the LightSquared plans for three spectrum deployment phases (though the L1 identified in this Figure represents only the main lobe of the C/A portion of the GPS L1 signals).

- Phase 0: One 5 MHz channel: 1550.2 MHz- 1555.2 MHz, 62 dBm effective isotropic radiated power (EIRP) per 5 MHz channel, per base station sector.

- Phase 1: Two 5 MHz channels: 1526.3 MHz -1531.3 MHz & 1550.2 MHz - 1555.2 MHz, 62 dBm EIRP per 5 MHz channel, per sector.

  Phase 2: Two 10 MHz channels: 1526 MHz -1536 MHz & 1545.2 MHz - 1555.2 MHz, 62 dBm EIRP per 10 MHz channel, per sector.

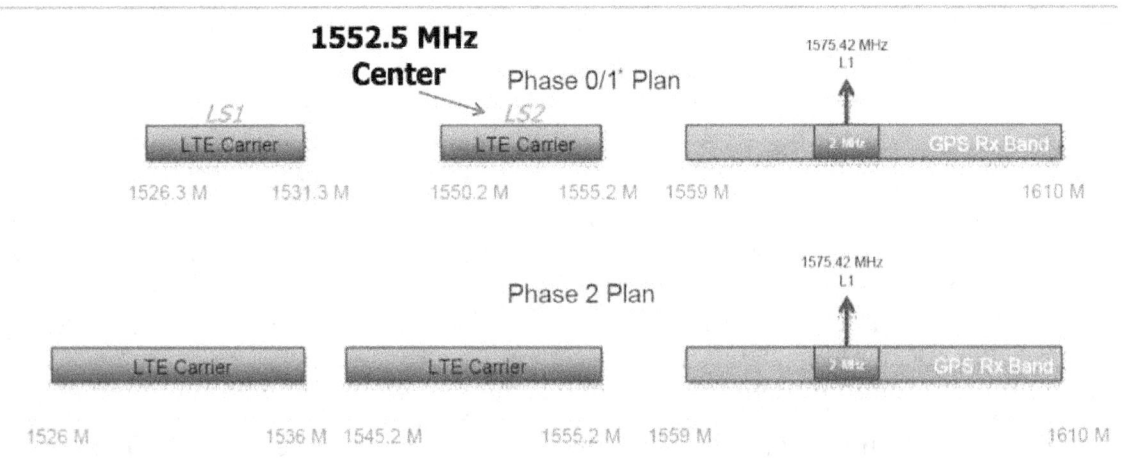

*Only upper 5-MHz LTE carrier is used in Phase-0. Both 5-MHz carriers are used in Phase-1

Figure 1: Lightsquared Downlink LTE L-Band and GPS Band

Figure From: LightSquared, "Preliminary results on Overload Characteristics of GPS Receivers in Proximity to LightSquared's L-band Terrestrial Base Stations (BTS) and User Equipment (UE)" 3GPP TSG-RAN4 #57AH R4-110470 Austin, TX, US 17 -21 Jan, 2011

Figure 1. LightSquared Signal Spectral Occupancy

LightSquared will utilize the prevalent fourth-generation cellular standard, known as Long Term Evolution (LTE), for their terrestrial network and has stated their intention to always operate ATCs at least 4 MHz separated from the start of the GPS L1 band (1559 MHz). It should be noted however, there is *no* regulatory requirement to maintain this guardband nor does LightSquared's MSS ATC authorization impose such a restriction. In addition, the FCC authorization permits use of ATC power levels as much as 10 dB in excess of what LightSquared intends to use and, as a consequence, tests could not be conducted at the maximum allowable ATC levels. At these allowable higher levels there may be additional deleterious effects, such as intermodulation products caused by ATC emissions that are as yet unobserved but can be confirmed with additional testing.

GPS application requirements obtained for this evaluation vary greatly in specificity, with very detailed requirements identified for aviation to much less information for other classes of GPS users. GPS application requirements were obtained primarily from the Technical Working Group (TWG) which reports to the LightSquared Working Group established at the direction of the Federal Communications Commission (FCC). The TWG categorized GPS applications under the following classes: aviation, cellular, general position/navigation, high precision, networks, and space. Key requirements for these categories of applications are contained in the Task 1 detailed report in Appendix B.

Task 2: Model Characterization of the Terrestrial Broadband Network

The ATC locations of sites planned for the initial deployment by LightSquared were provided to the NPEF. The separation distance between these base stations depends on type of morphology around each site as well as capacity and coverage considerations. The maximum number of LightSquared Network handsets a single ATC tower can support depends on the demand and service profile of each mobile device / handset. A typical site with the Phase 2 construct using two 10 MHz channels can support 1200 users in active state and a much higher number in dormant state. For the LightSquared Network deployment of base stations by 2015, LightSquared expects that the distance between base stations would typically be:

- Dense urban environment: 0.4-0.8 km

- Urban environment: 1-2 km

- Suburban environment: 2-4 km

- Rural environment: 5-8 km

Tower locations provided by LightSquared for their initial deployments were used in Task 6 as part of the aviation and space simulation scenarios.

Task 3: RF Interference in Operational Scenarios

The NPEF utilized the operational scenarios developed in the TWG and RTCA forums. TWG scenarios were developed for each of the receiver categories mentioned in Task 1. The scenarios considered most relevant to the NPEF test effort were those for aviation, space, and scientific applications. The aviation scenarios covered en Route, terminal and approach, and surface operations. The spaceborne scenario investigated radio occultation (RO) applications where the

GPS receiver antenna is directed towards the Earth limb in order to measure properties of the atmosphere and typical navigation applications.

Task 4: Receiver Performance Metrics

The NPEF documented several metrics useful to assess performance of a GPS receiver under interference conditions. These metrics include carrier to noise density ratio (C/N_0), pseudorange and carrier phase measurement quality, carrier phase measurement continuity, automatic gain control characteristics, and position/time quality. Additionally some applications measured the ability to acquire or reacquire the GPS L1 signal. While all these metrics have utility in evaluating performance effects, due to the time constraint for this effort receiver characterization under LightSquared interference conditions concentrated on C/N_0 and loss of position/time quality. Loss of position/time quality was referred to as loss of satellite tracking. For NASA, loss of tracking meant no data, rather than poorer quality data, was produced by the unit under test.

Task 5: Expected and Potential Effects on GPS Users

GPS susceptibility tests were conducted using various LightSquared signals and test environments. Conducted emissions testing was accomplished in laboratory environments, radiated emissions testing was performed in an anechoic chamber, and 'nominal' operations testing utilized the 'live sky' environments provided by the current GPS constellation. Test results were obtained from several different types of receivers with applications ranging from aviation to survey to space.

Tables 1 and 2 provide summaries of the standoff distances where civil receivers indicated a 1 dB degradation in C/N_0 and when satellite tracking was disrupted (loss of lock) in the presence of LightSquared emissions. The 1 dB degradation point (approximately 25% loss in effective signal power) is not necessarily a tolerable level of degradation from LightSquared emissions but is useful to highlight the onset of severity associated with these emissions. For example, some tested aviation receivers could not meet their WAAS word error rate requirements in the presence of LightSquared interference that caused a 1 dB degradation in C/No. These results are for a single LightSquared base station and do not address aggregate power from multiple base station scenarios (see Task 6 for specific applications). In lieu of listing specific receiver results, the Tables categorize receivers into functional areas and then provide ranges to cover the degradation observed for these receivers against each specific LightSquared signal type. (Note that the separation distances in these Tables are used to compare the relative sensitivity of different classes of receivers and are based on free space propagation path loss where the receiver is in the main beam of the LightSquared base station transmission.) In addition to the LightSquared-proposed spectrum deployment phases, results for a single 10 MHz Low channel are also provided in these Tables since there was initial exploratory evaluation of a modified LightSquared spectrum deployment that might prove viable as a mitigation approach for some GPS applications.

Results in these Tables demonstrate that for *all* GPS applications assessed during this NPEF effort, the LightSquared signal caused degradation at distances of approximately one kilometer to several hundred kilometers for LightSquared Phase 0, 1 and 2 configurations. These distances are in excess of the planned spacing between base stations for all but the most rural areas. Further, as shown in the Task 6 assessments, there is also an aggregate effect that compounds the degradations experienced from such emanations, i.e., the impacted area outside of a region of dense base station deployment will typically be much larger than the impacted area around a single station. For the 10 MHz Low channel, several receivers were found to operate very well while others demonstrated performance degradation at several hundred kilometers.

Additionally, the ability to acquire or reacquire GPS in the presence of LightSquared ATC was measured for some users. Analysis showed the distance from the LightSquared transmitter to acquire or reacquire GPS signals was always greater than the distance where loss of GPS L1 tracking itself occurred. Testing indicated that loss of the ability to acquire or reacquire GPS signals occurred at distances anywhere between 2 and 4 times greater than initial loss of GPS L1 solution.

It should also be noted that for some applications detailed receiver outputs could not be obtained. E911 and Bureau of Land Management are examples where their reporting from live sky testing at Holloman AFB was simply that at a given standoff distance the receivers stopped functioning or an erroneous position was output.

One final point concluded from these test efforts was confirmation that, for the LightSquared power levels tested, the LightSquared filters were able to satisfy their stated emission mask and constrain out of band LightSquared emissions to less than -100 dBW/MHz at 1559 MHz and above. Thus, for the LightSquared power levels tested, out-of-band emissions by LightSquared ATCs into the GPS band have been determined to *not* represent a significant interference source. Laboratory, anechoic chamber, and live sky testing confirmed that the primary sources of GPS receiver degradation are receiver front end overload and intermodulation interference generated in the antenna assembly or receiver that causes 3rd order intermodulation products to be formed in the GPS L1 band (for details see Task 5 in Appendix B).

Table 1. Distance in Kilometers for 1 dB Degradation Caused by a Single LightSquared Base Station

Application	Phase 0	Phase 1	Phase 2	10 MHz Low
Aviation	24.3 – 1.1	27.2 – 1.2	19.3 – 0.9	< 0.1
Maritime	NM	NM	NM	NM
High Precision** (Survey, Agriculture, Science)	TBR – 0.5	TBR – 6.8	TBR – 3.8	TBR -- < 0.1
Timing	NM	10.8	NM	NM
Space	121.6	305.5 – 19.3	NM	NM

**Data still being analyzed

Table 2. Distance in Kilometers for Loss of Satellite Tracking Caused by a Single LightSquared Base Station

Application	Phase 0	Phase 1	Phase 2	10 MHz Low
Aviation	10.8 – 0.4	12.2 – 0.5	8.6 – 0.3	< 0.1
Maritime	0.6-.2	1.6-.4	1.0-.3	< 0.1
High Precision (Survey, Agriculture, Science)	2.2 – 0.2	7.7 – 2.1	6.1 – 1.7	0.4 -- < 0.1
Timing	NM	< 0.1	NM	NM
Space	24.3	61.0 – 2.7	NM	NM

*NM- Not measured

Task 6: Simulation Activities

Simulation activities utilized the planned initial LightSquared network documented in Task 2, scenarios from Task 3, and susceptibility results from Task 5 to evaluate impacts to aviation and space applications.

An aviation impact assessment was undertaken using the initial LightSquared base station locations located in four markets. Assuming a maximum EIRP of 62 dBm per sector per carrier, the assessment indicated that aircraft avionics will experience interference levels over very large regions of the United States and some portions of Canada and Mexico for the Phase 0, Phase 1, and Phase 2 spectrum deployments that exceed the levels that the equipment is certified to tolerate. Of the subset of certified airborne GPS receivers tested, all appeared to demonstrate a tolerance to interference at the LightSquared frequencies that exceeds the applicable FAA and International Civil Aviation Organization (ICAO) standards by some amount. However, even when utilizing the measured interference tolerance of this small subset of equipment, the NPEF assessment indicates that the LightSquared Network initial deployment would cause severe operational impact over significant regions of the United States. For instance, Figure 2 depicts two contours where GPS would be unusable for an aircraft operating at 500 feet above the ground for two representative receivers subjected to the LightSquared Phase 0 and Phase 1 signals. A common airborne receiver used on transport-category aircraft would be unable to track any GPS satellites in the orange region, while both this receiver and a very popular general aviation airborne receiver would be unable to track any GPS satellites in the red region. Both receivers would be significantly degraded over much larger regions than depicted on the map. Additional analyses are contained in the RTCA LightSquared Report (DO-327[1]).

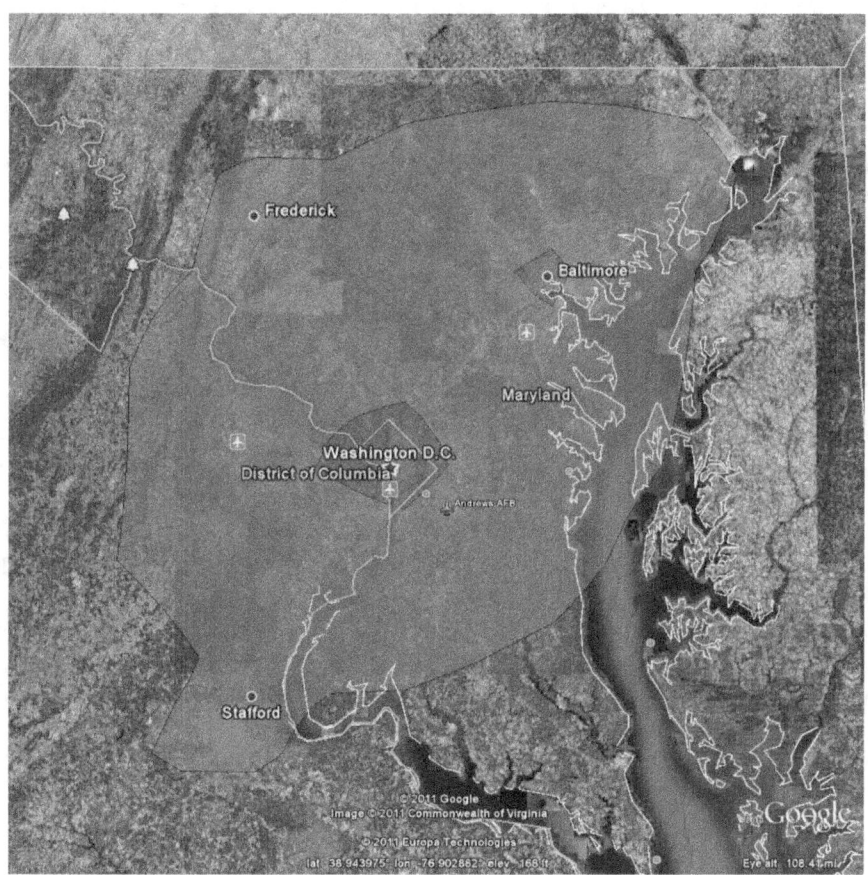

Figure 2. Upper Channel Received Power Levels 500 feet Above the Ground in the Baltimore-Washington Area for the Example LightSquared Network Deployment for Phase 0 or Phase 1.

---

[1] Assessment of the LightSquared Ancillary Terrestrial Component Radio Frequency Interference Impact on GNSS L1 Band Airborne Receiver Operations, RTCA/DO-327, 3 June 2011

Simulation and analysis for space-based receivers was performed based on testing performed at JPL on current and future generations of space-based GPS receivers. Analysis was conducted to determine the percentage of time that space-based occultation measurements would be disrupted within a 10-day simulation. Results indicated that, depending on the spacecraft orbit (orbits assumed were 400 and 800 kilometer orbits inclined at 72 degrees) and on assumed parameters for the LightSquared base stations, the percentage of time occultation measurements could be disrupted was on the order of 5-10% for the power levels planned for use by LightSquared, to as high as 12% if FCC authorized levels of transmit power are assumed. Note that these are outage percentages based on a 10-day period and that the outage percentages based only on when the spacecraft is in view of the United States would be significantly higher per satellite pass. Such degradation would represent a severe disruption of space-based GPS receivers for radio occultation measurement of the Earth's atmosphere and other science purposes. GPS receivers used for typical spacecraft navigation purposes with zenith pointed antennas are affected to a lesser degree (< 3% degradation for the worst case).

For high-precision GPS receivers used for Earth sciences and other applications requiring precise measurements, analysis was conducted to determine the required minimum separation distance between a terrestrial high-precision GPS receiver and a single LightSquared base station where there would be no discernible effect on received C/No. Results of the analysis showed that separation distances for the two receivers tested, assuming several different propagation models, ranged from approximately 1.5 to 4 kilometers for one receiver type to approximately 3 to12 kilometers for the other receiver model tested. Both models tested are used in the International GNSS Service (IGS) network. Given the ATC deployment density anticipated with the LightSquared terrestrial network, it is unlikely that such separation distances could be assured.

High-precision receivers are also used in many state and local networks. The National Geodetic Survey (NGS), an office of NOAA's National Ocean Service, manages a network of Continuously Operating Reference Stations (CORS) that provide Global Navigation Satellite System (GNSS) data consisting of carrier phase and code range measurements in support of three dimensional positioning, meteorology, space weather, and geophysical applications throughout the United States, its territories, and a few foreign countries. The sites are independently owned and operated. Each agency shares their data with NGS and NGS in turn analyzes and distributes the data free of charge. As of May 2010, the CORS network contains over 1,450 stations, contributed by over 200 different organizations, and the network continues to expand (See **Error! Reference source not found.**).

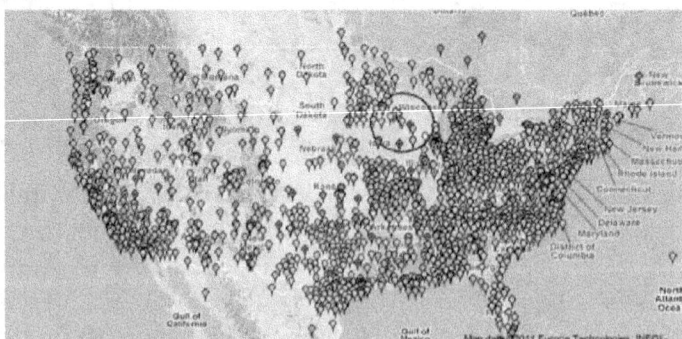

Figure 3. U.S. CORS Station Locations

Task 7: Work Plan, Test Planning & Field Test Activities

The testing discussed in Task 5 included participation by LightSquared personnel to observe and comment on test conduct. LightSquared visited both Zeta Associates Inc., who performed FAA sponsored aviation receiver tests, and JPL, who performed NASA sponsored space-based receiver testing. LightSquared visited White Sands Missile Range to observe chamber test conditions and also provided and operated a representative ATC base station in support of open-air ('live sky') testing conducted at Holloman Air Force Base. To ensure a high fidelity test, actual LightSquared filters with representative antennas and equipment were used to transmit the LightSquared signal. LightSquared did not identify or voice any concerns regarding any of the above described test configurations.

Task 8: Mitigation Measures Applicable to GPS Users

Four possible mitigation measures applicable to GPS were identified and assessed. These included:

- Additional filtering – adding filtering to GPS user equipment to suppress the LightSquared signals.

- Adaptive antennas – using adaptive array antennas to spatially suppress the LightSquared signals.

- GPS changes – increasing GPS and WAAS broadcast signal strength to compensate for the signal-to-noise degradation caused by the LightSquared Network.

- Operational solutions – keeping GPS users separated from LightSquared base stations and mobile subscriber handsets.

Of these measures, adding additional filtering was found to be the most viable but would most likely be costly where it could be applied and cannot be applied to all GPS users. Many fielded GPS receivers are self-contained or integrated into other products (e.g., mobile phones). For such equipment, it is likely to be more cost-effective to replace the equipment rather than modify a given unit. Some fielded GPS equipment that utilizes external antennas may be able to satisfactorily function with the addition of in-line filtering or a replacement antenna with additional self contained filtering. However, such add-on filtering solutions are not viable for a significant fraction of fielded equipment due to considerations such as performance (signal attenuation, increased thermal noise floor, phase and group delay variations with temperature and between frequencies, loss of narrow correlator benefits), cost, size, and weight. Further, in the case of the aviation application, the equipment and its installation procedure would also need to be recertified following the inclusion of an in-line filter.

For a new product, many additional degrees of freedom are opened for mitigation techniques. In this case, the entire receiver and antenna design could be optimized to meet an overarching set of requirements that included the need to tolerate high levels of out of band interference at the LightSquared frequencies. In addition to adding to the filtering distributed along the RF front-end signal path, there are other design modifications that may be necessary to facilitate coexistence with the proposed LightSquared network. These include the careful control of the unit's oscillator phase noise and spurs that may lead to reciprocal mixing problems, and the need to ensure that the signal path components do not saturate in the presence of the high-powered

LightSquared emissions. Unfortunately, redesign is not likely to result in the same level of performance provided by current receivers, especially those employing wide RF front-end passbands. Such receivers are expected to increase in usage and importance in the near future as GLONASS, Galileo, and Compass satellite navigation constellations plan to be interoperable with GPS.

Given the wide variety of operational uses for GPS, however, the design requirements on receiving equipment also varies widely and there are some applications for which a practical receiver design will **NOT** be possible once the added constraint of coexistence with 34,000 high-powered base stations broadcasting signals 20 MHz away from the L1 carrier is applied. High-precision equipment is among the most difficult to protect against the LightSquared emissions since these receivers typically process wideband GPS signals that require a wideband receiver passband and such equipment usually also has severe differential group delay requirements. For these types of receivers, filtering can typically significantly degrade or even destroy the very information required for the most demanding scientific and precision applications.

Task 9: Mitigation Measures Applicable to LightSquared

The NPEF examined several possible mitigation measures that could be implemented by LightSquared to reduce potential interference to GPS receivers while still providing a viable nationwide terrestrial broadband service as required by the FCC. Five possible mitigation measures were examined: 1) increasing the frequency separation of LightSquared's transmitted signal relative to the lower edge of the RNSS allocated band at 1559-1610 MHz (e.g., by using only the lower of the two proposed LightSquared channels); 2) reducing the transmitted power to reduce the magnitude of the interfering signal; 3) modifying the base station antenna (either by narrowing the vertical beamwidth or increasing the antenna tilt so that less area is covered by each transmitting antenna); 4) using exclusion zones to maintain a minimum separation distance where the installation is fixed; and 5) relocating the proposed LightSquared network operating frequencies to a band more suitable for high power terrestrial operations.

Of these possible mitigation techniques applicable to LightSquared, the two involving increased frequency separation present the most promise for the widest communities of GPS users. The mitigation technique that offers the greatest long-term benefit to the GPS community is the relocation of LightSquared's terrestrial operations to a band more suitable for such applications and less disruptive to adjacent band space services such as GPS.

Another approach examined involves limiting the LightSquared transmissions to the lower 5 or 10 MHz channel of their planned deployment. However, while this approach would protect a limited number of GPS applications other applications would still be susceptible to interference.[2] Using this approach it may be possible to protect classes of GPS receivers, primarily those with

---

[2] The 15 May 2011 report of the FCC Technical Working Group noted that their tests did not reflect the planned LightSquared power levels. In single frequency mode, the test sites operated at power levels of approximately 59 dBm EIRP per channel as opposed to the 62 dBm EIRP per channel currently planned for the initial commercial deployment. For two carrier tests, the MIMO gain will not be present, reducing the EIRP a further 3 dB per channel to approximately 56 dBm EIRP. It is not adequate to merely adjust the standoff distances to account for greater power because this does not account for intermodulation products which might be introduced at the highest radiated power. The effects shown with respect to GPS may have to be adjusted in further tests to reflect planned operating conditions.

greater receiver selectivity. However, some classes of GPS receivers would still not be protected under this mitigation technique. Receivers having wider RF front-end characteristics, such as those used for scientific and commercial uses requiring high precision measurements, and some receivers capable of receiving multiple signals from different GNSS systems (e.g., GLONASS) would remain susceptible. Additionally, the use of only the lower LightSquared channel would provide only a temporary solution to the existing interference problems as 4G LTE levels of service may not be possible. Thus, even if allowed, the FCC's objectives and service conditions on the LightSquared license would not be met.

Recommendations

Based on analysis described in the main body of this Report, the NPEF has developed the following technical recommendations for ESG consideration.

Recommendation 1: *LightSquared should not commence commercial services per its planned deployment for terrestrial operations in the 1525 – 1559 MHz Mobile-Satellite Service (MSS) Band due to harmful interference to GPS operations.*

Test results of the LightSquared Phase 0, Phase 1, and Phase 2 deployments of ATC transmitters utilizing the MSS band (1550.2 – 1555.2 MHz for Phase 0, 1526.3 – 1531.3/1550.2-1555.2 MHz for Phase 1, and 1526-1536/1545.2 – 1555.2 MHz for Phase 2) have demonstrated there are significant detrimental impacts to all GPS applications assessed as part of this NPEF effort. These impacts encompassed both US Government and commercial GPS applications. The potential degradation of GPS operation due to LightSquared emissions was further characterized via simulation that showed that completion of the network of high-powered base stations envisioned by LightSquared would result in degradation or loss of GPS function (ranging, position) at standoff distances of a few kilometers extending to space operations. Possible mitigations for GPS applications were identified and evaluated but were deemed impractical as they would require significant modification or complete redesign and replacement of currently fielded GPS equipment. The timeline to field new GPS receivers for some applications, from initial concept development through production, can take 10-15 years. Finally, there remain certain applications (e.g., high precision) that, even with modification, may not be able to perform their current mission in the presence of LightSquared's network transmitting in the 1525 – 1559 MHz band.

Recommendation 2: *The U.S. Government should conduct more thorough studies on the operational, economic and safety impacts of operating the LightSquared Network, to include additional ATC signal configurations not currently in LightSquared planned spectrum phases, effects on timing receivers, as well as transmissions from LightSquared handsets. As part of these studies the compatibility of ATC architectures in the MSS L-Band with GPS applications should be reassessed.*

Initial test results demonstrated that some applications (e.g. aviation) were able to operate with little to no degradation when only a 5 or 10 MHz channel (1526.3 – 1531.3 MHz or 1526 – 1536 MHz) in the lower portion of the MSS spectrum was utilized for the LightSquared broadcast.

However, for other applications, GPS loss of function still occurs at unacceptable distances to LightSquared towers. Use of only the lower portion of the L-band MSS spectrum is *not* one of the planned Phases for the LightSquared Network evolution so only limited testing has been conducted under this scenario. Additionally, no tests on LightSquared handset (or user terminal) transmissions were conducted as part of this NPEF study, due to non-availability of hardware.

LightSquared handsets will transmit in the band 1626.5 – 1660.5 MHz and the potential for interference to GPS receivers given the very close proximity to an arbitrary number of

LightSquared users remains to be evaluated. Evaluation of the LightSquared emissions effects on timing receivers was not thoroughly addressed during the course of this NPEF investigation. An additional evaluation period of at least six months would enable completion of a thorough assessment of the LightSquared Network and should be conducted to allow the EXCOM to make informed decisions on impacts, mitigations, and the way forward for all GPS users.

At the conclusion of this NPEF effort, significant technical concerns remain that operation of an ATC service can successfully coexist with GPS. Rigorous analysis of potential interference had been impossible prior to now due to non-availability of relevant commercial ATC equipment. This recommendation suggests there is a need for additional analysis to determine if ATC architectures can be accommodated in the MSS L-band without impacting GPS.

Appendix A: Assessment of LightSquared Terrestrial Broadband System Effects on Civil GPS Receivers and GPS-dependent Civil Government Applications

Task Statement

Assessment of LightSquared Terrestrial Broadband System Effects on Civil GPS Receivers and GPS-dependent Civil Government Applications

Scope

At the direction of the Executive Steering Group (ESG) of the National Executive Committee for Space-Based Positioning, Navigation, and Timing, herein referred to as the EXCOM, and with facilitation by the National Coordination Office (NCO), the National Space-Based PNT Systems Engineering Forum (NPEF) is tasked to conduct an assessment of the effects of LightSquared's planned deployment of terrestrial broadband systems to Global Positioning System (GPS) receivers and GPS-dependent systems and networks. The NPEF should engage with: 1) The LightSquared Working Group established at the direction of the Federal Communications Commission (FCC) and 2) GPS manufacturing and applications communities through relevant industry bodies (e.g. the U.S. GPS Industry Council and RTCA, Inc.). The NPEF is to investigate, assess, and determine the range of effects to GPS use based on operationally relevant scenarios that represent the current installed user base. While the NPEF tasks are to be conducted in cooperation with all involved entities to the extent possible, the NPEF is requested to produce an independent report to the ESG and EXCOM.

Background

Reference FCC Order DA 11-133, in the matter of LightSquared Subsidiary LLC "Request for Modification of its Authority for an Ancillary Terrestrial Component," adopted and released January 26, 2011 and NTIA January 12, 2011 letter to FCC Chairman.

Methodology and Assessment

1. Document LightSquared's Ancillary Terrestrial Component (ATC) and related user equipment signals and antenna specifications and characteristics, GPS receiver specifications and characteristics (e.g., Radionavigation-Satellite Service (RNSS) receiver characteristics submitted to the International Telecommunication Union (ITU)), and future spectrum environment considerations.

2. In cooperation with the LightSquared Working Group, develop a baseline model characterization of the planned initial and fully deployed broadband network, including ATC locations and siting assumptions/limitations. Identify user handset planning assumptions as appropriate.

3. In conjunction with federal and commercial GPS technical experts, develop operational scenarios representative of the full range of anticipated effects to GPS receiver use (including characterization by existing GPS receiver categories where possible) as well as deployed federal and commercial GPS-dependent systems or networks. The scenarios assessed shall consider federal and state government and commercial communities' current and planned use of GPS and GPS applications.

4. Develop appropriate metrics to quantitatively and qualitatively assess performance degradations from both technical and operational perspectives.

5. Analyze the expected and potential effects on GPS use for each of the developed scenarios including both current and future spectrum environment (e.g. 2025) considerations.

6. Coordinate simulation activities to further assess effects on GPS usage under various scenarios.

7. Coordinate work plan, test planning, and field test activities with the FCC, LightSquared, NTIA and the EXCOM departments and agencies to measure emissions and determine representative technical and operational GPS receiver effects as a function of distance from a LightSquared terrestrial base station

8. Assess potential mitigation techniques and their expected effectiveness/costs for various representative GPS receivers in each of the selected scenarios. Assessments should include analysis, simulation, and prototype testing (as practical).

9. Assess and recommend potential mitigation measures or techniques that are applicable to the LightSquared system based on the representative GPS receivers and the operational scenarios developed above including, for example, potential variations in emitted power, antenna gain pattern, and operating spectrum for the ATC base stations and mobile handsets.

Schedule and Deliverable

The NPEF is to complete the work under this Task Statement by May 31, 2011. An interim update will be provided to the ESG/EXCOM through the NCO Director by March 31, 2011. The final deliverable report will be produced in a publicly releasable version and For Official Use Only version as appropriate. The reports will detail the planned broadband system effects on GPS use and include details on potential technical and operational mitigation options for interoperability between the planned LightSquared network and federal and commercial GPS-dependent users, systems and networks. The report will include field measurements from the LightSquared ATC stations and mobile handset and an analysis of representative GPS receiver performance. Any classified concerns will be briefed to the NCO and ESG for discussion in an appropriate forum and venue. Issues of proprietary data will be handled on a case-by-case basis.

Appendix B: NPEF Tasks

**See companion pdf document.

Appendix B: NPEF Tasks

Table of Figures

List of Tables

Appendix B: NPEF Tasks

1. Subtask 1 -- Assessment of LightSquared Terrestrial Broadband System Effects on Civil GPS Receivers and GPS-dependent Civil Government Applications

Task Statement

Document LightSquared's Ancillary Terrestrial Component (ATC) and related user equipment signals and antenna specifications and characteristics, GPS receiver specifications and characteristics (e.g., Radionavigation-Satellite Service (RNSS) receiver characteristics submitted to the International Telecommunication Union (ITU)), and future spectrum environment considerations.

LightSquared Ancillary Terrestrial Component (ATC) Technical Parameters

LightSquared plans for three spectrum phases:

- Phase 0: One 5 MHz channel : 1550.2 MHz- 1555.2 MHz, 62 dBm EIRP per 5 MHz channel

- Phase 1: Two 5 MHz channel : 1526.3 MHz -1531.3 MHz & 1550.2 MHz - 1555.2 MHz, 62 dBm EIRP per 5 MHz channel

- Phase 2: Two 10 MHz channel : 1526 MHz -1536 MHz & 1545.2 MHz - 1555.2 MHz, 62 dBm EIRP per 10 MHz channel

Currently, LightSquared plans to transmit in L-band (1525 MHz -1559 MHz). LightSquared has stated that their intention is to always operate ATCs at least 4 MHz away from the GPS band, at 1559 MHz. Using LTE technology (OFDM, orthogonal frequency division multiplex modulation), each 10 MHz channel will have 1 MHz internal guard band, including 500 KHz on each side of the channel. LightSquared plans to deploy 20W per channel per sector. Each sector will have two transmit chains so a total power of 40W per sector per channel will be transmitted from each base station tower. Given there are three sectors, that results in a total of 120W per tower per channel. In LightSquared plans for spectrum Phases 1 and 2 there will be two channels so the result is 80W per sector or 240W per tower. Further, LightSquared plans to deploy a maximum of 62 dBm EIRP per channel and with two channels per sector, total EIRP per sector will then be 65 dBm per sector. Vertical cross polarization will be used for ATC transmissions.

Table 1-1. LightSquared Deployment Phases

Development Phase	Channel Quantity and Size	Channel Locations	Nominal BTS Channel EIRP
Phase 0	One (1) 5MHz FDD	DL: 1550.2-1555.2MHz UL: 1651.7-1656.7 MHz	32 dBW (25 dBW/MHz)
Phase 1A	Two(2) 5MHz FDD	**Channel 1** DL: 1526.3-1531.3MHz UL: 1627.0-1632.0 MHz **Channel 2** DL: 1550.2-1655.2 MHz UL: 1651.7-1656.7 MHz	32 dBW (25 dBW/MHz)
Phase 2	Two(2) 10 MHz FDD	**Channel 1** DL: 1526-1536 MHz UL: 1627.5-1637.5 MHz **Channel 2** DL: 1545.2-1555.2 MHz UL: 1646.7-1656.7 MHz	32 dBW (22 dBW/MHz)

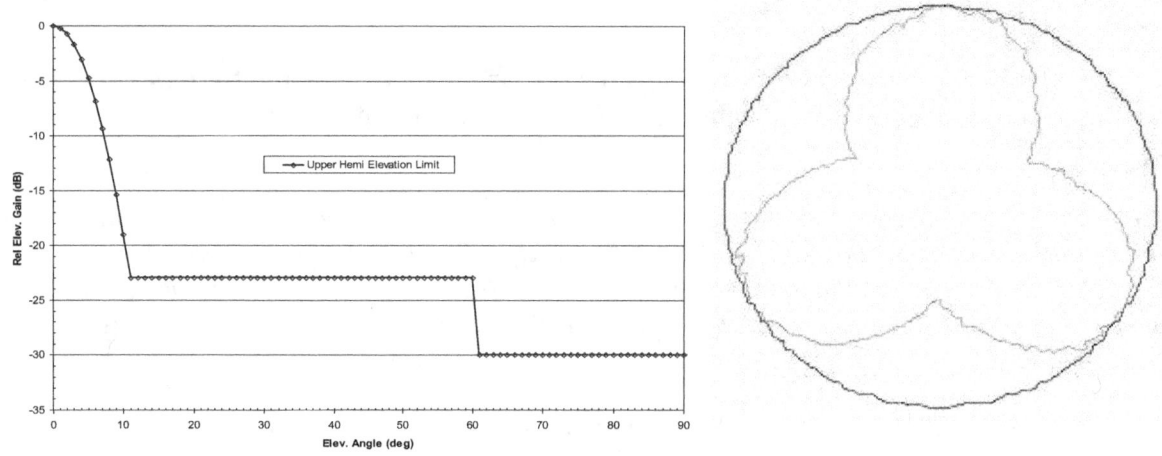

Rel. Az. Patterns (omni & 3-sector)

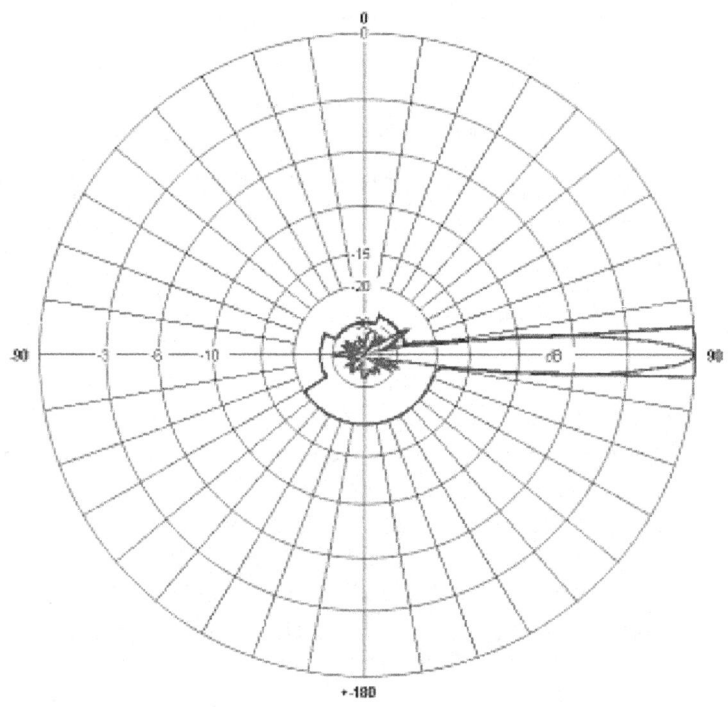

Relative Elev. Pattern (~7° beamwidth)

Blue limits = FCC pattern mask

Figure 1-1. ATCt Base Station Transmit Antenna Patterns

ATCt Base Station

- Max. fundamental EIRP: 42 dBW (total in occupied bandwidth)

- Max. unwanted EIRP: -100 dBW/MHz (1559-1610 MHz)

- *Modulation: 4 MSPS RRC QPSK, 5.0 MHz occupied bandwidth

- *Highest carrier freq. 1552.7 MHz

- *Antenna height: 30 m   (* from SC-222 WP053)

The distance between transmitters depends on type of morphology around each site as well as other capacity and coverage considerations. LightSquared expects that the distance between transmitters would typically be:

- Dense urban environment: 0.4-0.8 km

- Urban environment: 1-2 km

- Suburban environment: 2-4 km

- Rural environment: 5-8 km

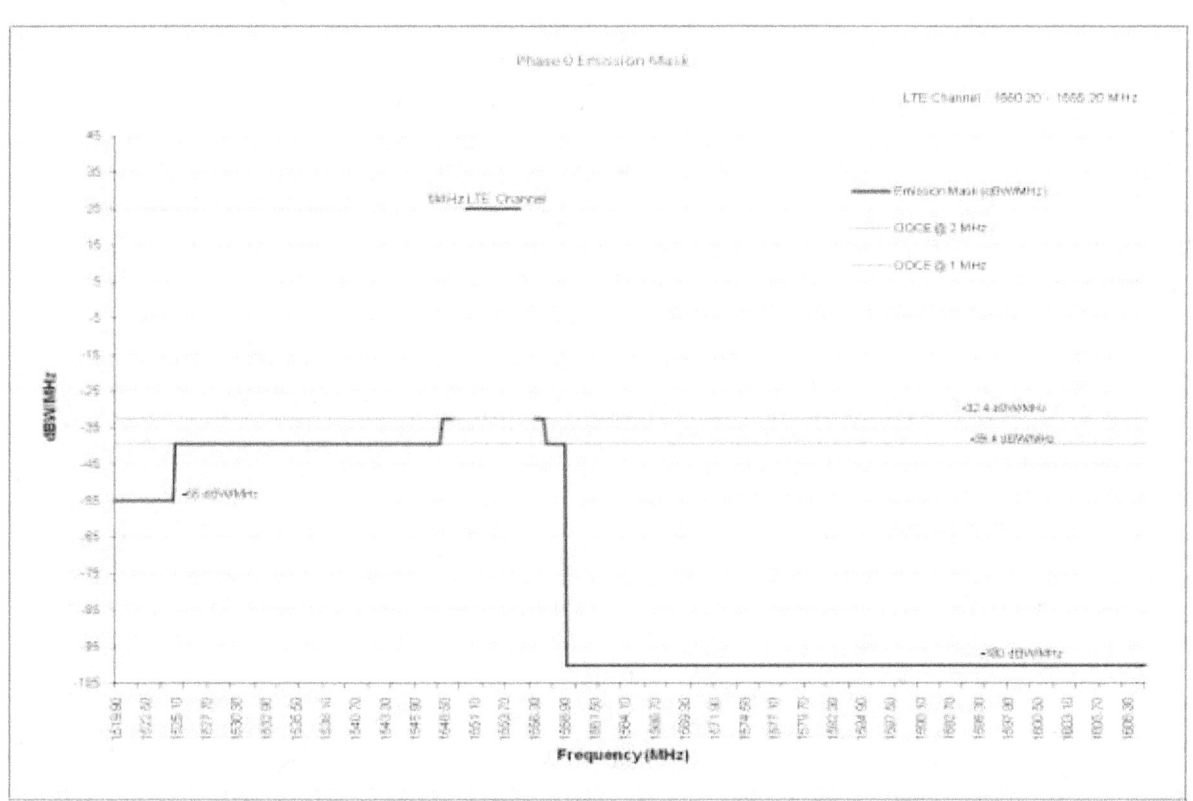

Figure 1-2. LightSquared Planned Spectrum Phases

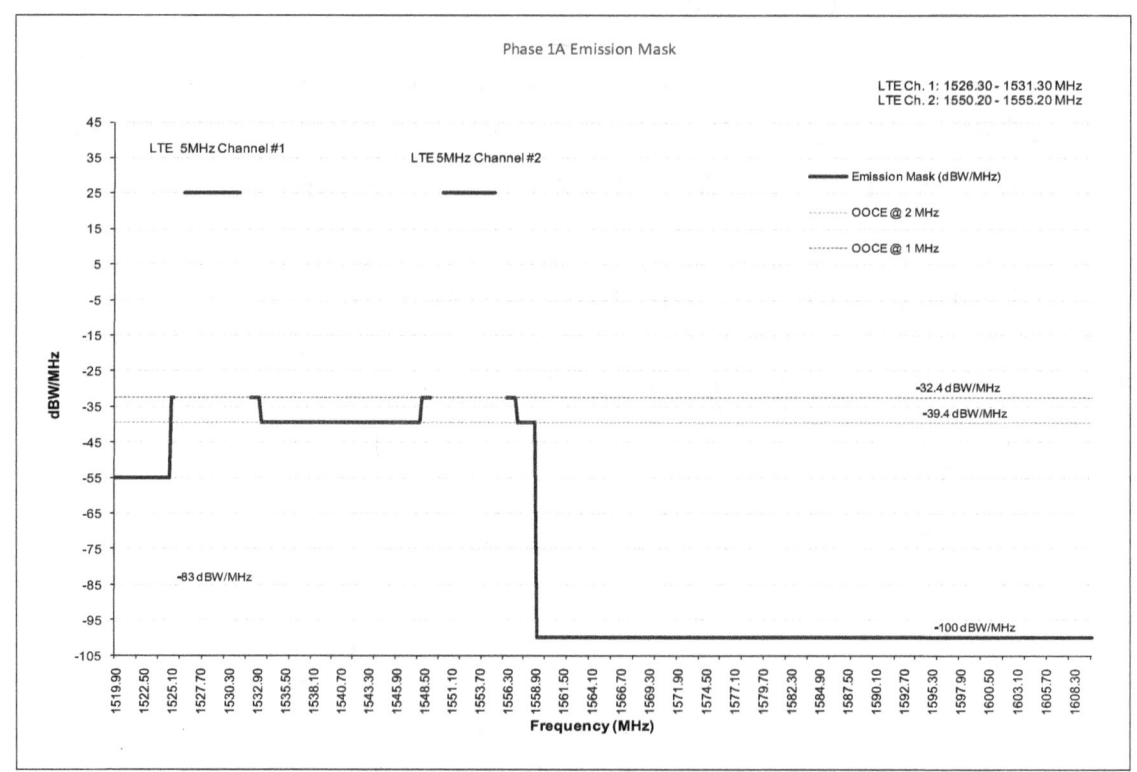

Figure 1-3. LightSquared Planned Phase 1 Base Station Mask

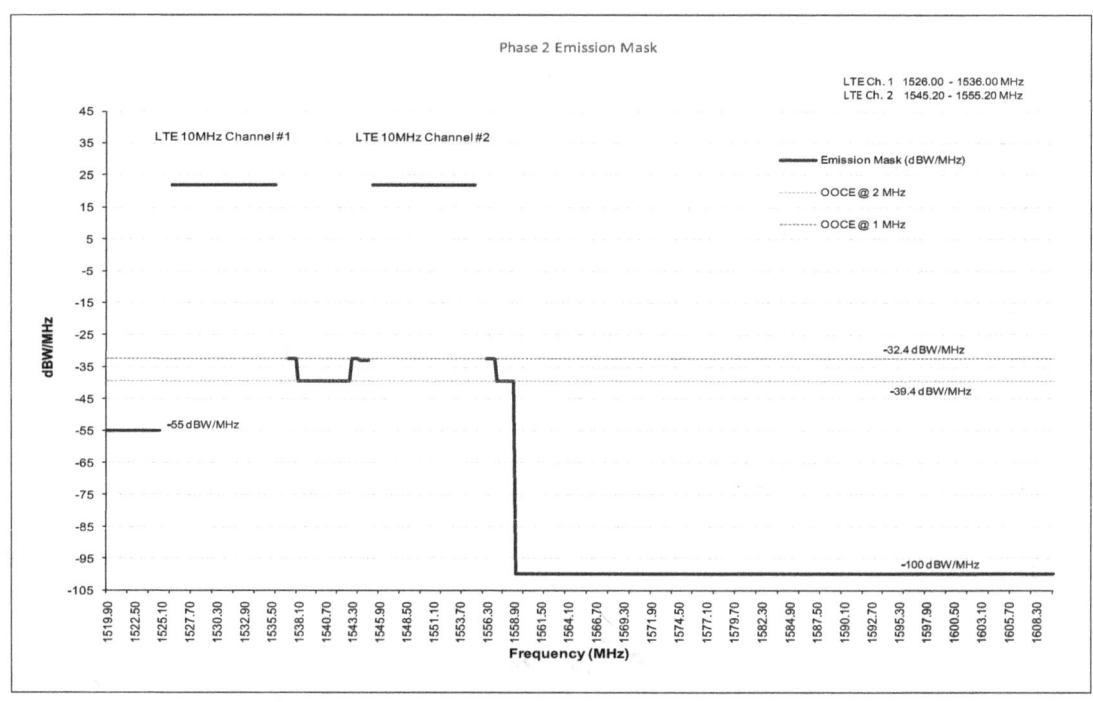

Figure 1-4. LightSquared Planned Phase 2 Base Station Mask

LightSquared User Handset Technical Parameters

When communicating with LightSquared towers, LightSquared mobile devices will transmit in the L-band (1626.5 MHz -1660.5 MHz). LightSquared will use 10% of the total channel bandwidth as a guard band. For example, each 10 MHz channel will have 1 MHz guard band; 500 kHz on each side of the channel. LightSquared anticipates that some future devices may also utilize additional terrestrial cellular bands for transmission, but the specific bands are not yet confirmed. Linear polarization will be used for handset transmissions with a maximum 23 dBm EIRP.

ATCt Mobile Terminal

- Maximum fundamental EIRP: -7 dBW**

- Maximum unwanted EIRP: -90 dBW/MHz (1559-1605 MHz)

- Modulation: LTE (OFDM)**, 5 MHz occupied bandwidth

- Carrier frequency: 1654.2 MHz**

- Antenna height: 1.8 m (est.)

(** from LightSquared RTCA brief (McCall), 10 Feb 2011)

As with the ATC, LightSquared plans three spectrum phases for the deployment of handsets:

- Phase 0: One 5 MHz channel: 1651.7 MHz - 1656.7 MHz, 23 dBm maximum EIRP per user and smallest bandwidth a user can transmit is 180 KHz;

- Phase 1: Two 5 MHz channels: 1627.8 MHz - 1632.8 MHz & 1651.7 MHz - 1656.7 MHz, 23 dBm maximum EIRP per user and smallest bandwidth a user can transmit is 180 KHz; and

- Phase 2: Two 10 MHz channels: 1627.5 MHz - 1637.5 MHz & 1646.7 MHz - 1656.7 MHz, 23 dBm maximum EIRP per user and smallest bandwidth a user can transmit is 180 KHz.

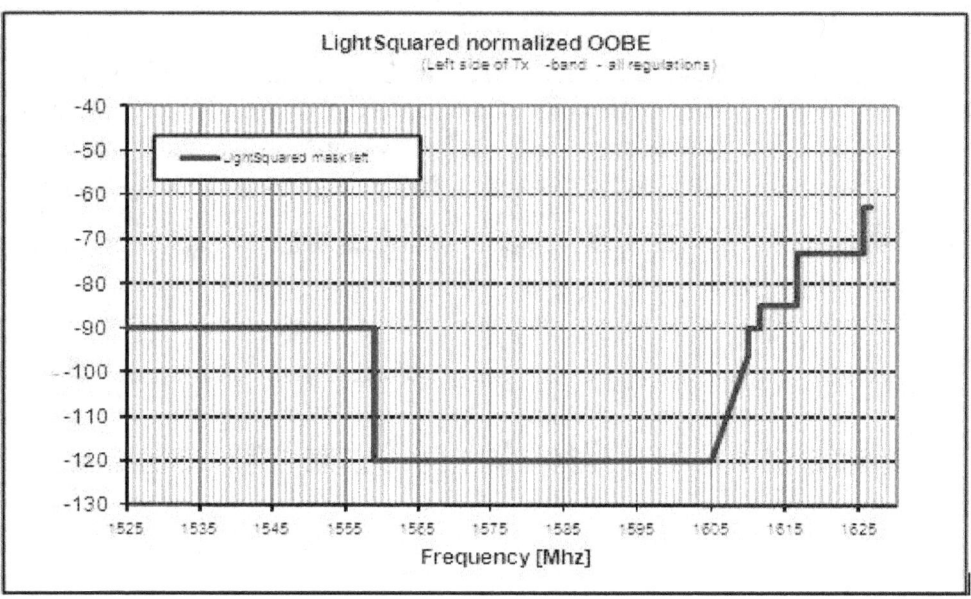

Figure 1-5. LightSquared OOBE Requirements (normalized dBm/Hz left side from 1626.5 MHz for LTE 10 MHz)

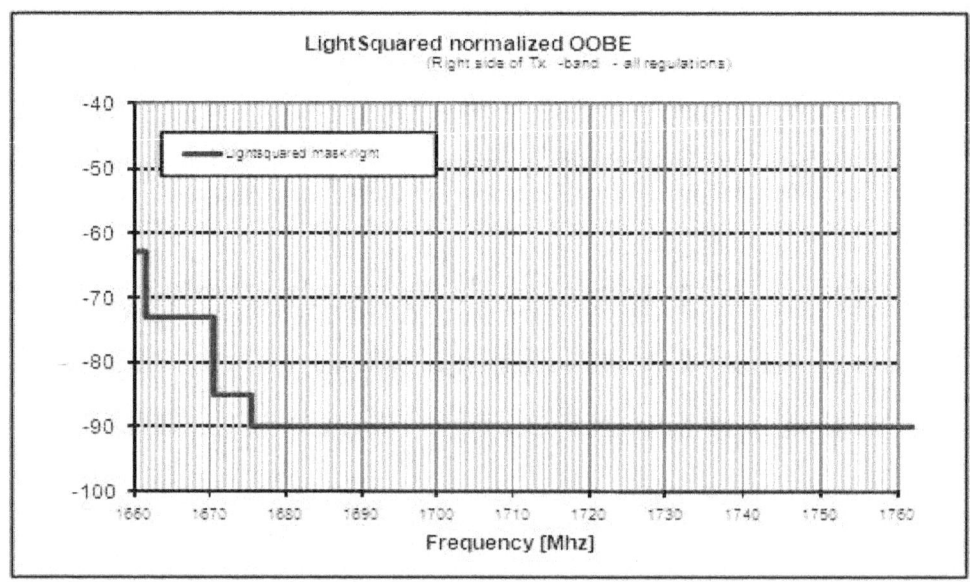

Figure 1-6. LightSquared OOBE Requirements (normalized to dBm/Hz right side from 1660.5 MHz for LTE 10 MHz)

GPS Receiver Specifications and Characteristics

Seven categories of receivers that are representative of the non-military use of GPS in the United States have been identified: aviation, cellular, general location/navigation, high precision, timing, space-based receivers and networks. Each category includes augmented and non-augmented devices. Public safety receivers are included in precision timing and in general location/navigation applications. Receivers used in science are included in the high precision category. Commercial and global maritime distress and safety receivers are included in general location/navigation. Technical characteristics for each of these categories of GPS receivers are provided below.

Aviation

See Appendix 1-A: GNSS Aviation Receivers – Performance Characteristics and Operational Scenarios

Cellular

Baseline Performance Specifications: AGPS receivers in cellular telephones designed for operation with air link technologies covered by the specifications of the 3rd Generation Partnership Project (3GPP), are designed to comply with core performance specification 3GPP TS 25.171. *"Requirements for support of Assisted Global Positioning System (A-GPS) Frequency Division Duplex (FDD)."*

Baseline Conformance Specifications: AGPS receivers designed for operation with airlink technologies covered by the specifications of 3GPP are tested for conformance to test specification 3GPP TS 34.171 *"Terminal conformance specification; Assisted Global Positioning System (A-GPS); Frequency Division Duplex (FDD)."*

GPS Receiver Sensitivity, Assisted Mode: AGPS receiver sensitivity is specified in terms of location accuracy relative to the received signal level. For example, current 3GPP TS 34.171 test requirements call for a location accuracy of 100 meters 95% of the time and a Time to First Fix (TTFF) of between 16 and 20 seconds (the TTFF is dependent upon the specific 3GPP airlink technology supported by the cellular telephone). 3GPP TS 34.171 calls for the cellular telephone to comply with the accuracy metrics listed above at a signal level of -147 dBm and will be tested down to -162 dBm. In addition to 3GPP standards, the TWG will utilize accuracy and availability standards prescribed in the FCC's rules and within OET 71.

GPS Receiver Sensitivity, Unassisted (Autonomous) Mode: Like the assisted mode above, the sensitivity of an unassisted GPS receiver can also be specified in terms of location accuracy. However, neither the 3GPP TS 25.171 core performance specification nor the 3GPP TS 34.171 conformance test specification defines a minimum performance value for this mode. Given sufficient measurement time, an unassisted GPS receiver in a cellular telephone should be able to comply with the accuracy metrics associated with the assisted mode.

General Location/Navigation

Position Accuracy: Dependent upon operational scenario

Velocity: 0.2 meters / second

Acquisition and Tracking Sensitivity: Dependent upon operational scenario

Acquisition Time: 1.0 seconds (Hot Start); 38.0 seconds (Warm Start); 45.0 seconds (Cold Start)

High Precision

Acquisition signals: GPS (L1 C/A, L1C, WAAS L1), (L2 semi-codeless , L2C),
(L5, WAAS L5), L-Band (OmniStar, StarFire)

Signal acquisition time (s): TBD

Sensitivity (dBm):

- GPS Point of mean time between cycle slips < 600(s)   (usable for RTK)
- GPS Point of loss of lock
- WAAS Point of BER > 1E-6
- WAAS Point of loss of lock
- L-Band Point of BER > 1E-6
- L-Band Point of loss of lock

Precision Timing

Time to "Good Clock" (s):

- Cold: (Position known and fixed, no almanac or time)
- Warm: (Position known and fixed, almanac + (time +/- min))
- Hot: (Position known and fixed, ephemeris + (time +/- us))

Steady state time accuracy: ITU G.810 MTIE, TDEV

Steady state frequency accuracy: ITU G.810 ADEV, MDEV

Phase noise (dBc): TBD

Networks

The performance characteristics of networks vary greatly by network type. This information is still being gathered.

Space-Based Receivers

Measurement precision: The occultation experiment requires the phase rate be measured with 0.8 mm/s accuracy. Data are output at 100 Hz. Typical 1-second measurement precisions are 0.3 mm for the ionospheric error free combination of dual carrier phase measurements. The unknown delay variation through the receiver filters must be less than 1 nanosecond over 0 to 40 degrees C.

Applications: Precision measurements from space orbit, including vertical location of satellites with sub-cm error, use for gravity recovery with integrated K+Ka bands transmit/receive capability, measurement of atmospheric refractivity during GPS limb soundings, ionospheric science measurements of electron content and ionospheric scintillation, ground-based carrier-based frequency transfer.

General description of receiver: Tracks C/A code, L2C code (some receivers), Y1 and Y2 codes using semi-codeless, L5 code (receivers being built now). Receiver can be upgraded in orbit. New software is routinely uploaded after launch. Firmware in FPGAs is modified after launch to add new signal capability.

Observables produced: Time-tagged pseudo-range, carrier phase, and effective C/N_0 are produced for each of the codes mentioned above. Also, the onboard solution consisting of the position, the receiver clock offset (and their time derivatives), along with the satellites used in the solution, the formal error, and the solution Chi-squared are all output.

Appendix 1-A: GNSS Aviation Receivers – Performance Characteristics and Operational Scenarios

1. Overview

This appendix describes receiver performance characteristics and operational scenarios for civil aviation applications of GNSS. The focus is on receivers relied upon to allow civilian aircraft to navigate in instrument meteorological conditions (IMC)[1]. These receivers include those installed on aircraft, and those used on the ground for satellite-based or ground-based augmentation systems (SBAS/GBAS).

Currently-available airborne GPS receivers allow civilian aircraft to navigate using GPS for all phases of flight, from en route to precision approach. Over 10,000 GPS-based instrument approach procedures in the United States have been published to date.

2. Airborne Equipment

2.1 Antennas

Minimum performance standards for current-generation airborne GNSS antennas for use in the United States are provided in [1 – 4]. Harmonized requirements are included within the

---

[1]GPS is used on many aircraft for other purposes, including photogrammetry and flight test instrumentation. These applications are not addressed here.

International Civil Aviation Organization (ICAO) Standards and Recommended Practices (SARPs) [5].

The majority of airborne antennas are active. Some key performance requirements include:

- Passive element gain - The minimum specified gain of the passive antenna component for elevation angles at or above 5 degrees is -5.5 dBic. RTCA recommended installed antenna gain models for minimum and maximum gain for the purposes of interference analysis are provided in [6] and summarized in Figure 1-7 and Figure 1-8 below.

- Axial ratio - Although airborne antennas are nominally right hand circularly polarized, axial ratio is only controlled at boresight (zenith), where it is specified to be less than 3.0 dB. Like most low-profile GNSS antennas, airborne antennas tend to be approximately linearly (vertical) polarized at low elevation angles with typical axial ratios exceeding 15 dB near the horizon.

- Active antenna subassembly gain – at least 26.5 dB from the passive antenna output port to the output port of the active antenna.

- Input 1 dB compression – see Figure 1-9 below for minimum performance, with the level referenced to the output of the passive antenna

- Filtering requirements – see Figure 1-10 for minimum attenuation vs frequency (note that the active antenna is required to provide a 3-dB bandwidth of at least 15 MHz).

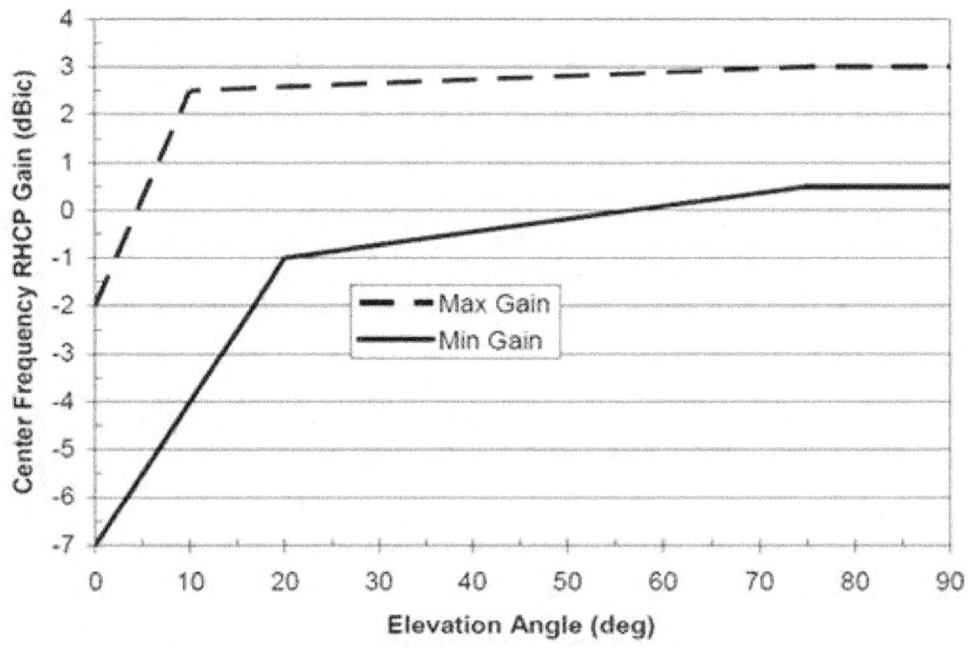

Figure 1-7. Minimum and Maximum Installed Airborne Antenna Gain Above the Horizon

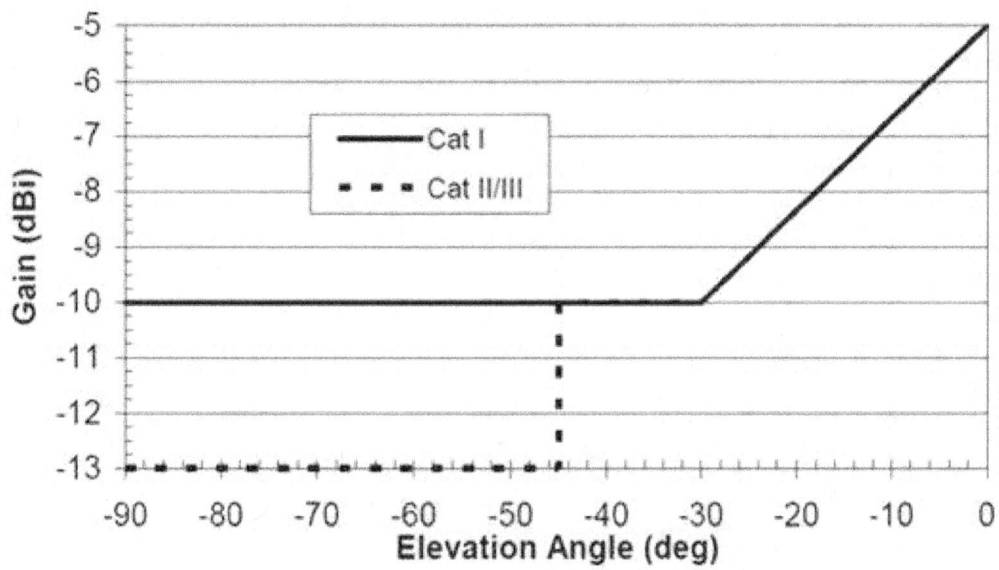

Figure 1-8. Maximum Installed Airborne Antenna Gain Below the Horizon

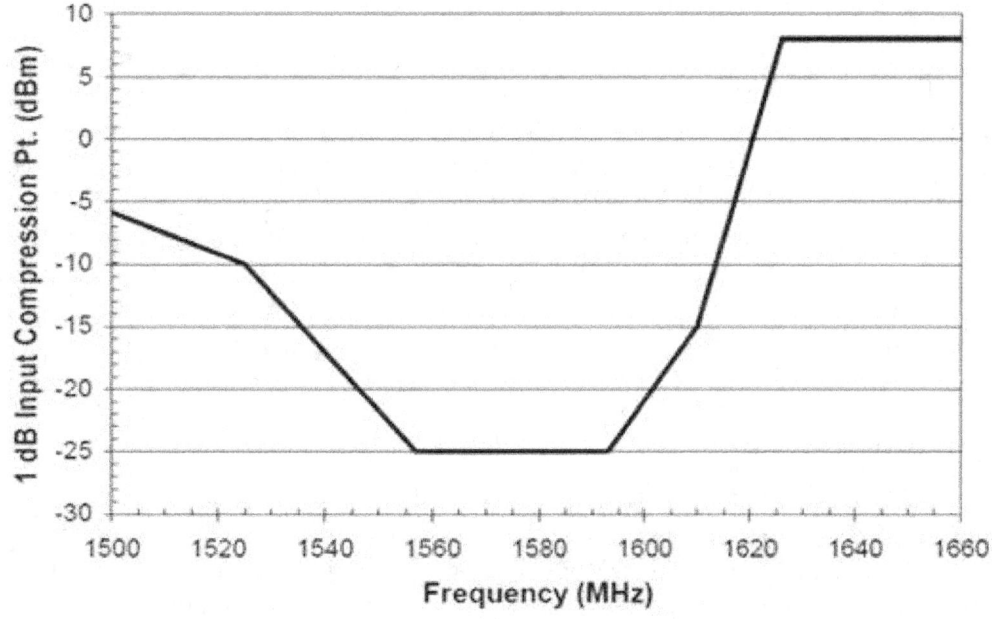

Figure 1-9. Input 1 dB Compression Point for Active Airborne Antenna

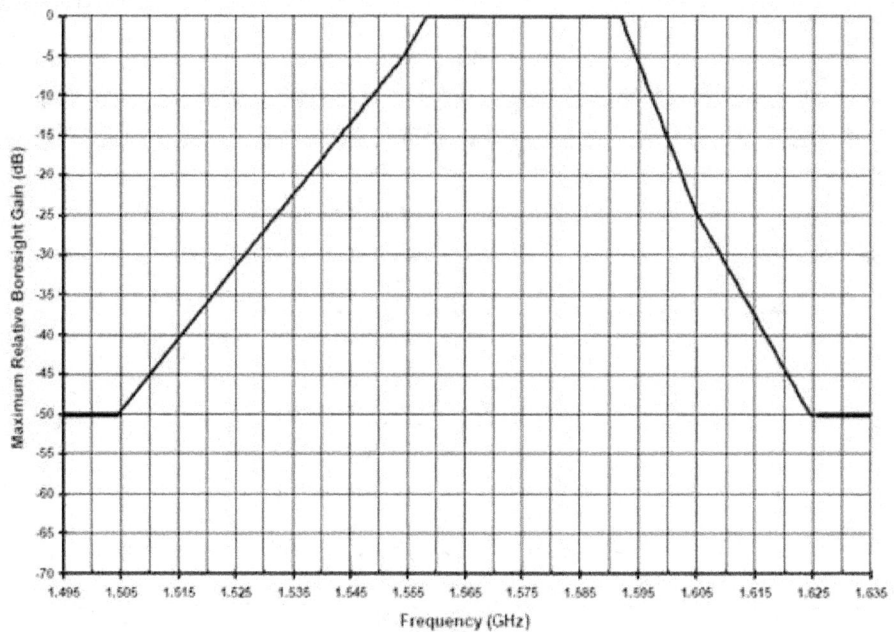

Figure 1-10. Antenna Frequency Selectivity Requirements

To satisfy operational performance requirements, airborne antennas must comply with many other low-level specifications that are too numerous to summarize here. See [3,4]. These include specifications on group delay differential vs. frequency, group delay differential vs. direction of signal arrival, environmental conditions, burnout protection, power supply interfaces. Airborne antennas also must be low-profile. Maximum and minimum cabling losses between the airborne antenna and the receiver would also need to be considered in light of the signal operating environment. A common form factor for airborne GPS antennas is specified in [7]. This form factor calls for a conformal antenna that is $4.7 \times 2.9 \times 0.75$ in^3, with the height dimension (0.75 in) only accounting for the portion of the unit protruding above the fuselage.

2.2 Airborne Receivers

Current-generation civilian airborne receivers used for IMC navigation all rely on the GPS C/A-code signal broadcast at 1575.42 MHz (L1), and typical receivers have 3-dB pre-correlation bandwidths ranging from 2 to 20 MHz. WAAS-capable airborne receivers additionally rely on L1 C/A-like signals that are broadcast by geostationary satellites, which provide differential corrections and integrity data to the aircraft from a ground network. LAAS airborne receivers are provided differential corrections and integrity data from a very high frequency (VHF) datalink.

Well over 100,000 airborne GPS receivers have been sold to date in the United States. Approximately 60,000 of these include both GPS and WAAS functionality. Typical GPS equipment for large air transport aircraft are redundant (two or three) multi-mode receivers (MMRs). These receivers are referred to as multi-mode, because they also provide other navigation sensor functionality (e.g., Instrument Landing System [ILS], very high frequency omnirange [VOR], and marker beacon). They are connected via an aircraft bus to external antennas, flight displays, flight management systems, autopilot, and other avionics that require position, velocity, or timing (PVT) inputs (e.g., automatic dependent surveillance broadcast [ADS-B] equipment and terrain awareness warning systems [TAWS]).

General aviation and business/regional aircraft may include distributed navigation systems similar to those employed by air transport aircraft. However, a more common configuration for general aviation aircraft is the use of a panel mount unit. A typical panel-mount unit integrates GPS/SBAS with ILS/VOR, and VHF communications functionality.

Minimum performance standards for airborne GNSS receivers are provided in [8-11] for standalone airborne equipment, in [12 - 14] for GPS/Wide Area Augmentation System (WAAS) equipment, and in [15, 16] for GPS/Local Area Augmentation System equipment. Performance requirements are far too numerous to describe completely here, so the interested reader is urged to refer to the referenced standards. Some particularly challenging performance requirements include:

- Root-mean-square (RMS) pseudorange measurement error ≤ 15 centimeters at minimum GPS C/A-code signal levels (-128.5 dBm out of a reference 3 dBil user antenna as specified in [17] adjusted by the minimum airborne antenna gain of -5.5 dBic at 5 degree elevation angle as specified in [3, 4]).

- SBAS message loss rate less than 1 message per 1000 at minimum specified SBAS C/A-code signal level. (One SBAS message is 250 bits in length, and the SBAS signal data is sent at 250 bits/second as specified in [14]).

The standards also include detailed test procedures that include laboratory testing with a signal simulator. In the acquisition-reacquisition tests [11,14], only five signals are simulated, and the tests always include one satellite (GPS or WAAS, depending on the specific test) at minimum specified power levels (minimum specified signal-in-space level adjusted by minimum airborne antenna gain at 5 degrees elevation angle). When testing receiver measurement accuracy additional satellites at the minimum satellite power are permitted. However, the measurement accuracy is tested in the pseudorange domain and is *not* dependent on the satellite geometry. It is not permissible to lose track of any satellite during testing, and indeed the quality of the tracking and data demodulation must meet numerous performance requirements including the RMS pseudorange error and SBAS message loss rate requirements described above. See [11, 14, 16] for details.

As with the airborne antennas, requirements for airborne receivers have been harmonized internationally within the ICAO SARPs [5]. A summary of the high-level performance requirements for each phase of flight supported by current generation equipment is provided in Table 1-2. It should be noted that the most challenging requirements are the very stringent integrity levels, which for instance only permit two or fewer occurrences out of 10 million Category I precision approach operations for the GPS sensor to provide position errors exceeding the associated horizontal and alert levels, without an alert to the pilot within 6 seconds.

Table 1-2. ICAO GNSS Performance Requirements

Operation	Horizontal/ Vertical Accuracy (95%)	Integrity Level	Horizontal/ Vertical Alert Limit	Time-to-alert	Continuity	Availability
En-route	3.7 km N/A	$1 - 1 \times 10^{-7}$ /h	3.7 to 7.4 km N/A	5 min	$1 - 1 \times 10^{-4}$/h to $1 - 1 \times 10^{-8}$/h	0.99 to 0.99999
Terminal	0.74 km N/A	$1 - 1 \times 10^{-7}$ /h	1.85 km N/A	15 s	$1 - 1 \times 10^{-4}$/h to $1 - 1 \times 10^{-8}$/h	0.999 to 0.99999
Non-precision approach	220 m N/A	$1 - 1 \times 10^{-7}$ /h	556 m N/A	10 s	$1 - 1 \times 10^{-4}$/h to $1 - 1 \times 10^{-8}$/h	0.99 to 0.99999
Approach with vertical guidance (APV)-I	16 m 20 m	$1 - 2 \times 10^{-7}$ /approach	40 m 50 m	10 s	$1 - 8 \times 10^{-6}$ in any 15 s	0.99 to 0.99999
Approach with vertical guidance (APV)-II	16 m 8 m	$1 - 2 \times 10^{-7}$ /approach	40 m 20 m	6 s	$1 - 8 \times 10^{-6}$ in any 15 s	0.99 to 0.99999
Category I	16 m 4 to 6 m	$1 - 2 \times 10^{-7}$ /approach	40 m 10 to 35 m	6 s	$1 - 8 \times 10^{-6}$ in any 15 s	0.99 to 0.99999

Source: [5]

Airborne equipment are required to meet all of the applicable performance specifications in the presence of interference up to those levels shown in Figure 1-11 for standalone GPS/WAAS, and GPS/LAAS airborne equipment and Figure 1-12 for older airborne supplemental navigation GPS equipment. (Note that these interference levels are system level, i.e., they must be met by the receiver/antenna combination for the installed equipment, and are referenced to the output port of the passive antenna whether the antenna is passive or active). For interference centered at frequencies within the range of 1553.8 – 1593.8 MHz, the maximum tolerable interference levels for standalone GPS, GPS/WAAS and GPS/LAAS avionics specified in [11,14,16] are a function of the bandwidth of the interference (presumed to be noise-like with a rectangular power spectral density). The bottom curve in Figure 1-11 over this range of frequencies is for continuous-wave (CW; i.e., tone) interference, and the top curve in this figure for interference with 1 MHz bandwidth. For interference at center frequencies outside of the range of 1553.8 – 1593.8 MHz, only CW levels are specified.

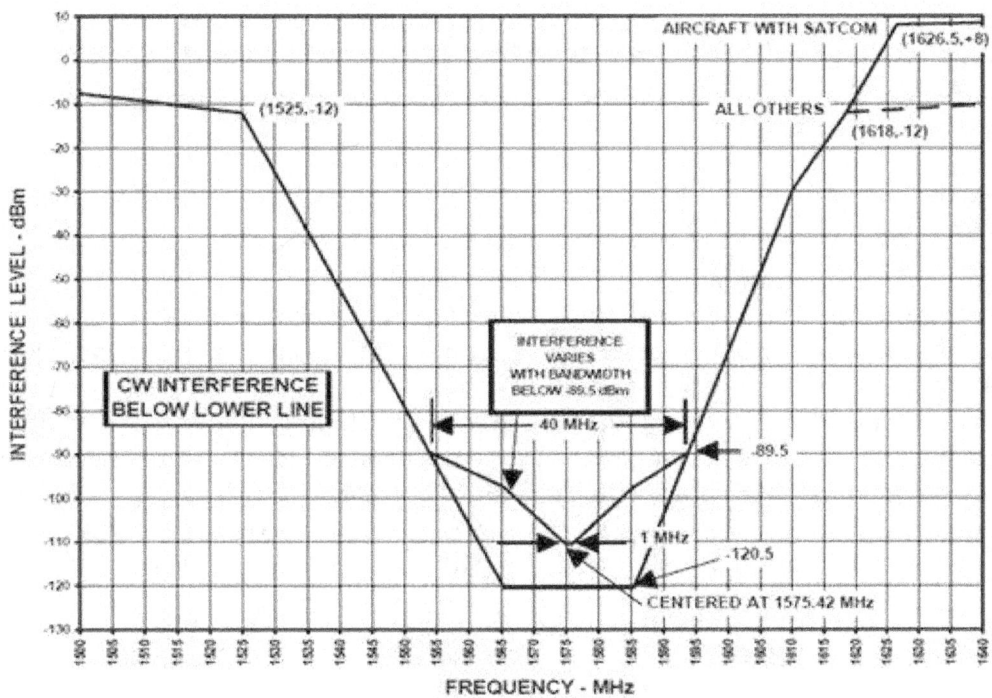

Figure 1-11. Maximum Tolerable Interference Levels for Airborne GPS/WAAS Equipment
(referenced to the passive antenna output port)

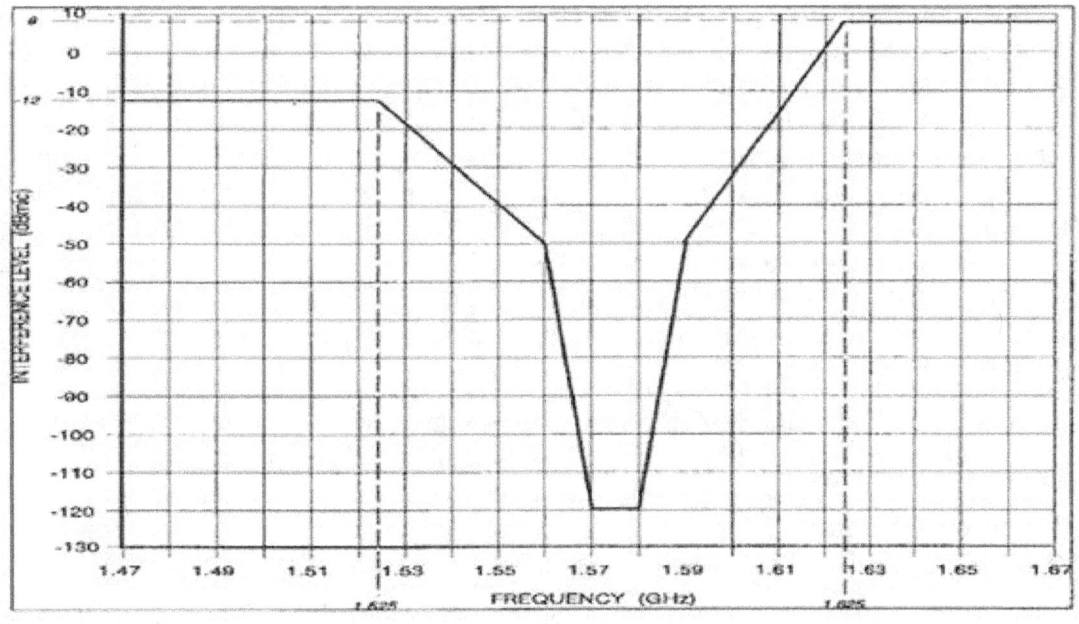

Figure 1-12. Maximum Tolerable CW Interference Levels for Airborne Supplemental
Navigation GPS Equipment [8]

2.3 Integrated Equipment

Airborne GPS receivers may be used to provide PVT data to other on-board equipment, including TAWS and ADS-B equipment. Such installations may place additional requirements upon the GPS receiver output.

3. Ground Equipment

To meet the integrity requirements for aircraft navigation, ICAO defines several types of augmentations. Aircraft-based augmentation systems (ABAS) include methods to provide integrity using redundant GPS measurements (i.e., receiver autonomous integrity monitoring [RAIM]) or other on-board sensors (e.g., inertial, barometer-altimeter). The other types of augmentation require GPS receivers on the ground in conjunction with processing facilities to generate differential corrections and integrity data to be supplied to the aircraft. Satellite-based Augmentation Systems (SBAS) provide this functionality using a ground network with GPS receivers widely dispersed over a large geographic region. Ground-based augmentation systems (GBAS) provide this functionality using redundant GPS receivers located on an airport.

GPS receivers are used also for timing purposes for critical Federal Aviation Administration systems.

3.1 WAAS Network

The U.S. SBAS program is referred to as WAAS. The WAAS is a safety critical system that augments GPS by providing additional ranging with geostationary earth orbit (GEO) satellites, improved accuracy with differential corrections, and safety with integrity monitoring. The WAAS system consists of 38 reference stations, three master stations, and six Ground uplink Subsystems supporting three L1/L5 GEO satellites. WAAS Reference Stations (WRSs) are located throughout the Continental United States, Hawaii, Alaska, and Puerto Rico and internationally with stations in Mexico and Canada. Reference stations are located primarily at FAA Air traffic control facilities but some are located at flight service stations, airports and for remote stations in specially constructed shelters. The WRSs utilize the Omni directional NW2225 antenna and G-II reference receiver. Each of the redundant WRS receivers includes the capability to track the GPS and SBAS L1 C/A-code signals and additionally the GPS L1 and L2 P(Y)-code signals using semi-codeless processing techniques. Further details on this equipment are provided in the next sections.

Ground uplink subsystems used with the WAAS GEOs are located at commercial earth station terminals at Woodbine (Maryland), Brewster (Washington), Littleton (Colorado), Napa (California), Santa Paula (California) and Paumalu (Hawaii). These sites also utilize the NW2225 antenna as well as high gain/high directional antennas for L1 and L5 downlink signals. The L1 signal processing in the GUST receiver is the same as with the G-II reference receiver.

WAAS has been operating since 1998 and has been supporting safety of life operations since 2003. The system, at present, supports en route through category I-equivalent (referred to as "LPV") precision approach operations, see, e.g., [18, 19].

3.1.1 WAAS Antenna Assemblies

3.1.1.2 Omni Directional Antenna Characteristics

WAAS Reference Stations (WRSs) and Ground Uplink Subsystems (GUSs) both utilize the NW2225 antenna. The requirements this antenna must satisfy are documented in unit and system level WAAS documentation. Table 1-3 provides an excerpt from this documentation for key L1 antenna requirements useful for evaluation of interference effects. Additionally, Figure 1-13 provides actual performance of the antenna's integrated Filter/LNA for frequencies near the L1 passband.

Table 1-3. Key L1 Antenna Characteristics for NW2225

Antenna pattern gain for RHCP signal
Gain L1
    Elevation = 5°
    Elevation = 90° (Zenith)
	
	≥ -9.0 dBic
	≥ 3.0 dBic

Axial ratio	4.0 dB, Max.
RF Gain	48 ± 3 dB
Maximum Input Signal w/o Damage	+20 dBm, CW
1 dB Compression Point	+10 dBm, Min,
Noise Figure	≤ 2.0 dB @25° C
Attenuation ≥ -80 dB Attenuation near L1 -80 dB	Non-operating frequencies @ ± 50 of 1575.42 MHz (Max)

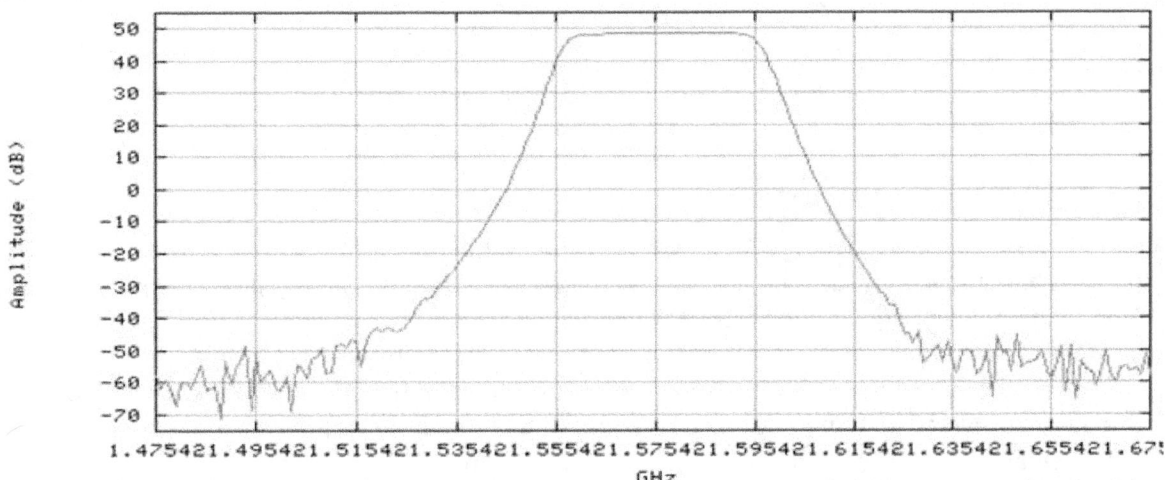

Figure 1-13. WAAS Antenna (NW2225) L1 Signal Conditioning Performance

1-17

3.1.1.2 Downlink Antenna Characteristics

The GUS also uses a High Directional/High Gain antenna for receiving the L1 and L5 downlink signals from the WAAS GEO satellites. Key performance requirements for this antenna are reflected in Figure 1-14 where the max gain has been normalized to zero dB. The gain of the antenna at boresight is nominally 28 dB.

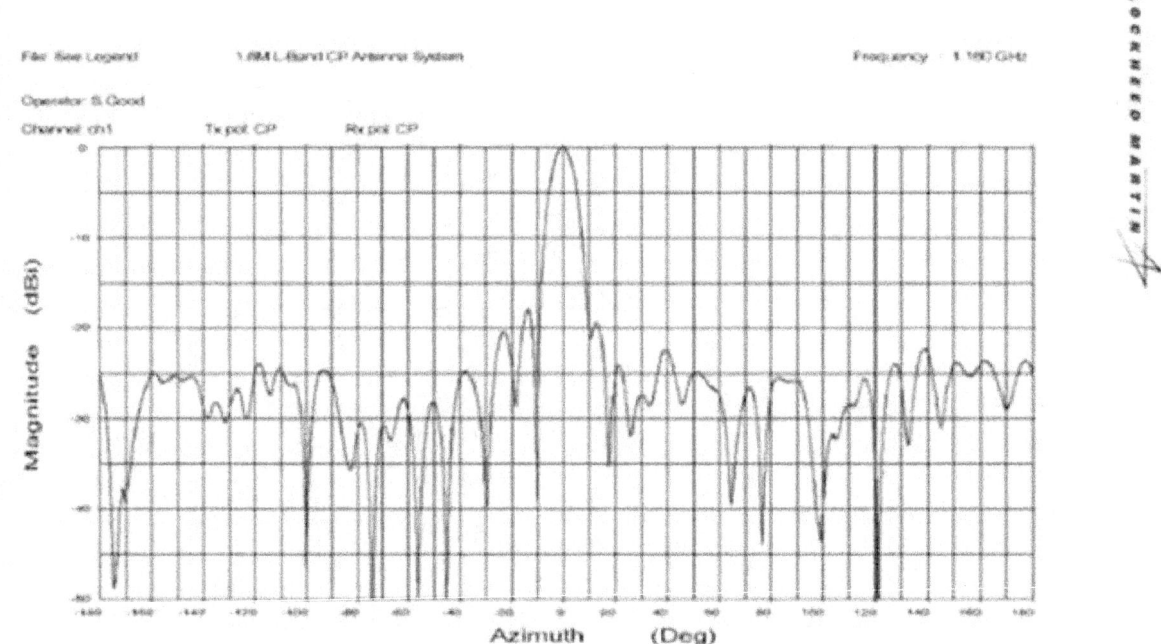

Figure 1-14. GUS Antenna Gain Pattern

3.1.2 WAAS Network Receivers

L1 signal processing provided by the receiver is essentially identical for reference station and ground uplink applications in WAAS. As with the WAAS antenna, signal processing requirements relevant to RF interference performance are documented in unit and system level WAAS documentation. This documentation contains other requirements too numerous to list in this document related to signal acquisition, accuracy and data demodulation performance. For receiver performance pertaining to interference, the specifications require the receiver provide filter attenuation for out-of-band emissions of 50 dB or greater. For out-of-band emissions within ± 50 MHz of the L1, L2 and L5 center frequencies, the receiver provides filter attenuation characteristics as specified in Figure 1-15. The receiver may achieve these attenuation characteristics through a combination of RF and IF filters.

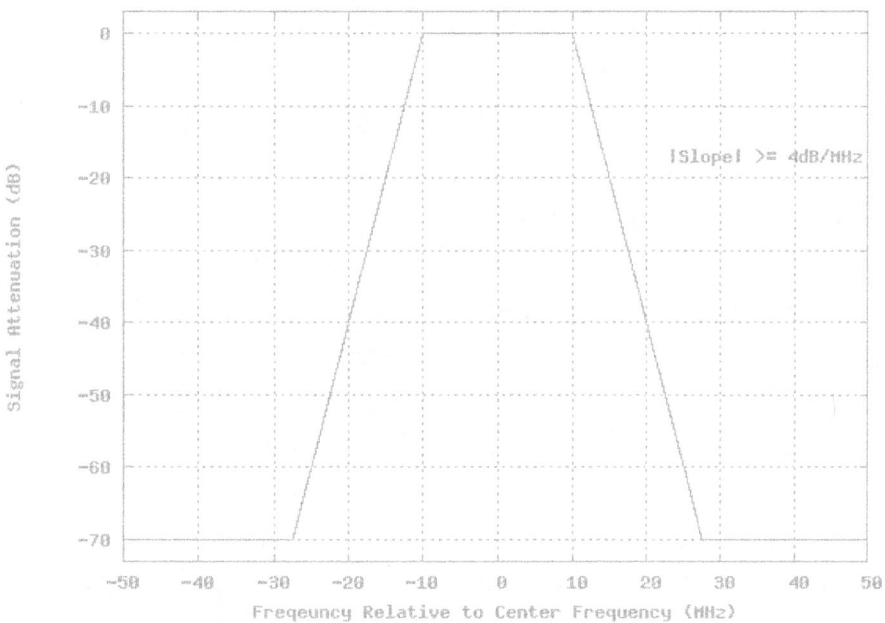

Figure 1-15. RF Attenuation Near L1 L2 and L5 Passbands

Out-of-band rejection characteristics are intended to be satisfied with the combination of antenna and receiver filtering and receiver processing gain. Therefore, after initial signal acquisition and steady-state operation has commenced with the receiver, a GPS/WAAS antenna/receiver can operate in the presence of a single CW interferer that does not exceed the interference to signal power ratio by more than the levels shown in Table 1-4 (further illustrated in Figure 1-16). The interference signal is relative to the minimum GPS/WAAS signal levels. The signal suppression allocations are as follows: 80 dB for the antenna filter, 50 dB for receiver out of band, and 24 dB for receiver in-band processing gain. Note that CW was specified for out-of-band emissions to constrain test requirements.

Table 1-4. Out of Band Rejection Characteristics

Interference Frequency, f (MHz)	Interference to Signal Power Ratio (dB)
800 < f ≤ 1106.45	≥150 dB
1106.45 < f ≤ 1166.45	+150 − 2*(f-1106.45) dB
1237.6 < f ≤ 1297.6	+30 + 2*(f - 1237.6) dB
1297.6 < f ≤ 1505.42	≥150 dB
1505.42 < f ≤ 1565.42	+150 - 2*(f-1505.42) dB
1585.42 < f ≤ 1645.42	+30 + 2*(f - 1585.42) dB
1645.42 < f < 2000 for L1	≥150 dB
1645.42 < f < 1700 for L2	≥150 dB

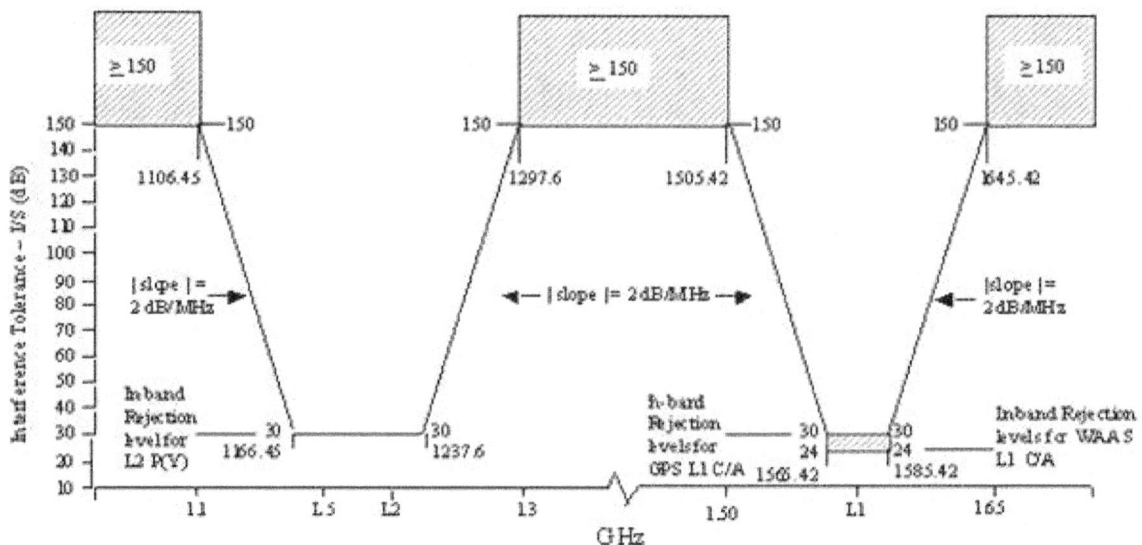

Figure 1-16. Out of Band Rejection Characteristics for CW Interference

3.2 GBAS

The U.S. GBAS program was originally referred to as the Local Area Augmentation System (LAAS) but recently changed in name to adhere to international terminology. A Category I (CAT I) Non-Federal GBAS built by Honeywell International received System Design Approval (SDA) from the FAA on September 3, 2009. The Port Authority of New York/New Jersey has purchased and installed the first system at Newark Liberty International Airport. This system is expected to become operational in the near future. Several different prototype systems are installed at other locations in the United States. The FAA's GBAS Program Office is working in conjunction with industry towards the operational validation of Category II/III GBAS standards and specifications.

Current CAT I Non-Federal GBASs conform to the specifications in [20], which provide numerous performance requirements that must be met with identical maximum interference levels as those in use for GPS avionics described earlier in this document.

3.3 Timing

GPS timing receivers are used for critical purposes at numerous facilities in the national airspace system (NAS). These include Trimble Resolution T receivers for the ADS-B stations being deployed by ITT. TrueTime and Symmetricom GPS timing receivers are used for timing for several automation systems. These are commercial timing products that should be covered by the TWG's timing receiver category.

4 Operational Scenarios

The following operational scenarios are extracted from [6]. For each operational scenario, all applicable performance requirements from [14, 16] must be met in the presence of both LightSquared emissions (considering constraints on the siting of the base stations near airports to protect mobile satellite services) and all known other interference sources as identified in [6].

4.1 En Route/Terminal Area

For the en route flight phase aircraft are generally constrained to be at an altitude of at least 500 feet above structures or terrain in uncongested areas and at least 1000 feet above structures or terrain in congested areas. In the terminal area on the initial approach segment the flight path is a minimum of 1000 feet above any obstacles. On the intermediate approach segment the flight path is a minimum of 500 feet above obstacles. In these phases of flight, GNSS may be used for horizontal guidance in IMC operations. For off-board sources, the minimum RFI source separation distance to the closest terrestrial source is defined as 500 feet.

4.1.1 En Route Acquisition

The aircraft in this scenario is assumed to have been in normal, en route GNSS navigation for a sufficient time to have up-to-date satellite ephemeris data, stored position, velocity, and receiver clock bias/drift information. Normal navigation is then somehow interrupted for a short time (e.g. by a momentary aircraft power failure) and the receiver must re-establish navigation by a full "warm-start" acquisition. For this scenario, the aircraft is assumed to be in level flight at a representative limiting-case altitude of 18,000 feet (5.5 km).

4.1.2 En Route Tracking/Data Demodulation

For the en route tracking / demodulation scenario, the aircraft is assumed to be in level flight at a representative limiting-case altitude of 18,000 feet (5.5 km) above ground level. Both GPS and SBAS (e.g., WAAS) satellite signals are considered. The usefulness of the SBAS signals for integrity and error correction depends on the aircraft position being within an area covered by SBAS ground reference stations. Certain components of total RFI vary as a function of location, (e.g., GNSS self-interference, terrestrial RFI). Given these two aspects, the en route GPS and SBAS scenario link analyses may be performed at different limiting-case locations.

4.1.3 Terminal Area Tracking/Data Demodulation

For this terminal area scenario, the aircraft is assumed to be in level flight with its GNSS antenna at an intermediate value between the en route and Category I precision approach scenarios. The airborne GPS antenna height is 1756 feet (535.2 m).

4.2 Non-precision Approach Tracking/Data Demodulation

For non-precision approach operations, [6] recommends using a 100 foot (30.5 m) separation to a ground-based obstacle (source of interference) and the Category I airborne antenna gain pattern below the aircraft (see Figure 1-8).

4.3 Category I Precision Approach Tracking/Data Demodulation

For category I (CAT I) precision approach, [6] recommends using a 96.7 foot (29.5 m) obstacle clearance surface (OCS) distance (distance to closest possible ground-based interference source) and a 175 foot (53.3 m) above-ground GNSS airborne antenna height.

4.4 Category II/III Precision Approach Tracking/Data Demodulation

For a CAT II/III precision approach, [6] recommends using a 70 foot (21.3 m) OCS distance (distance to closest possible ground-based interference source) and a 85.1 foot (25.9 m) above-ground GNSS airborne antenna height. Such operations require a CAT II/III GBAS to be installed at the airport.

4.5 Surface Acquisition and Tracking/Data Demodulation

This operational scenario encompasses surface operations where the aircraft is at the gate or taxiing. For this scenario, the GNSS aircraft antenna height is assumed to be 4 m (a nominal height for a regional or business jet). The aircraft is either stationary or in a slow taxi. GNSS receiver signal tracking and acquisition should be tested in the scenario.

5 Future Considerations

Work is currently underway domestically and internationally towards the development of multi-frequency, multi-GNSS standards. Such standards will support additional signals in the 1559 – 1610 MHz band, including the Galileo open service and GPS L1C signals that use a multiplexed binary offset carrier modulation (MBOC). The power spectral density of MBOC is much broader than the GPS L1 C/A-code and may require wider bandwidth avionics.

Future GNSS avionics, in order to accrue the benefits of new civil signals on other frequencies (e.g., GPS L5 at 1176.45 MHz), will require new airborne multi-band antennas. These will likely be stacked patch antennas, and it is possible that their gain performance at L1 will suffer in comparison to existing antennas. Additionally, in the future, GNSS avionics may be required to meet more demanding performance requirements. These factors, together, will tighten current slim margins on interference budgets (see, e.g., [6]) for airborne GNSS equipment.

REFERENCES:

[1] FAA, *Passive Airborne Global Positioning System Antenna*, Technical Standard Order (TSO) C144a, Federal Aviation Administration, Washington, D.C., 30 March 2007. (This FAA regulatory document invokes the performance requirements in RTCA DO-228, Change 1).

[2] RTCA, *Minimum Operational Performance Standards for Global Navigation Satellite System (GNSS) Airborne Antenna Equipment*, Washington, D.C., RTCA DO-228, including Change 1, January 11, 2000.

[3] FAA, *Active Airborne Global Navigation Satellite System (GNSS) Antenna*, Technical Standard Order (TSO) C190, Federal Aviation Administration, Washington, D.C., 30 March 2007. (This FAA regulatory document invokes the performance requirements in RTCA DO-301).

[4] RTCA, *Minimum Operational Performance Standards for Global Navigation Satellite System (GNSS) Airborne Active Antenna Equipment for the L1 Frequency Band*, Washington, D.C., RTCA DO-301, December 13, 2006.

[5] ICAO, Annex 10 to the Convention of International Civil Aviation, Montreal, Canada, Jul. 12, 2010, vol. I, Radio Navigation Aids, Amendment 85.

[6] RTCA, *Assessment of Radio Frequency Interference Relevant to the GNSS L1 Frequency Band*, Washington, D.C., RTCA DO-235B, March 13, 2008.

[7] ARINC, *Global Navigation Satellite System (GNSS) sensor*, Annapolis, MD, ARINC Characteristic 743A-4, Dec. 2001.

[8] FAA, Airborne Supplemental Navigation Equipment Using the Global Positioning System (GPS), Technical Standard Order (TSO) C129a, Federal Aviation Administration, Washington, D.C., 20 February 1996. (This FAA regulatory document invokes the performance requirements in RTCA DO-208, Change 1).

[9] RTCA, *Minimum Operational Performance Standards for Airborne Supplemental Navigation Equipment Using Global Positioning System (GPS)*, Washington, D.C., RTCA DO-208, July 1991.

[10] FAA, *Airborne Supplemental Navigation Sensors for Global Positioning System Equipment using Aircraft-Based Augmentation*, Technical Standard Order (TSO) C196, Federal Aviation Administration, Washington, D.C., 21 September 2009. (This FAA regulatory document invokes the performance requirements in RTCA DO-316).

[11] RTCA, *Minimum Operational Performance Standards for Global Positioning System/Aircraft-based Augmentation System Airborne Equipment*, Washington, D.C., RTCA DO-316, 14 April 2009.

[12] FAA, *Airborne Navigation Sensors Using the Global Positioning System Augmented by the Satellite Based Augmentation System*, Technical Standard Order (TSO) C145c, Federal Aviation Administration, Washington, D.C., 2 May 2008.

[13] FAA, *Stand-Alone Airborne Navigation Equipment Using the Global Positioning System Augmented by the Satellite Based Augmentation System*, Technical Standard Order (TSO) C146c, Federal Aviation Administration, Washington, D.C., 9 May 2008.

[14]   RTCA, *Minimum Operational Performance Standards for Global Positioning System/Wide Area Augmentation System Airborne Equipment*, Washington, D.C., RTCA DO-229D, Dec. 13, 2006.

[15]   FAA, *Ground Based Augmentation System Positioning and Navigation Equipment*, Technical Standard Order (TSO) C161a, Federal Aviation Administration, Washington, D.C., 17 December 2009.

[16]   RTCA, *Minimum Operational Performance Standards for Global Positioning System Local Area Augmentation System Airborne Equipment*, Washington, D.C., RTCA DO-253C, December 16, 2008.

[17]   U.S. Air Force, GPS Directorate, Los Angeles Air Force Base, *Navstar GPS Space Segment/User Navigation User Interfaces*, El Segundo, CA, IS-GPS-200D, Mar. 2006.

2.   Subtask 2 - Model Characterization of the Terrestrial Broadband Network

Task Statement

In cooperation with the LightSquared Working Group, develop a baseline model characterization of the planned initial and fully deployed broadband network, including ATC locations and siting assumptions/limitations. Identify user handset planning assumptions as appropriate.

LightSquared Ancillary Terrestrial Component (ATC) Technical Parameters

LightSquared plans for three spectrum phases for its broadcast signal:

- Phase 0: One 5 MHz channel : 1550.2 MHz- 1555.2 MHz, 62 dBm EIRP per 5 MHz channel

- Phase 1: Two 5 MHz channel : 1526.3 MHz -1531.3 MHz & 1550.2 MHz - 1555.2 MHz, 62 dBm EIRP per 5 MHz channel

- Phase 2: Two 10 MHz channel : 1526 MHz -1536 MHz & 1545.2 MHz - 1555.2 MHz, 62 dBm EIRP per 10 MHz channel

LightSquared has stated that their intention is to always operate ATCs at least 4 MHz away from the GPS band edge at 1559 MHz. Using LTE technology (OFDM, orthogonal frequency division multiplex modulation), each 10 MHz channel will have 1 MHz internal guard band, including 500 KHz on each side of the channel. LightSquared plans to deploy 20W per channel per sector. Each sector will have two transmit chains so a total power of 40W per sector per channel will be transmitted from each base station tower. Given there are three sectors, that results in a total of 120W per tower per channel. In LightSquared plans for spectrum Phases 1 and 2 there will be two channels so the result is 80W per sector or 240W per tower. Further, LightSquared plans to deploy a maximum of 62 dBm EIRP per channel and with two channels per sector, total EIRP per sector will then be 65 dBm per sector. Vertical cross polarization will be used for ATC transmissions.

Table 2-1. LightSquared Spectrum Deployment Phases

Development Phase	Channel Quantity and Size	Channel Locations	Nominal BTS Channel EIRP
Phase 0	One (1) 5MHz FDD	DL: 1550.2-1555.2MHz UL: 1651.7-1656.7 MHz	32 dBW (25 dBW/MHz)
Phase 1A	Two(2) 5MHz FDD	**Channel 1** DL: 1526.3–1531.3MHz UL: 1627.8-1632.8 MHz **Channel 2** DL: 1550.2-1555.2 MHz UL: 1651.7-1656.7 MHz	32 dBW (25 dBW/MHz)
Phase 2	Two(2) 10 MHz FDD	**Channel 1** DL: 1526-1536 MHz UL: 1627.5-1637.5 MHz **Channel 2** DL: 1545.2-1555.2 MHz UL: 1646.7-1656.7 MHz	32 dBW (22 dBW/MHz)

The distance between transmitters depends on type of morphology around each site as well as other capacity and coverage considerations. The maximum number of LightSquared network handsets a single ATC tower can support depends on the demand and service profile of each mobile device / handset, a typical site with two 10MHz channels can support 1200 users in active state and a much higher number in dormant state. LightSquared expects that the distance between transmitters would typically be:

- Dense urban environment: 0.4-0.8 km

- Urban environment: 1-2 km

- Suburban environment: 2-4 km

- Rural environment: 5-8 km

LightSquared User Handset Technical Parameters

When communicating with LightSquared towers, LightSquared mobile devices will transmit in L-band (1626.5 MHz -1660.5 MHz). LightSquared intends to use 10% of the total channel bandwidth as a guard band. For example, each 10 MHz channel will have 1 MHz guard band; 500 kHz on each side of the channel. LightSquared anticipates that some future devices may also utilize additional terrestrial cellular bands for transmission, but the specific bands are not yet confirmed. Linear polarization will be used for handset transmissions, with a maximum 23 dBm EIRP.

ATCt Mobile Terminal

- Maximum fundamental EIRP: -7 dBW

- Maximum unwanted EIRP: -90 dBW/MHz (1559-1605 MHz)

- Modulation: LTE (OFDM), 5 MHz occupied bandwidth

- Carrier frequency: 1654.2 MHz

- Antenna height: 1.8 m (est.)

As with the ATC, LightSquared plans three spectrum phases for its user handsets:

- Phase 0: One 5 MHz channel: 1651.7 MHz - 1656.7 MHz, 23 dBm maximum EIRP per user and smallest bandwidth a user can transmit is 180 KHz

- Phase 1: Two 5 MHz channels: 1627.8 MHz - 1632.8 MHz & 1651.7 MHz - 1656.7 MHz, 23 dBm maximum EIRP per user and smallest bandwidth a user can transmit is 180 KHz

- Phase 2: Two 10 MHz channels: 1627.5 MHz - 1637.5 MHz & 1646.7 MHz - 1656.7 MHz, 23 dBm maximum EIRP per user and smallest bandwidth a user can transmit is 180 KHz

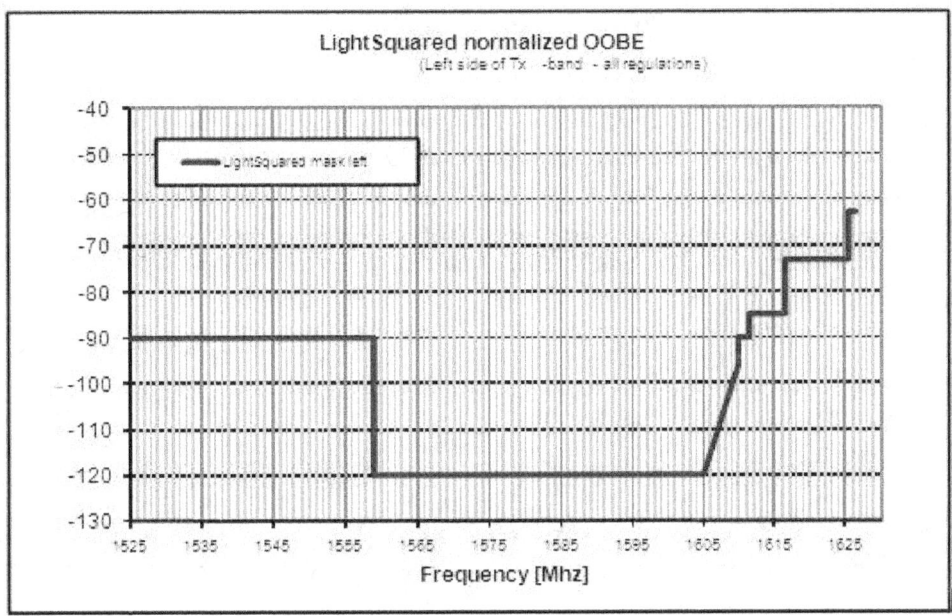

Figure 2-1. LightSquared OOBE requirements (normalized dBm/Hz from 1626.5 MHz) for LTE 10 MHz

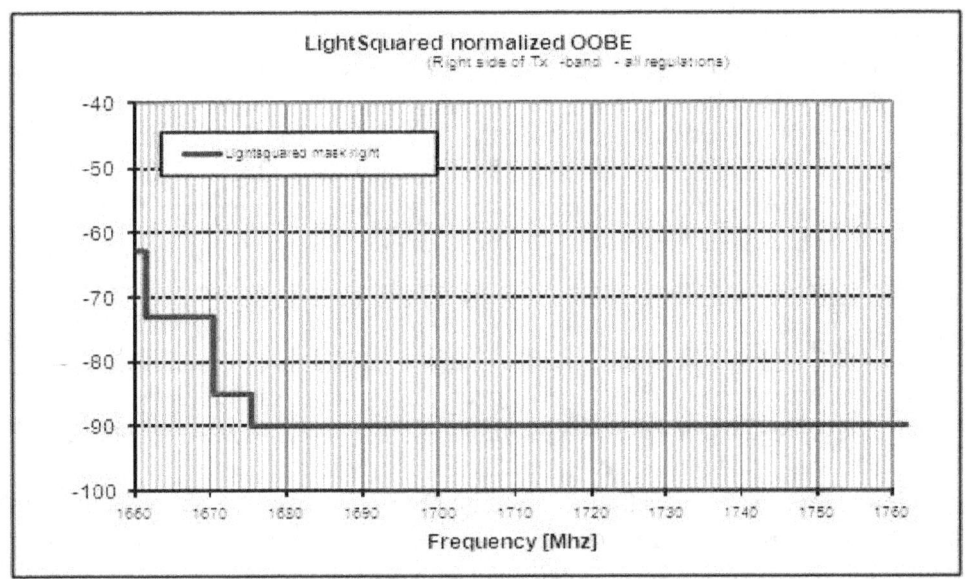

Figure 2-2. LightSquared OOBE requirements (normalized to dBm/Hz from 1660.5 MHz) for LTE 10 MHz

3. Subtask 3 - RF Interference in Operational Scenarios

Task Statement

In conjunction with federal and commercial GPS technical experts, develop operational scenarios representative of the full range of anticipated effects to GPS receiver use (including characterization by existing GPS receiver categories where possible) as well as deployed federal and commercial GPS-dependent systems or networks. The scenarios assessed shall consider federal and state government and commercial communities' current and planned use of GPS and GPS applications.

Operational Scenarios

Aviation

The following operational scenarios are extracted from [6]. For each operational scenario, all applicable performance requirements from [14, 16] must be met in the presence of both LightSquared emissions (considering constraints on the siting of the base stations near airports to protect mobile satellite services) and all known other interference sources as identified in [6].

En Route/Terminal Area

For the en route flight phase aircraft are generally constrained to be at an altitude of at least 500 feet above structures or terrain in uncongested areas and at least 1000 feet above structures or terrain in congested areas. In the terminal area on the initial approach segment the flight path is a minimum of 1000 feet above any obstacles. On the intermediate approach segment the flight path is a minimum of 500 feet above obstacles. In these phases of flight, GNSS may be used for horizontal guidance in IMC operations. For off-board sources, the minimum RFI source separation distance to the closest terrestrial source is defined as 500 feet.

En Route Acquisition

The aircraft in this scenario is assumed to have been in normal, en route GNSS navigation for a sufficient time to have up-to-date satellite ephemeris data, stored position, velocity, and receiver clock bias/drift information. Normal navigation is then somehow interrupted for a short time (e.g. by a momentary aircraft power failure) and the receiver must re-establish navigation by a full "warm-start" acquisition. For this scenario, the aircraft is assumed to be in level flight at a representative limiting-case altitude of 18,000 feet (5.5 km).

En Route Tracking/Data Demodulation

For the en route tracking / demodulation scenario, the aircraft is assumed to be in level flight at a representative limiting-case altitude of 18,000 feet (5.5 km) above ground level. Both GPS and SBAS (e.g., WAAS) satellite signals are considered. The usefulness of the SBAS signals for integrity and error correction depends on the aircraft position being within an area covered by SBAS ground reference stations. Certain components of total RFI vary as a function of location, (e.g., GNSS self-interference, terrestrial RFI). Given these two aspects, the en route GPS and SBAS scenario link analyses may be performed at different limiting-case locations.

Terminal Area Tracking/Data Demodulation

For this terminal area scenario, the aircraft is assumed to be in level flight with its GNSS antenna at an intermediate value between the en route and Category I precision approach scenarios. The airborne GPS antenna height is 1756 feet (535.2 m).

Non-precision Approach Tracking/Data Demodulation

For non-precision approach operations, [6] recommends using a 100 foot (30.5 m) separation to a ground-based obstacle (source of interference) and the Category I airborne antenna gain pattern below the aircraft.

Category I Precision Approach Tracking/Data Demodulation

For category I (CAT I) precision approach, [6] recommends using a 96.7 foot (29.5 m) obstacle clearance surface (OCS) distance (distance to closest possible ground-based interference source) and a 175 foot (53.3 m) above-ground GNSS airborne antenna height.

Category II/III Precision Approach Tracking/Data Demodulation

For a CAT II/III precision approach, [6] recommends using a 70 foot (21.3 m) OCS distance (distance to closest possible ground-based interference source) and a 85.1 foot (25.9 m) above-ground GNSS airborne antenna height. Such operations require a CAT II/III GBAS to be installed at the airport.

Surface Acquisition and Tracking/Data Demodulation

This operational scenario encompasses surface operations where the aircraft is at the gate or taxiing. For this scenario, the GNSS aircraft antenna height is assumed to be 4 m (a nominal height for a regional or business jet). The aircraft is either stationary or in a slow taxi. GNSS receiver signal tracking and acquisition should be tested in the scenario.

Cellular

Cellular Telephone AGPS Use Cases

The three primary use case examples for GPS receivers in cellular telephones are: E911 Location; Location-Based Services; and Real-Time Navigation. This is not an all-inclusive list, but the three groups above are representative of typical AGPS use in the context of cellular telephones. Each of these three use cases is associated with unique signal level and propagation aspects, driven, in part, by device orientation and proximity to the user.

E911 Location

During an E911 call, the cellular telephone is expected to obtain a fix within 20 seconds to an accuracy of 50 meters 67% of the time and an accuracy of 150 meters 95% of the time. These performance criteria are in alignment with FCC E911 requirements. During an E911 call, the cellular telephone must be capable of meeting the location accuracy requirements described above while the device is held to the user's ear, which may affect the manufacturer's selection of antenna design and location.

Location-Based Services (LBS)

This use case provides cellular telephone users with information concerning businesses, activities, events, etc., located or taking place near the user's current location. Typically, in this use case the cellular telephone is oriented such that the display is easy to read, which may imply that the GPS antenna is facing away from the sky.

Real-Time Navigation

This use case allows the user to utilize his cellular telephone as a navigation device. Like location-based services above, the cellular telephone will typically be oriented such that it does not have a direct view of the sky. In addition, the cellular telephone may be situated inside a moving vehicle where the GPS signal strength is further compromised and fading is prevalent.

Cellular Telephone Non-AGPS Use Case

E911 Roaming

In instances where a cellular telephone is roaming onto another system, the telephone may not be able to receive network assist information from the roaming network. In these instances, E911 location information is determined by the cellular phone in an independent fashion using GPS in an autonomous mode.

General Location/Navigation

PND Use Case 1: Suburban

Suburban, tree lined environment mounted on dash of vehicle. Frequent changes of direction, obscuration of signals by the roof of the car, signal attenuation through windscreen, mild dynamics. Unit needs the ability to lock on to the correct road and navigate turns successfully. Need to distinguish between adjacent roads and ramps.

PND Use Case 2

Urban Canyon Urban canyon environment mounted on dash of vehicle. Frequent changes of direction, obscuration of signals by the roof of the car, blockage of satellites in view by tall buildings, signal attenuation through windscreen, mild dynamics. Unit needs the ability to lock on to the correct road and navigate turns successfully. Need to distinguish between adjacent roads and ramps.

Outdoor Use Case: Golfing

Open area environment. Unit is held in the hand of a user who is walking and standing. Some dynamics associated with walking with the device, partial obscuration of signals by user's body. Unit needs the ability to measure distance, track user's position, and navigate to waypoints successfully.

Outdoor Use Case: Deep Forest

Deep forest environment. Unit is held in the hand of a moving user. Some dynamics associated with walking with the device, obscuration of signals by forest canopy and body of user. Unit needs the ability to measure distance, track user's position, and navigate to waypoints successfully.

Fitness Use Case: Arm Swing Environment

Unit under test mounted on the arm of a user who is swinging their arms in a manner consistent with distance running. The unit will experience frequent heading changes and the signal will be obscured by the body at times. Stressful dynamics are associated with the arm swing. Unit needs the ability to measure distance, track user's position/velocity, and navigate to waypoints successfully.

High Precision and Precision Timing Receivers

The only operational scenario for High Precision GPS usage is stationary and would primarily reflect the distance between the LightSquared base station transmitter and the GPS receiver. The distance at which unacceptable interference would occur would be the primary consideration for High Precision GPS receivers.

Type 1: Single point mode (no Augmentation)

- Performance Measures:
- Time To First Fix (s)
- Position accuracy (m)
- Velocity accuracy (m/s)
- Time accuracy (ns)
- PVT availability (% of time, or coverage area)

Type 2: WAAS Augmentation

- Time To First Fix (s)
- Position accuracy (m)
- Velocity accuracy (m/s)
- Time accuracy (ns)
- PVT availability (% of time, or coverage area)

Type 3: DGPS+RTK (code and carrier)

- Time To First Fix (s)
- Position accuracy (m)
- Velocity accuracy (m/s)
- Time accuracy (ns)
- PVT availability (% of time, or coverage area)

Networks

The performance characteristics of networks vary greatly by network type. This information is still being gathered. *(See the final TWG Report on 15 June 2011 for this information)*.

Space-Based Receivers

Terrestrial-based scenario:

The BlackJack family of space-based receivers are each ground tested using rooftop antennas at the Jet Propulsion Laboratory for performance and burn-in for approximately 2000 hours before launch. Testing can also occur at various sites throughout the U.S. where spacecraft integration is accomplished.

Space-based Scenario:

A "worst case" scenario after launch has the occultation antenna, with up to 18 dBi antenna gain, directed toward the earth limb at the Eastern 1/3 of the continental USA. Six satellites are planned for an orbit at 520 km altitude, 24 degrees inclination, with six more at 800 km and 72 degrees.

REFERENCES:

[1]   FAA, *Passive Airborne Global Positioning System Antenna*, Technical Standard Order (TSO) C144a, Federal Aviation Administration, Washington, D.C., 30 March 2007. (This FAA regulatory document invokes the performance requirements in RTCA DO-228, Change 1).

[2]   RTCA, *Minimum Operational Performance Standards for Global Navigation Satellite System (GNSS) Airborne Antenna Equipment*, Washington, D.C., RTCA DO-228, including Change 1, January 11, 2000.

[3]   FAA, *Active Airborne Global Navigation Satellite System (GNSS) Antenna*, Technical Standard Order (TSO) C190, Federal Aviation Administration, Washington, D.C., 30 March 2007. (This FAA regulatory document invokes the performance requirements in RTCA DO-301).

[4]   RTCA, *Minimum Operational Performance Standards for Global Navigation Satellite System (GNSS) Airborne Active Antenna Equipment for the L1 Frequency Band*, Washington, D.C., RTCA DO-301, December 13, 2006.

[5]   ICAO, Annex 10 to the Convention of International Civil Aviation, Montreal, Canada, Jul. 12, 2010, vol. I, Radio Navigation Aids, Amendment 85.

[6]   RTCA, *Assessment of Radio Frequency Interference Relevant to the GNSS L1 Frequency Band*, Washington, D.C., RTCA DO-235B, March 13, 2008.

[7]   ARINC, *Global Navigation Satellite System (GNSS) sensor*, Annapolis, MD, ARINC Characteristic 743A-4, Dec. 2001.

[8]   FAA, Airborne Supplemental Navigation Equipment Using the Global Positioning System (GPS), Technical Standard Order (TSO) C129a, Federal Aviation Administration, Washington, D.C., 20 February 1996. (This FAA regulatory document invokes the performance requirements in RTCA DO-208, Change 1).

[9]   RTCA, *Minimum Operational Performance Standards for Airborne Supplemental Navigation Equipment Using Global Positioning System (GPS)*, Washington, D.C., RTCA DO-208, July 1991.

[10]   FAA, *Airborne Supplemental Navigation Sensors for Global Positioning System Equipment using Aircraft-Based Augmentation*, Technical Standard Order (TSO) C196, Federal Aviation Administration, Washington, D.C., 21 September 2009. (This FAA regulatory document invokes the performance requirements in RTCA DO-316).

[11]   RTCA, *Minimum Operational Performance Standards for Global Positioning System/Aircraft-based Augmentation System Airborne Equipment*, Washington, D.C., RTCA DO-316, 14 April 2009.

[12]   FAA, *Airborne Navigation Sensors Using the Global Positioning System Augmented by the Satellite Based Augmentation System*, Technical Standard Order (TSO) C145c, Federal Aviation Administration, Washington, D.C., 2 May 2008.

[13]   FAA, *Stand-Alone Airborne Navigation Equipment Using the Global Positioning System Augmented by the Satellite Based Augmentation System*, Technical Standard Order (TSO) C146c, Federal Aviation Administration, Washington, D.C., 9 May 2008.

[14]   RTCA, *Minimum Operational Performance Standards for Global Positioning System/Wide Area Augmentation System Airborne Equipment*, Washington, D.C., RTCA DO-229D, Dec. 13, 2006.

[15]   FAA, *Ground Based Augmentation System Positioning and Navigation Equipment*, Technical Standard Order (TSO) C161a, Federal Aviation Administration, Washington, D.C., 17 December 2009.

[16]   RTCA, *Minimum Operational Performance Standards for Global Positioning System Local Area Augmentation System Airborne Equipment*, Washington, D.C., RTCA DO-253C, December 16, 2008.

[17]   U.S. Air Force, GPS Directorate, Los Angeles Air Force Base, *Navstar GPS Space Segment/User Navigation User Interfaces*, El Segundo, CA, IS-GPS-200D, Mar. 2006.

4. Subtask 4 - Receiver Performance Metrics

Task Statement

Develop appropriate metrics to quantitatively and qualitatively assess performance degradations from both technical and operational perspectives.

Overview

The metrics used to assess performance of a receiver depend on both its intended application and the type of output the unit provides. Regardless of the type of unit under test, a signal quality metric such as carrier to noise density ratio (C/N_0), if available, is valuable to include in an evaluation because this type of metric can be extended to determine how GNSS signals at varying elevation angles will be affected in a given receiver and antenna system so performance under varying constellation and environmental conditions can be predicted.

Although the metrics of interest for a particular receiver ultimately depend both on its available output and on its operational requirements, some types that can be used in evaluating degradation effects are listed here.

- Signal strength or quality

- Pseudorange and carrier phase measurement quality

- Carrier phase measurement continuity

- Automatic gain control characteristics

- Position/Time quality

Quantities related to these metrics are collected or calculated at a rate of 1 Hz or higher (each metric as possible by receiver) and then correlated in time to LightSquared signal power present at a specified point in the receive chain (for example, at the input to the antenna filter/LNA). Position quality results may be presented as scatter plots of positions collected at various LightSquared power levels and compared to similar constellation/environment conditions without LightSquared signals present. Other results may be plotted or tabulated according to LightSquared power levels with any significant receiver degradation events indicated as appropriate. More detail on each type of metric follows.

Signal strength or quality

The preferred measurement of signal strength or quality is carrier to noise density ratio (C/N_0) but any related metric may provide insight into how the receiver perceives its operating environment at different LightSquared signal power levels. Although the presence of a strong LightSquared signal at the edge of the GNSS L1 frequency band may invalidate some receiver assumptions in computing a signal quality indicator, it still may be pertinent because some receivers use this type of indicator to determine whether required levels for acquisition and/or tracking are being met. Still, concerns regarding signal quality indicator validity may be addressed through further analysis of corresponding pseudorange and carrier phase noise.

Pseudorange and Carrier Phase Measurement Quality

A typical measure of pseudorange or carrier phase measurement quality is standard deviation of error, which is a quantity output by some receivers but can be computed for any receiver that outputs the pseudorange and/or carrier measurements with adequately high precision (typically within 0.001m). This type of metric can serve along with the signal strength or quality metric to observe changes in degradation as the received LightSquared signal strength changes.

Carrier Phase Measurement Continuity

Carrier phase measurement continuity metrics such as lock time and carrier phase cycle slips may be evaluated if the intended application of the unit under test involves carrier phase measurement processing, as in pseudorange smoothing or carrier-based positioning. Measurements may not be usable if excessive cycle slips or losses of lock occur in such applications, even if a receiver shows it is able to track satellites.

Automatic Gain Control Characteristics

For receivers that output information on automatic gain control (AGC), this metric adds insight into receiver response to LightSquared power near the edge of the GPS L1 band. Performance of some types of receivers may be limited by how the AGC reacts to the presence of strong interference and it can be useful to see if any AGC characteristics (e.g. gain, A/D bin distribution) are correlated with degradation seen in other metrics.

Position/Time Quality

Although position quality depends on other factors in addition to the presence of RFI, position quality metrics with and without the LightSquared signal present can be compared for receivers that can accommodate testing the same simulated GNSS scenario multiple times. This type of metric can be useful for receivers that do not output the lower level measurements used in the other metrics. Standard deviations of latitude, longitude and height are appropriate metrics for a laboratory scenario in which all GNSS signals are simulated at similar power levels. Position dilution of precision (PDOP) is an additional metric appropriate for scenarios in which simulated satellite power levels vary by elevation angle according to antenna characteristics and environmental conditions. If using live GNSS signals with and without LightSquared signals present, position quality comparison still can be done since the constellation tends to repeat each sidereal day – this, however, typically is not as consistent as repeating a simulated scenario.

Timing receivers also can undergo related types of tests involving standard deviation of time and time dilution of precision (TDOP), particularly if lower level measurements related to other metrics are not available.

5.   Subtask 5 - Analysis of Effects to GPS Applications

Task Statement

Analyze the expected and potential effects of GPS use for each of the developed scenarios including current and future spectrum environment (e.g. 2025) considerations.

Overview

GPS susceptibility tests were conducted with various LightSquared signals and test environments. Testing was accomplished with conducted emissions in laboratory environments and radiated emissions in anechoic chamber and with Live Sky environments. During the course of this testing, over a dozen different types of receivers for applications ranging from aviation, survey to space were tested. **Table 5-1** provides the LightSquared power level where receivers indicated 1 dB degradations in C/No and when satellite tracking was disrupted (loss of lock). These results are for a single LightSquared base station and do not attempt to address aggregate power from multiple base stations (this is accomplished for specific applications in Task 6.) In addition to the Phase 0 through 2 LightSquared signal types, results from 10 MHz low are also provided in this Table. The results represented in this Table were generally taken from a single test environment versus providing a range of results for various test efforts. For example, the aviation receiver results were obtained from conducted emissions tests conducted at Zeta even though many of these same receivers were also used in Chamber and Live Sky testing. For completeness though, all test reports are included in this Subtask.

The summary Table for Task 5 in the main body of document was derived from these results using free space loss calculation and assuming a per channel EIRP of for LightSquared of 62 dBm and frequency of 1550 MHz.

Table 5-1. Degradation Effects * Caused by LightSquared Signals

Receivers	Phase 0	Phase 1	Phase 2	10 MHz Low
Aviation (conducted emissions)				
#1	-36/-28	-36/-28	-33/-24	-1/+3
#2	-62/-55	-63/-56	-60/-53	-2/+1
#3	-50/-48	-50/-48	-48/-45	-2/+2
#4	-35/-27	-38/-34	-38/-34	-4/+2
#5	-38/-21	NM	NM	NM
#6	-36/>-16	NM	NM	NM
#7	-30/-17	NM	NM	NM
Maritime (chamber tests)				
Timing (chamber tests)				

#8	NM	-55/-17 dBm	NM	NM
High Precision (chamber & live sky tests)				
#9	-32/-21	-54/-50	-46/-42	-27/-20
#10	-28/-21	-52/-47	-46/-42	-7 dBm/NA
#11	TBR/-24	TBR/-41	TBR/-39	TBR/-20
#12	-53/-41	-57/-52	-56/-50	-39/-27
#13	-43/-32	-51/-46	-50/-44	-20/-6
#14	TBR/-23	TBR/-43	TBR/-40	TBR/-21
#15	NM	-60/-46	NM	NM
#16	NM	-69/-43	NM	NM
Space (conducted emissions)				
TRIG	-76/-62	-84/-70	NM	NM
IGOR	NM	-60/-48	NM	NM

*data entries represent levels for (-1 dB C/No)/(Loss of tracking) values

TBR – data still being analyzed

Conducted Emissions Testing

FAA

Test Environment

GPS simulated signals were generated using a Spirent STR2760 or an Advanced Global Navigation Simulator (AGNS) calibrated to provide known signal levels (changed simulators because STR2760 power supply failed). For MOPS-based tests, broadband white noise was generated using an HP346B noise source that was amplified and then attenuated with a programmable attenuator to provide a controlled amount of additional noise. This broadband noise emulates the degradation of numerous sources that are not present for conducted tests and includes the energy of all other GNSS signals and sky noise.

The simulated GPS constellation used consists of 24 satellites plus one or two SBAS GEOs generating L1 C/A code, appropriate for MOPS-based tests and consistent with GPS SPS PS and DO-229 (SBAS simulated only for SBAS message loss tests). The constellation was generated from the Yuma almanac file from April 8th, 2009, with PRNs 01, 06, 18, 24, 25, 26, 32 removed and the GPS week changed to 1634. The power level of the simulated GPS signals depended on the type of test. For the ground-based receiver tests (Receivers #5, 6 & 7), the level was set to the SPS minimum of -128.5 dBm, assuming 0 dBi antenna gain. For the aviation receiver MOPS-based tests, one satellite was at -120 dBm and the rest were at -134 dBm, representing maximum and minimum levels at the input to a representative antenna filter/LNA. Note that in the MOPS-based tests, the receivers were allowed to track for approximately 15 to 30 minutes with all satellites at -120 dBm before dropping power of all but one to -134 dBm at the start of the test.

Although the tests of ground-based receivers did not include additional noise, the MOPS-based tests of aviation receivers required additional broadband white noise according to the MOPS-based test plan [1]. For the carrier-to-noise ratio (CNR) degradation test to determine a 1-dB degradation point, -173.5 dBm/Hz external noise was specified, which required adding 4.1 dB additional noise to the system. For the SBAS message loss tests, -170.5 dBm/Hz external noise was specified, which required adding 5.6 dB additional noise to the system. These noise levels are intended to emulate the highly stressful RF environment in which MOPS-compliant receivers are required to operate.

C/No 1 dB Degradation and Loss of Tracking Results

The 1 dB carrier to noise density (C/No) degradation and loss of tracking results for ground-based receivers are shown in Table 5-2. These were obtained with the Phase 0 LightSquared configuration and GPS signals at the SPS minimum level of -128.5 dBm. Note that Receiver #5 1-dB degradation result is at a point when the automatic gain control became unstable and caused a greater than 1 dB drop in C/No. Also Receiver #6 did not lose lock up to the maximum level tested, 16 dBm. Plots of the Phase 0 test results for Receivers #5, 6, & 7 are in **Figure 5-1**, Figure 5-2 and Figure 5-3, respectively.

Table 5-2. LightSquared Phase 0 Signal Power (dBm) for 1 dB C/No Degradation and Loss of Satellite Tracking

Receiver	1-dB C/No degradation	Loss of tracking
#5	-38*	-21
#6	-36	> -16**
#7	-30	-17

* G-II AGC gain shifted and C/No degraded by more than 1 dB at this level
** LGF did not lose lock at Phase 0 levels tested

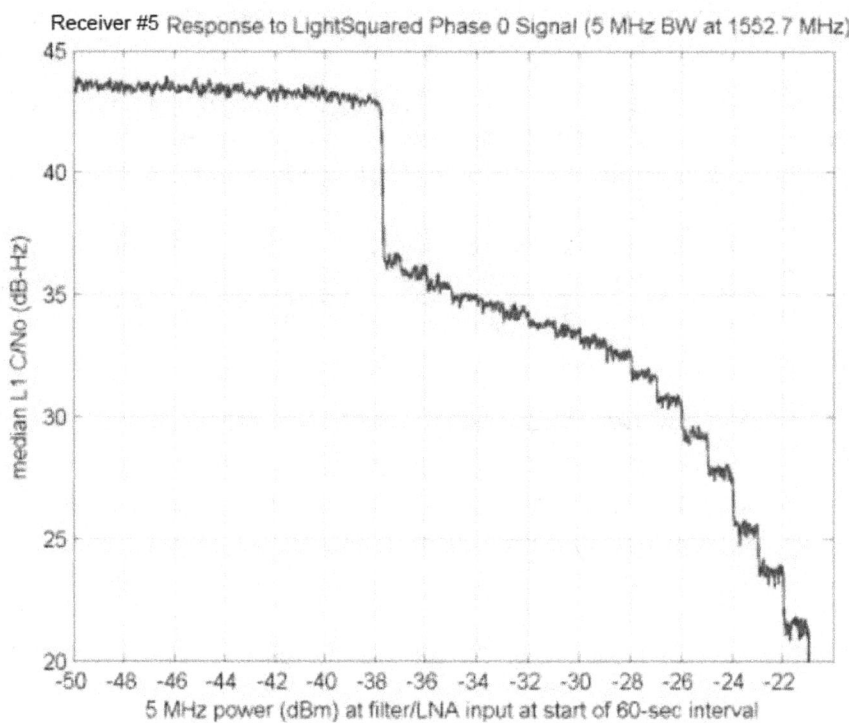

Figure 5-1. Receiver #5 C/No Response to LightSquared Phase 0 Signal

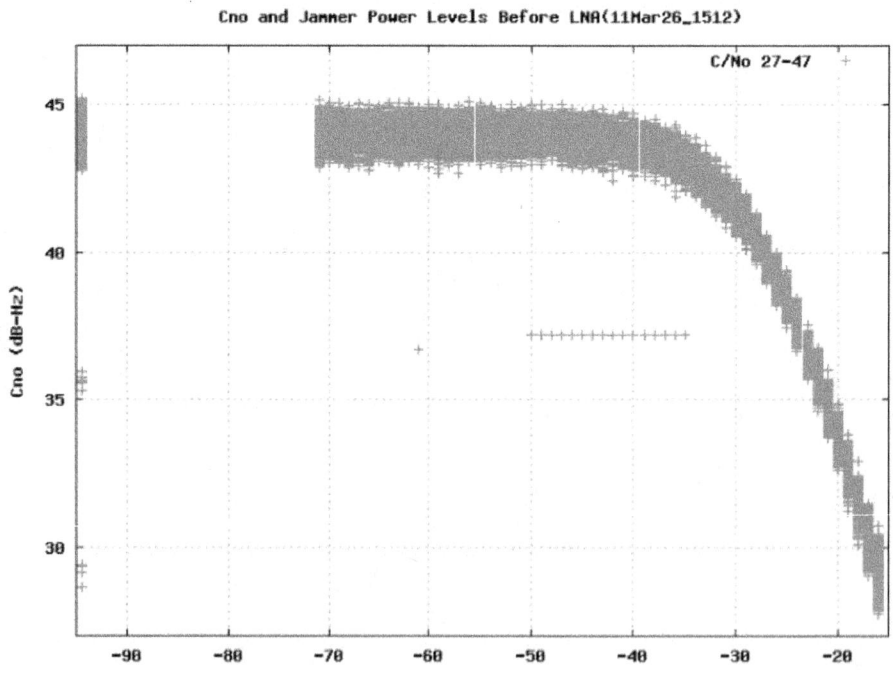

Figure 5-2. Receiver #6 C/No Response to LightSquared Phase 0 Signal

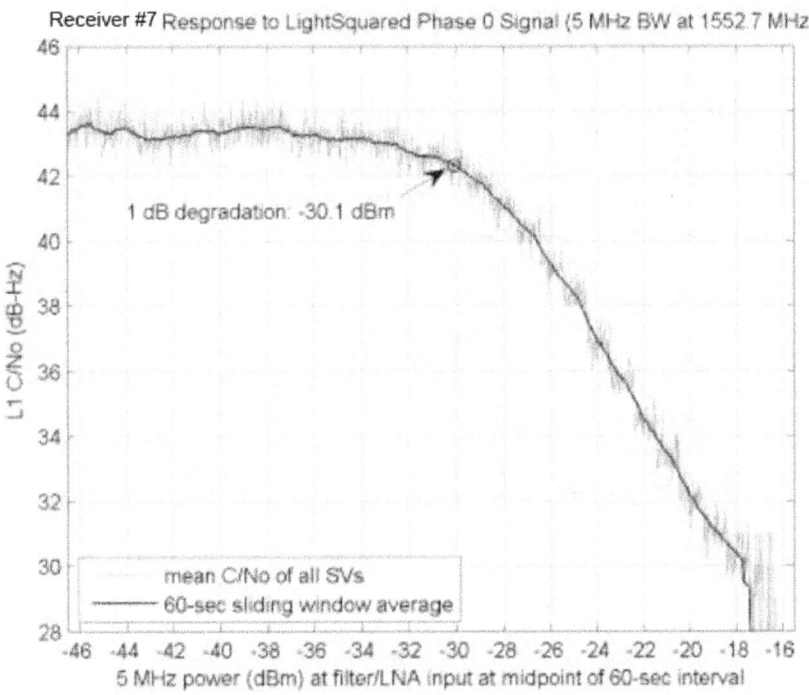

Figure 5-3. Receiver #7 C/No Response to LightSquared Phase 0 Signal

The 1 dB degradation and loss of tracking results for the aviation receivers obtained in the MOPS environment are shown in Table 5-3 and Table 5-4, respectively. The results cover LightSquared Phase 0, 1 and 2 configurations as well as two configurations using 5 MHz and 10 MHz bandwidths in the lower channel; the two low-channel configurations are the Phase 1 and 2 configurations without the upper channel included. Note these tests used GPS signals at low power, -134 dBm, and were conducted with the noise generator providing and equivalent external noise level of -173.5 dBm/Hz. Corresponding plots of the aviation receiver results are provided in Figure 5-4 through Figure 5-23.

Table 5-3. Signal Power (dBm/channel) for 1 dB C/No Degradation Caused by LightSquared Signals

Receiver	Phase 0	Phase 1	Phase 2	5 MHz Low	10 MHz Low
#1	-35.9	-35.9	-33.3	+3.4	-1.1
#2	-61.9	-62.5	-59.7	+3.7	-1.7
#3	-50.2	-50.0	-47.7	+2.9	-1.7
#4	-35.4	-38.2	-37.7	-1.0	-4.4

Table 5-4. Signal Power (dBm/channel) for Loss of Satellite Tracking Caused by LightSquared Signals

Receiver	Phase 0	Phase 1	Phase 2	5 MHz Low	10 MHz Low
#1	-28	-28	-24	+10*	+3
#2	-55	-56	-53	+9	+1
#3	-48	-48	-45	+10	+2
#4	-27	-34	-34	+7	+2

* Receiver #1 was at low C/No but maintained lock at +10 dBm

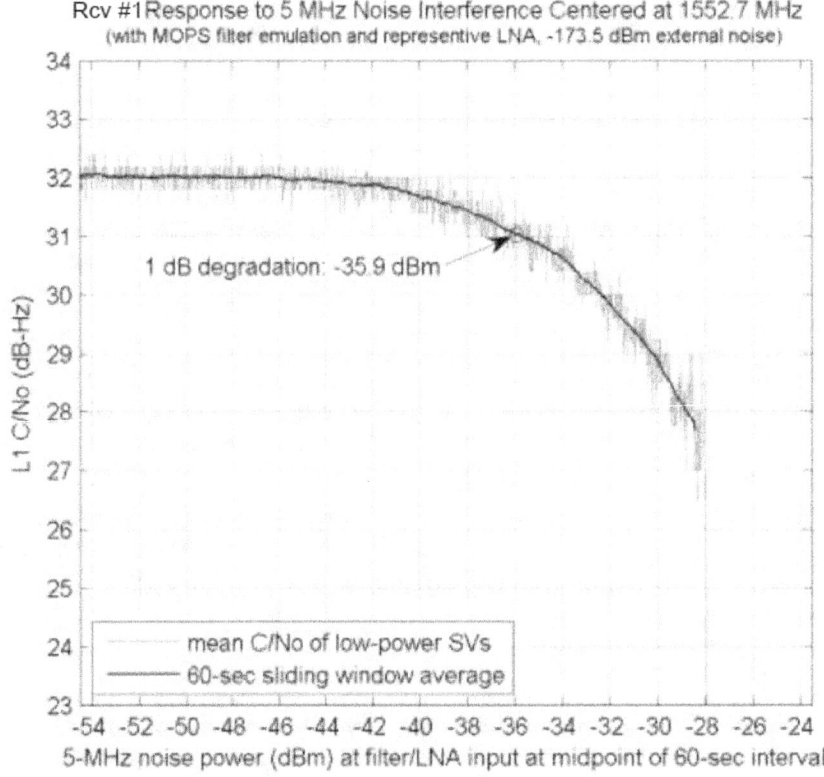

Figure 5-4. Receiver #1 5MHz BW Noise at 1552.7 MHz (Phase 0)

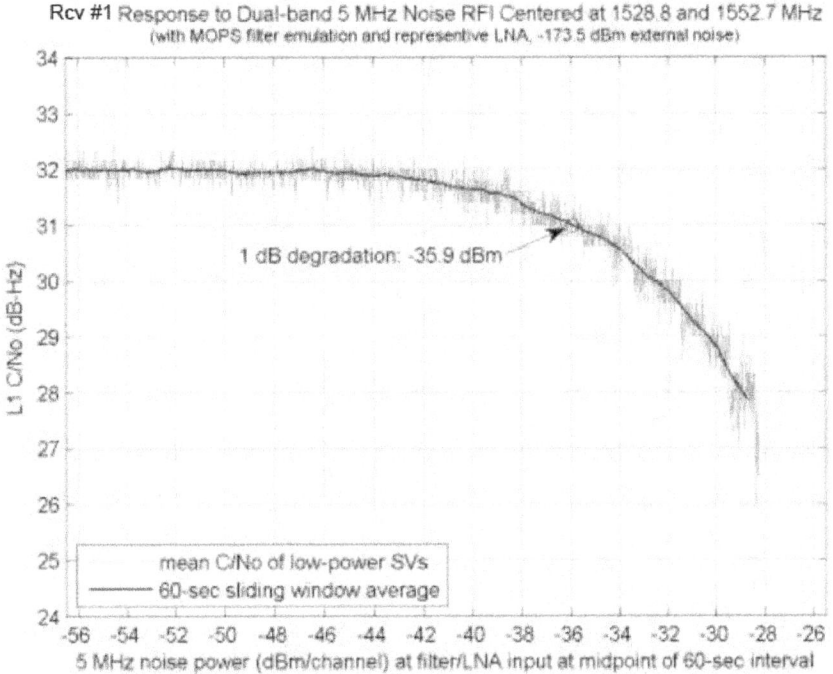

Figure 5-5. Receiver #1 Dual 5 MHz BW Noise (Phase 1)

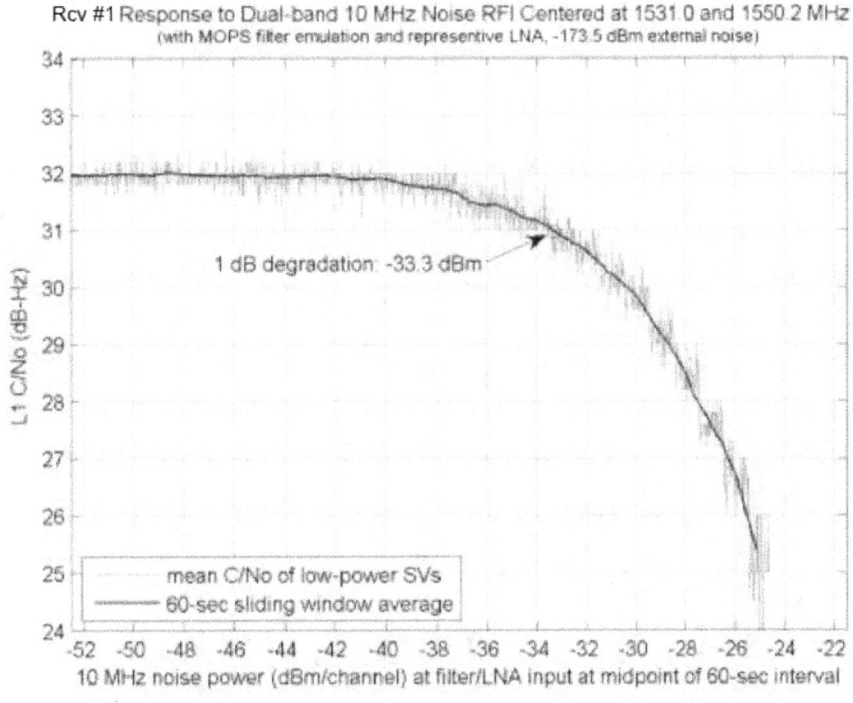

Figure 5-6. Receiver #1 Dual 10 MHz BW Noise (Phase 2)

5-7

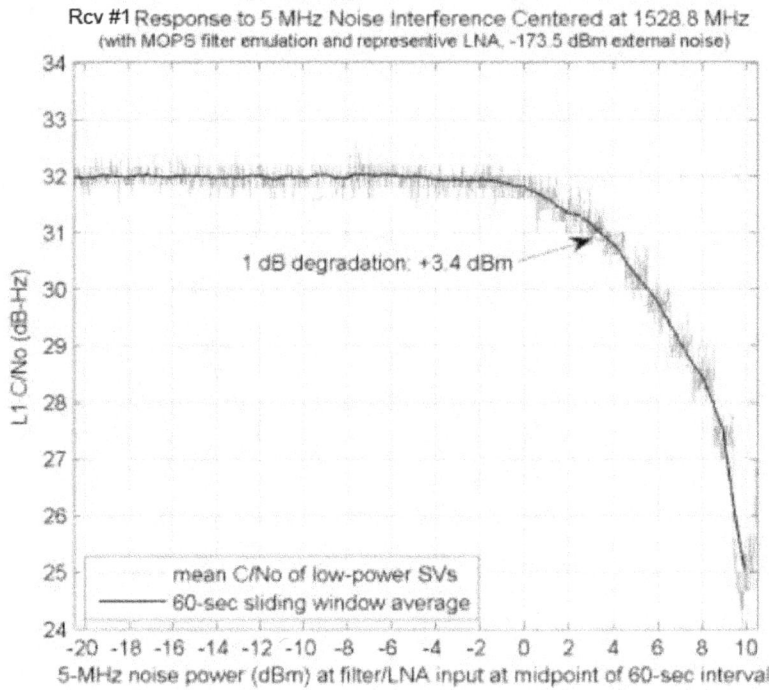

Figure 5-7. Receiver #1 5MHz BW Noise at 1528.8 MHz (5 MHz Low)

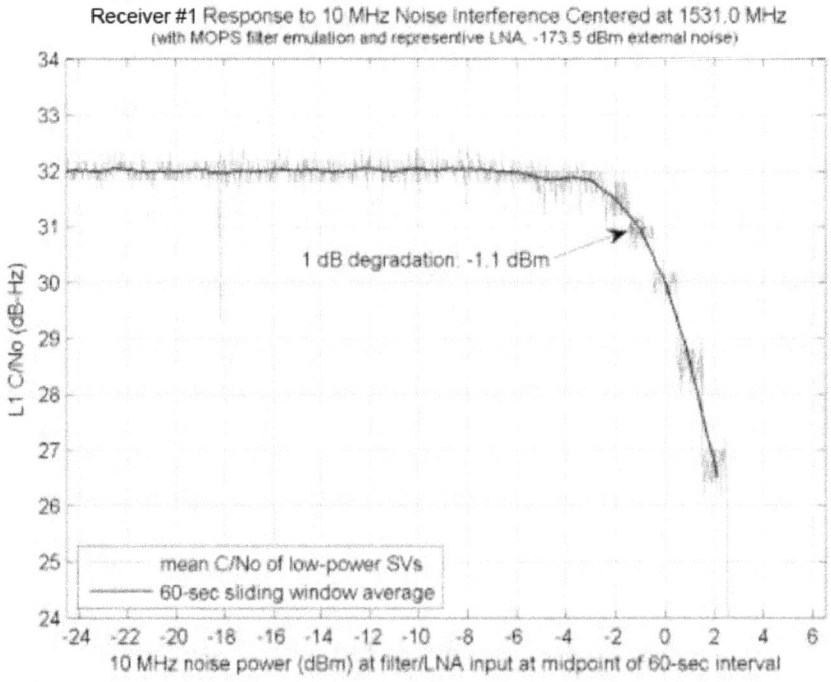

Figure 5-8. Receiver #1 10 MHz BW Noise at 1531.0 MHz (10 MHz Low)

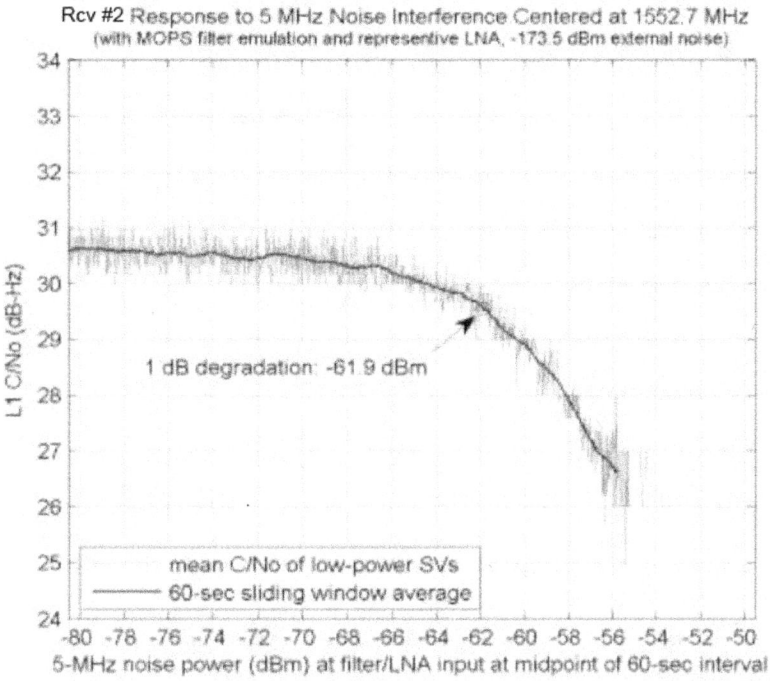

Figure 5-9. Receiver #2 5MHz BW Noise at 1552.7 MHz (Phase 0)

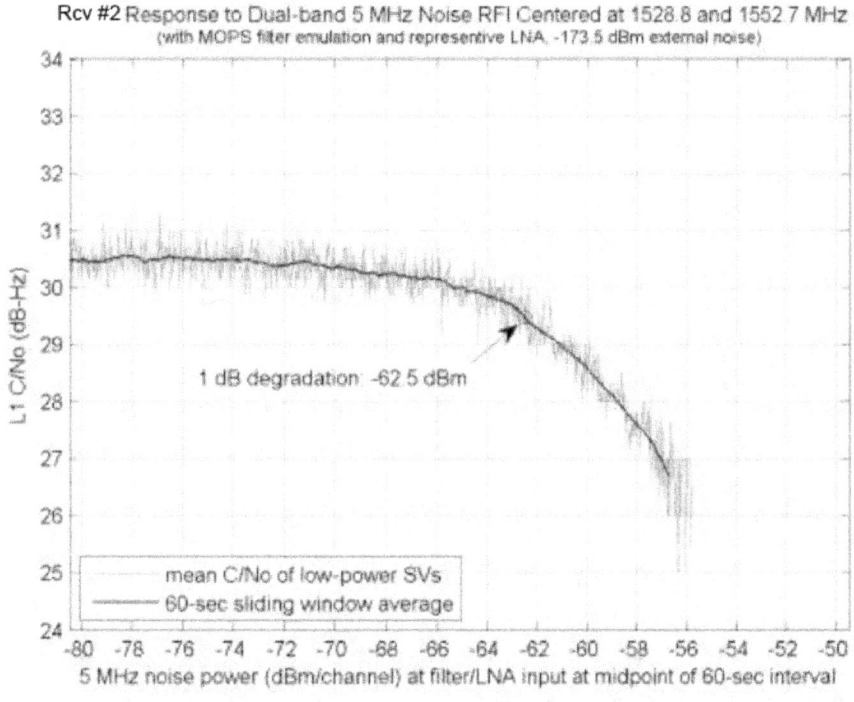

Figure 5-10. Receiver #2 Dual 5 MHz BW Noise (Phase 1)

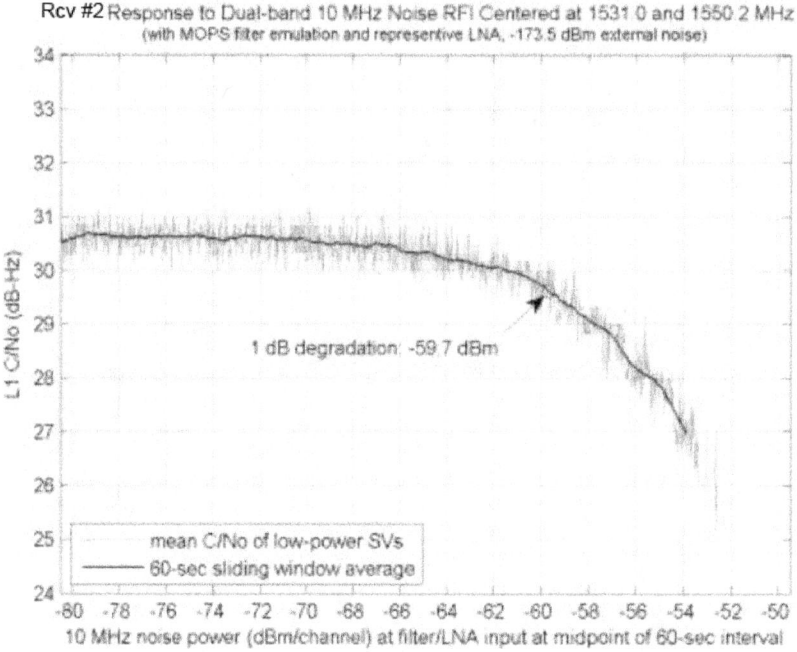

Figure 5-11. Receiver #2 Dual 10 MHz BW Noise (Phase 2)

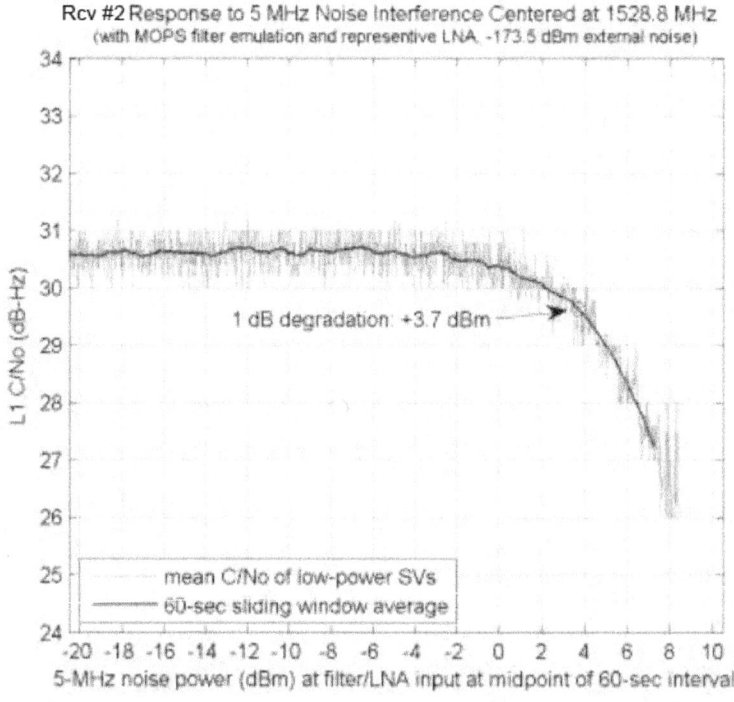

Figure 5-12. Receiver #2 5MHz BW Noise at 1528.8 MHz (5 MHz Low)

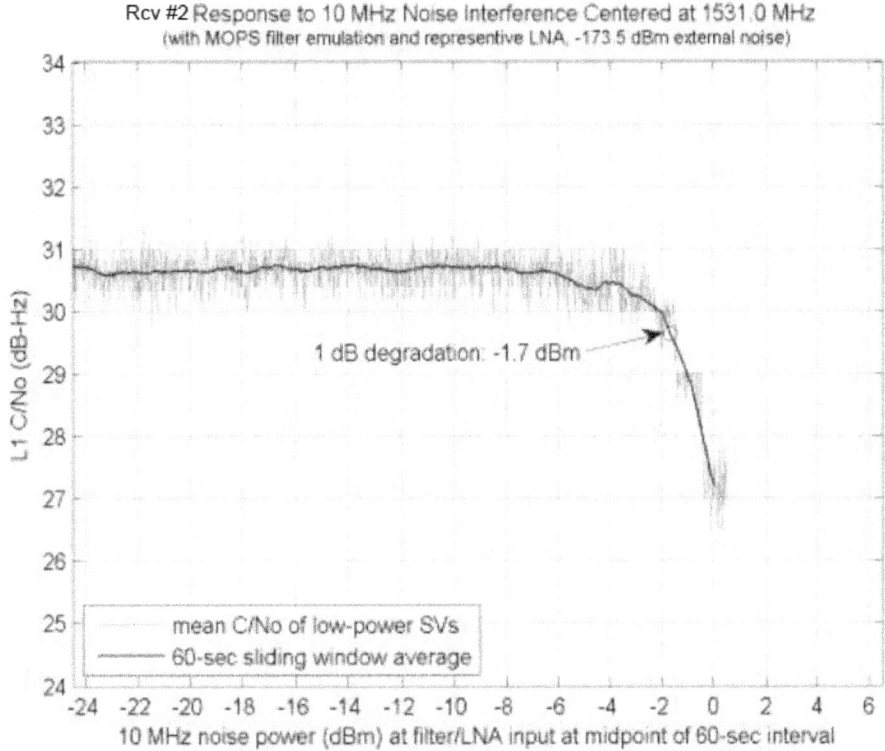

Figure 5-13. Receiver #2 10 MHz BW Noise at 1531.0 MHz (10 MHz Low)

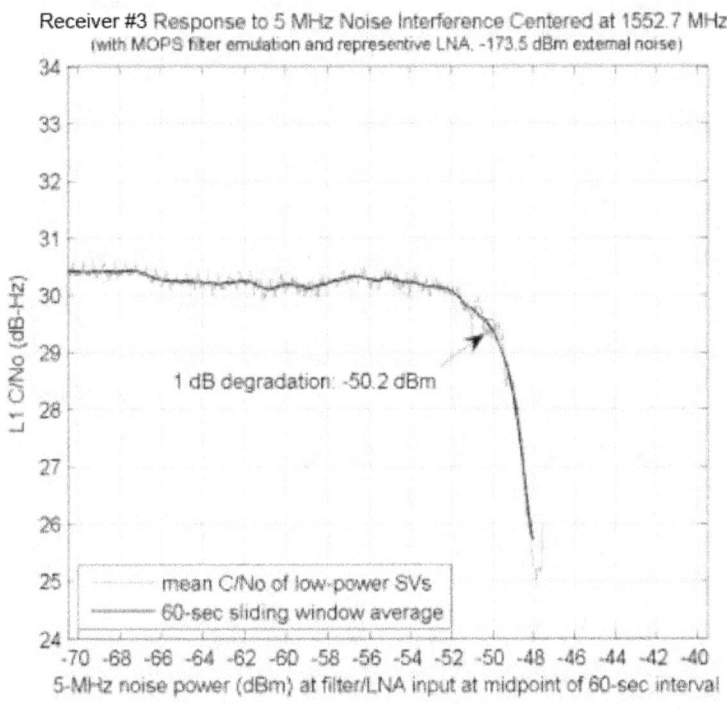

Figure 5-14. Receiver #3 5MHz BW Noise at 1552.7 MHz (Phase 0)

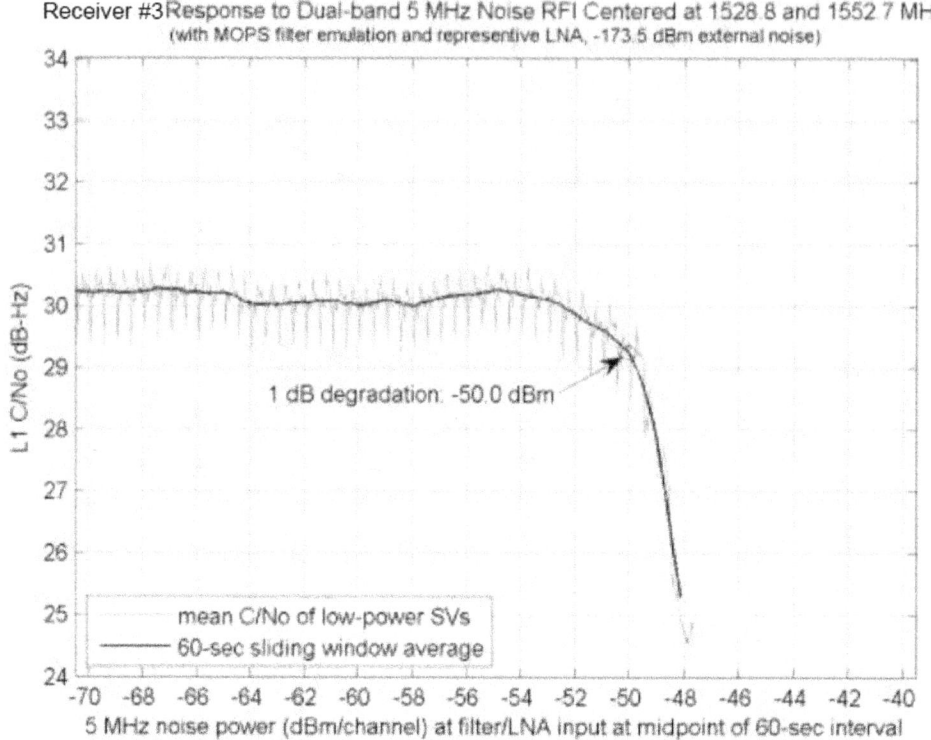

Figure 5-15. Receiver #3 Dual 5 MHz BW Noise (Phase 1)

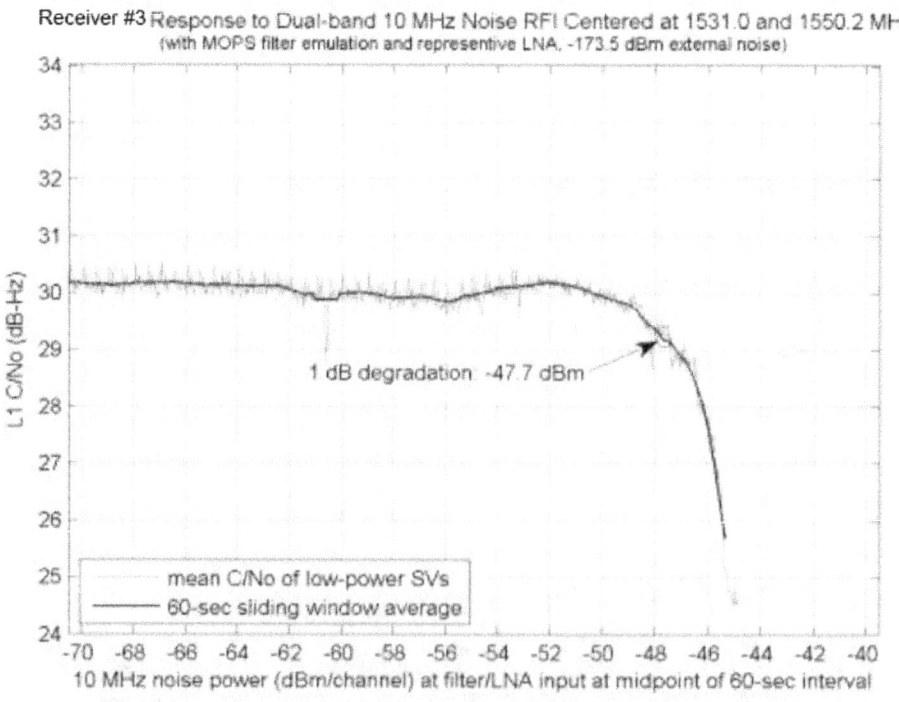

Figure 5-16. Receiver #3 Dual 10 MHz BW Noise (Phase 2)

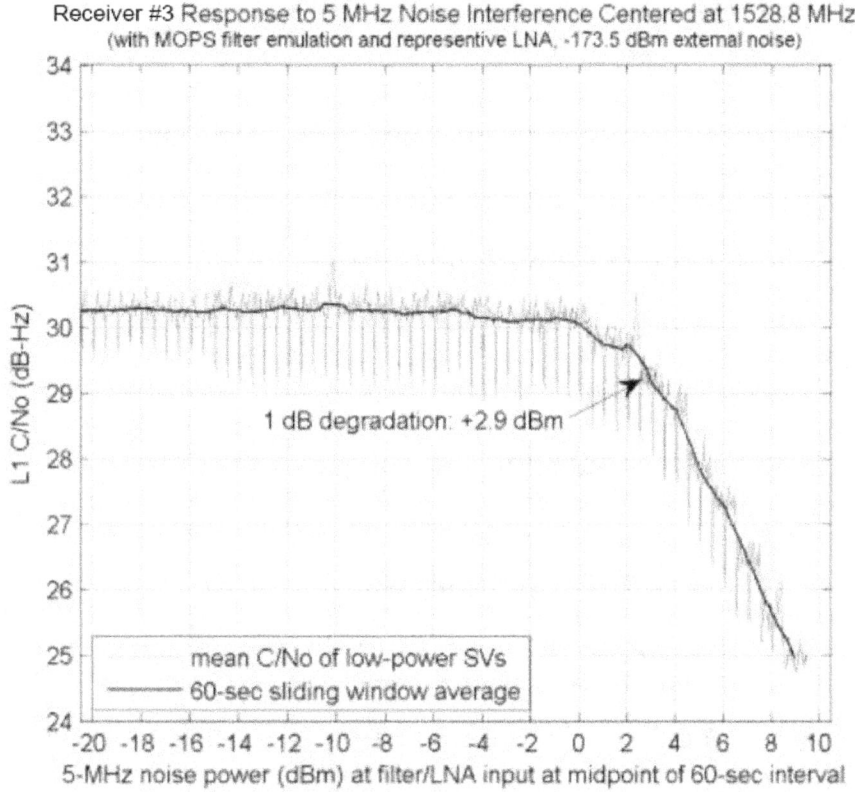

Figure 5-17. Receiver #3 5MHz BW Noise at 1528.8 MHz (5 MHz Low)

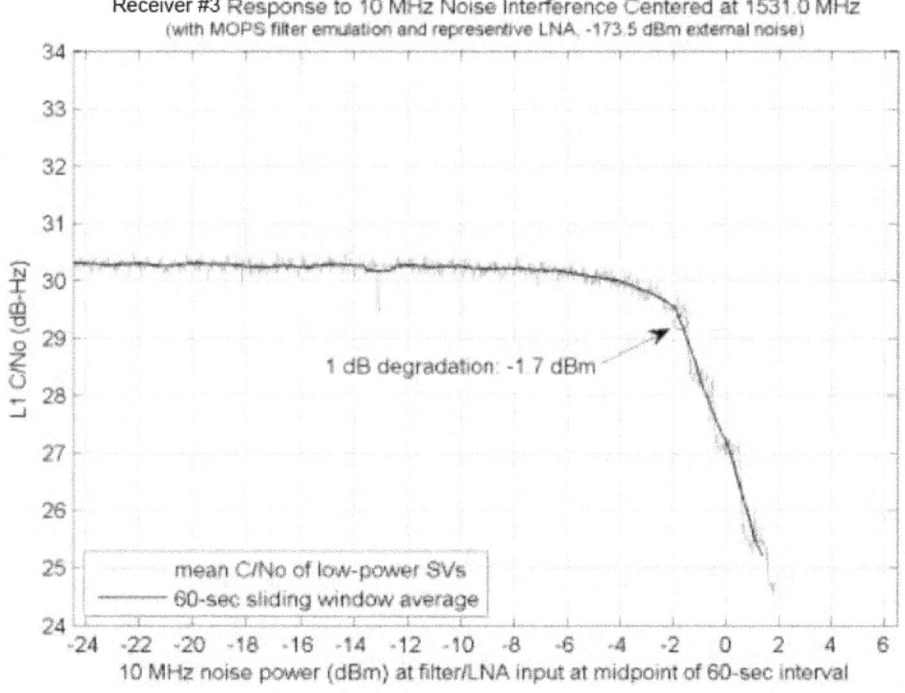

Figure 5-18. Receiver #3 10 MHz BW Noise at 1531.0 MHz (10 MHz Low)

5-13

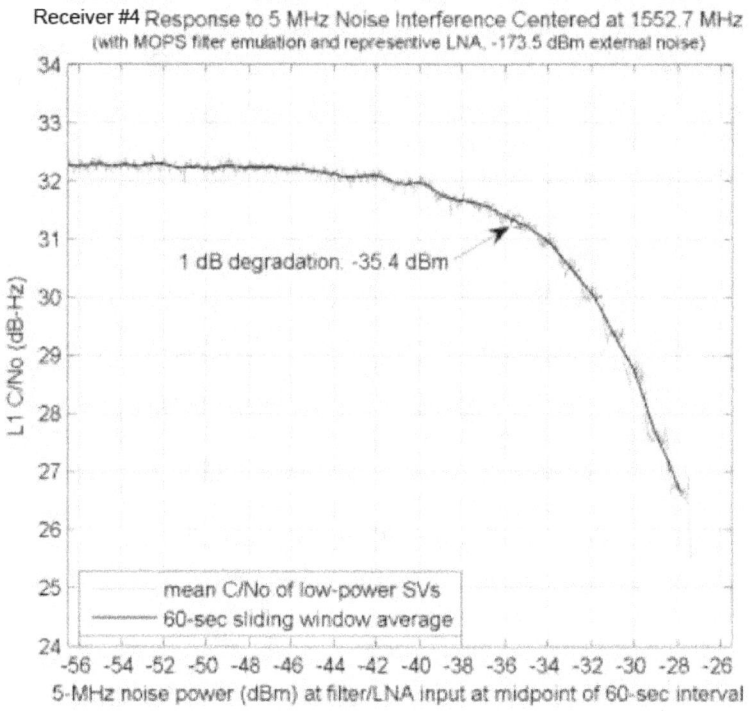

Figure 5-19. Receiver #4 5MHz BW Noise at 1552.7 MHz (Phase 0)

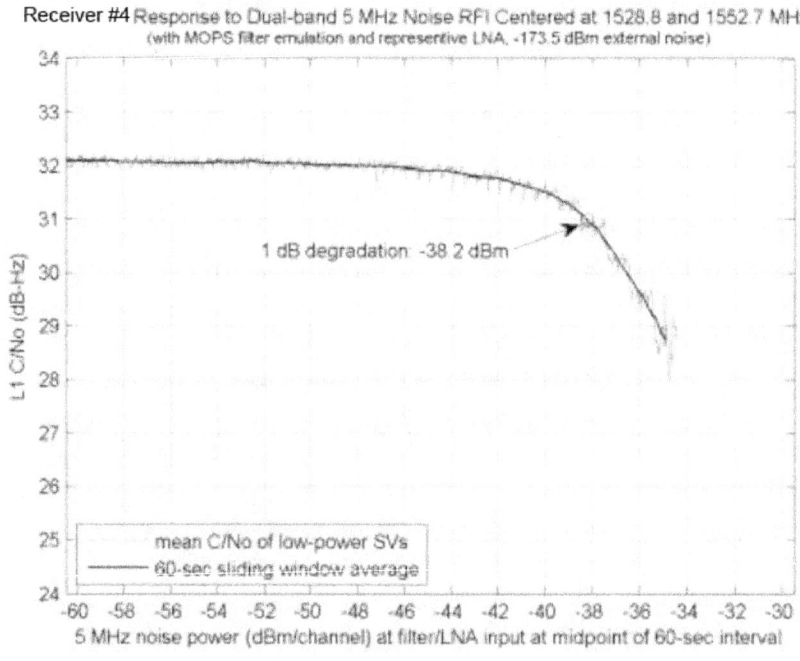

Figure 5-20. Receiver #4 Dual 5 MHz BW Noise (Phase 1)

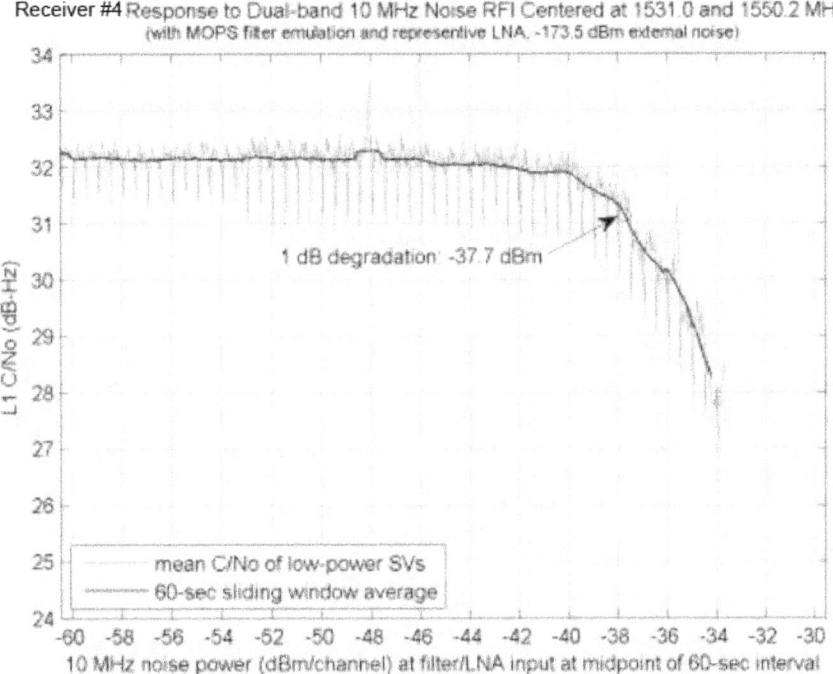

Figure 5-21. Receiver #4 Dual 10 MHz BW Noise (Phase 2)

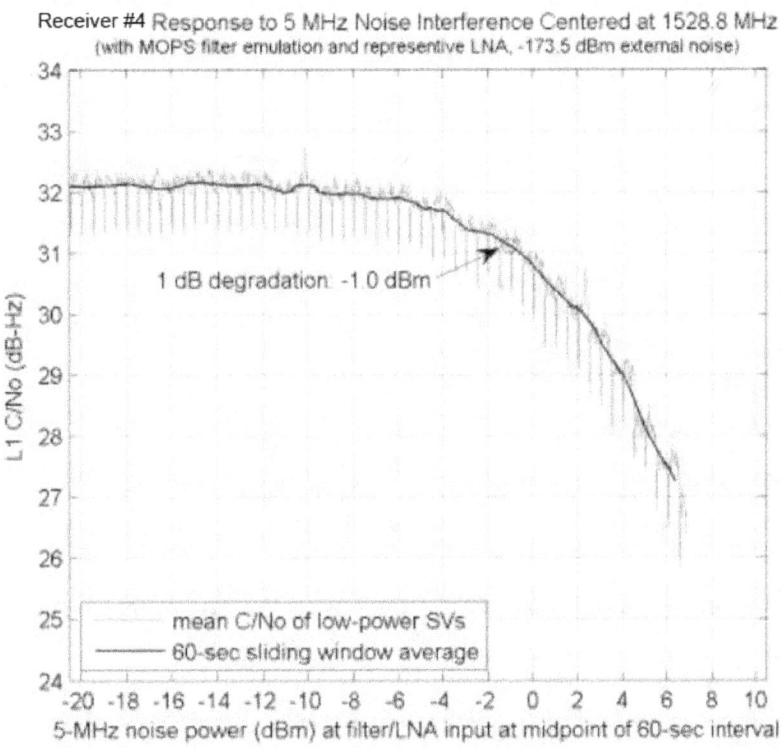

Figure 5-22. Receiver #4 5MHz BW Noise at 1528.8 MHz (5 MHz Low)

5-15

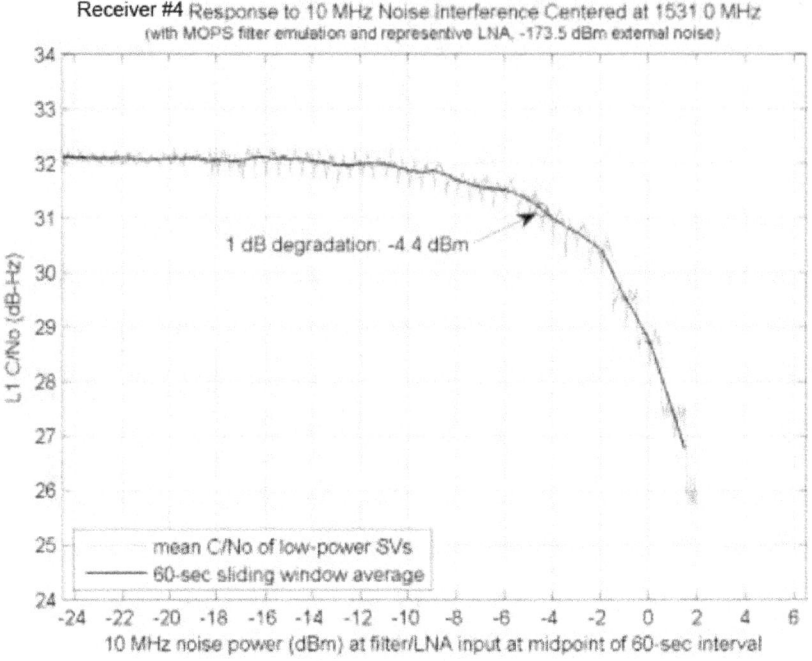

Figure 5-23. Receiver #4 10 MHz BW Noise at 1531.0 MHz (10 MHz Low)

References

[1] Assessment of the LightSquared Ancillary Terrestrial Component Radio Frequency Interference Impact on GNSS L1 Band Airborne Receiver Operations, RTCA Paper No. 084-11/SC159-993, RTCA, Inc., May 2011.

NASA

Click here for the NASA/JPL Test Report

Chamber Testing

Chamber Test Plan

(The GPS LightSquared Test Plan Draft, 28 March 2011, is an FOUO document and not releasable)

FAA Testing to Evaluate the Impact of LightSquared Signals on GPS Operation

Anechoic Chamber Tests

Introduction

The Federal Aviation Administration (FAA) participated in testing of Global Positioning System (GPS) receivers operating in the presence of a communication signal proposed by a company called LightSquared (LSQ.) The LSQ signal is a high power multi-carrier signal proposed for

5-16

use in the spectrum immediately adjacent to the GPS spectrum. Terrestrial transmitters are planned to be installed throughout the continental United States (CONUS) to provide mobile communications services.

The GPS community has raised concerns that GPS receivers may perform poorly or not at all when in the presence of the LSQ signal. The US government therefore conducted a group of tests in order to identify and quantify the effects of the LSQ signal on GPS receivers.

This report provides an initial look at the outage analysis for tests in the anechoic chamber only. Later reports will be generated as required for various other tests conducted in support of the evaluation of LSQ effects.

Background

In November of 2010, the Federal Communications Commission (FCC) granted a conditional waiver to LightSquared that permits them to operate high power ground transmitters in a band of the radio frequency (RF) spectrum previously reserved for low-power satellite downlink signals.

Objective

The goal of testing is to identify and quantify the effects of the LSQ signal on GPS receivers. These results will be used to determine the impact area of LSQ transmitters on GPS receivers. Government organizations propose that these results be used by the FCC to help determine whether the LSQ application should ultimately be accepted or rejected. This document reports the results on receivers operated by the FAA during these tests.

Test Description

The FAA participated in two test events sponsored by the US Air Force. These consisted of a test in an anechoic chamber using simulated GPS and LSQ signals, and a live-sky test using actual GPS signals and a simulated LSQ signal. These tests were conducted during the month of April 2011. A number of government and commercial participants brought receivers and data recording equipment to these tests in order to evaluate performance in the LSQ signal environment.

Equipment

The FAA brought a mix of representative civilian GPS receivers to the test. These included aviation, survey and general purpose receivers. Data were collected using the available interface for each receiver. In some cases these interfaces provide extensive amounts of data and in other cases simply a position and validity flag. A complete list of the receivers is provided in Table 5-5, and it includes the interface type and parameters available. Specific receivers used for the different tests are identified in each test section below.

All aviation certified receivers were connected to the one of two antennas.

Table 5-5. – Complete List of FAA Receivers and Data

Receiver	Type	Interface	Parameters Available
#1	Aviation certified – Air Carrier	ARINC - 429 Serial port	Position, Altitude, Validity, Number SVs, more
#19	Aviation handheld	Serial port	Position, Number SVs
#20	Aviation certified - GA	ARINC - 429	Position, Validity
#3	Aviation certified - GA	ARINC - 429	Position, Validity
#4	Aviation certified - GA	ARINC - 429	Position, Altitude, Validity, Number SVs
#25	Scientific	Serial port	Position, Altitude, Validity, Number SVs, more
#21	Scientific	Serial port	Position, Altitude, Validity, Number SVs, more
#5	Aviation certified reference receiver	Serial port	Position, Altitude, Validity, Number SVs, more
#22	Aviation certified	ARINC - 429	Position, Altitude, Validity, Number SVs, more
#23	General Purpose	Serial port	Position, Altitude, Validity, Number SVs, more
#24	Survey	Serial port TCP/IP	Position, Altitude, Validity, Number SVs, more

Data Collection

Data were collected over a four day period, from April 4 – 7, 2011. Test periods were approximately ten hours per day, with additional time for setup and coordination. Tests were organized into several test events, each with a different configuration of the LSQ signal. These are listed in Table 5-6. A shorthand notation is used for each test configuration. It identifies the bandwidth as either 5 MHz or 10 MHz, and the frequency range, which can be in the lower band (1520-1540 MHz) or upper band (1540-1559 MHz.) The Short Description in Table 5-6 uses this notation, and corresponds to the characteristics in the Signals column. In the Signals column, the frequency and bandwidth are provided, as well as the polarization of the signal, which can be right-hand, polarized (RP) or left-hand polarized (LP). The list includes single and dual frequency configurations.

Test configurations 1 through 8, as identified in Table 5-6, were run twice each during Test Days 1 and 2. These were all ramp tests, in which the power was varied over time from a low power to the maximum LSQ power. Acquisition tests at constant power levels were tests 9 through 16, which were run on Day 3. Day 4 was used to run tests 17 through 26, which were dual-channel configurations.

The LSQ signal was generated using a laboratory-quality vector signal generator and power amplifier to produce the signal, and actual LSQ antennas to transmit it. The transmitting equipment was located in a room on the second floor adjacent to the chamber. The transmit antennas were set up on the second level of the chamber, pointed down toward the center of the room, where the antennas were located. Figure 5-24 and Figure 5-25 show the inside of the chamber configured for testing. Figure 5-24 is the view from the east side, looking across the antenna farm to the LSQ antenna on the second level. Figure 5-25 is the opposite view, looking down from the LSQ antenna to the Government data collection area.

Receiver and data collection equipment were located on the bottom level inside the chamber. One side was used by the government test team, and the other by the commercial team comprised of representatives of private industry. A diagram of the equipment layout in each data collection area is provided in Figure 5-26 and Figure 5-27.

Figure 5-28 shows the location of the antennas used in the test, oriented such that the bottom of the figure corresponds to the west part of the chamber. The colored shapes are used to identify the location and owner of each. FAA antennas are shown, in orange, as numbers 6 and 32.

A laser rangefinder was used to precisely measure the distance from the LSQ transmit antenna to each of the test antennas. The antennas were 44 and 48.7 feet from the transmit antenna, respectively.

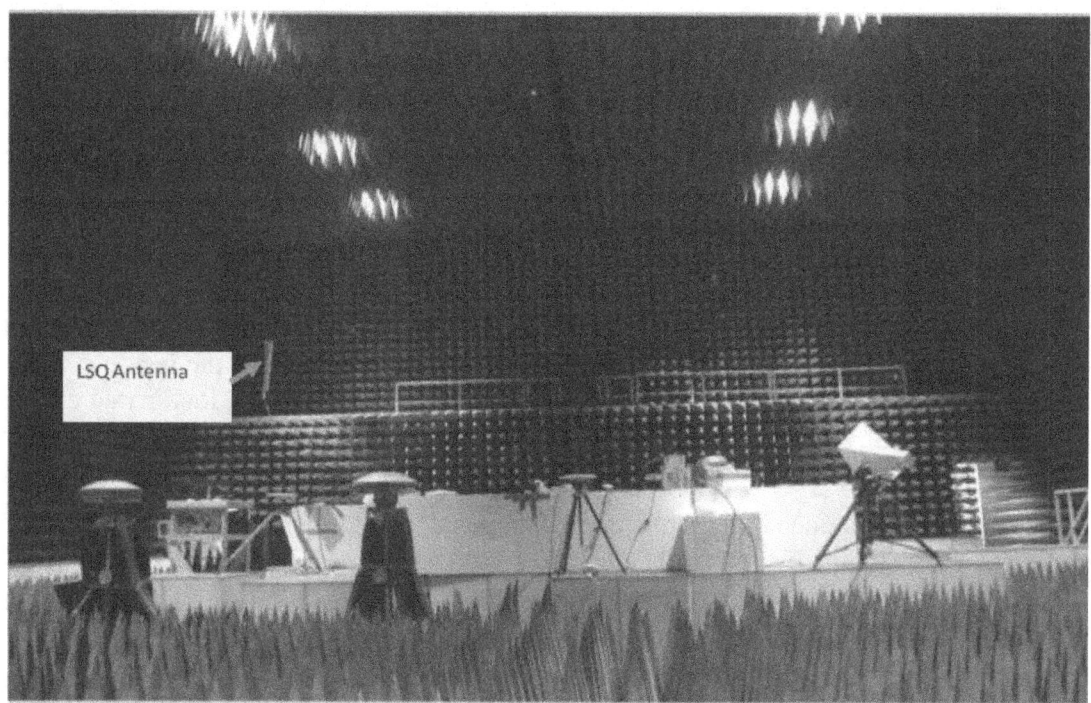

Figure 5-24. Chamber View Looking toward LSQ Antenna

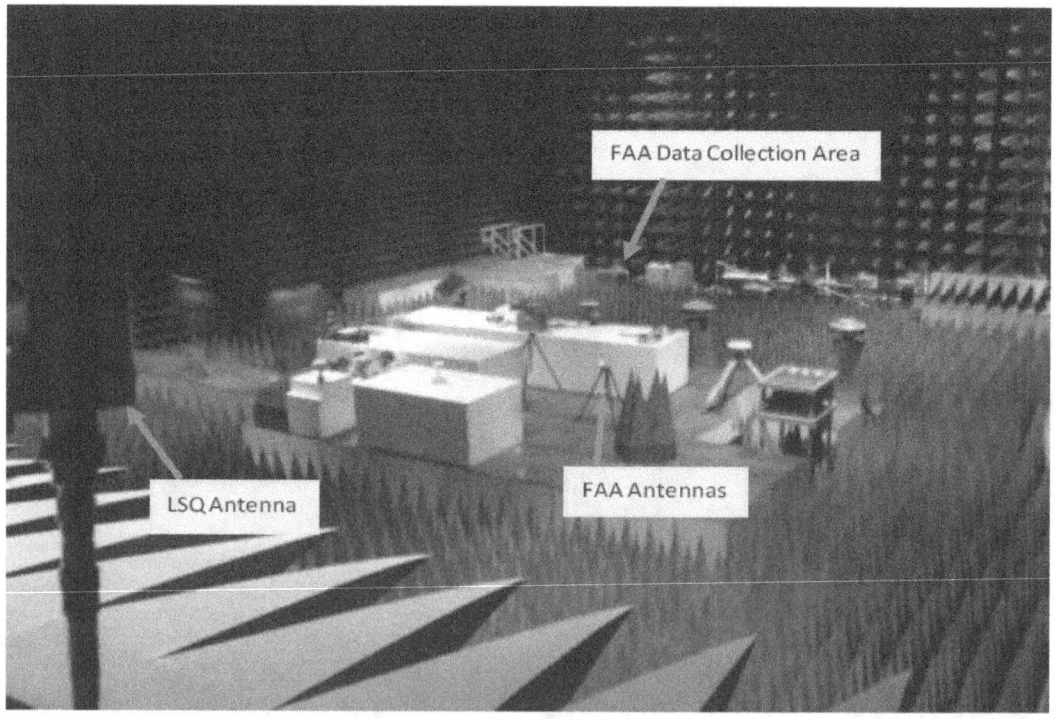

Figure 5-25. Chamber View Looking down from LSQ Antenna

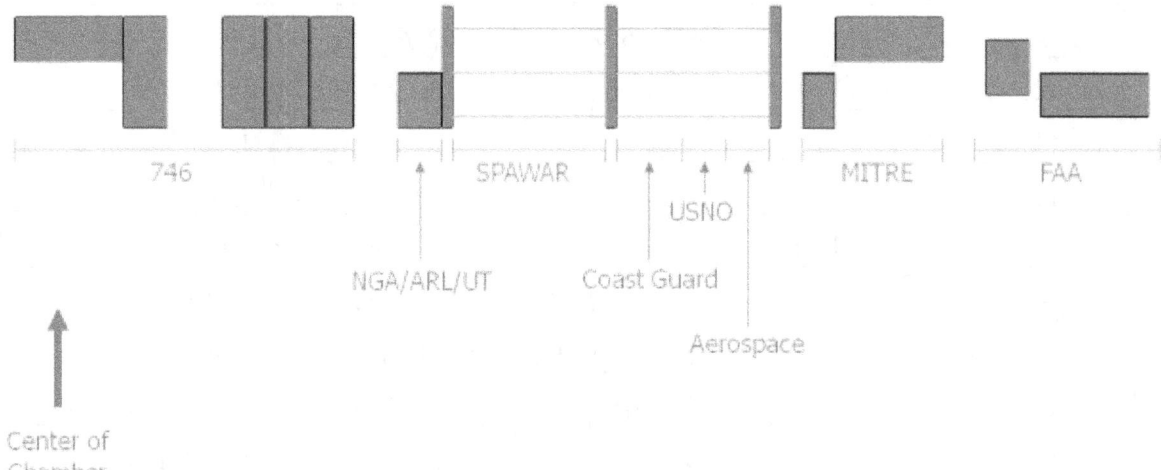

Figure 5-26. Equipment Areas on East Side of Chamber

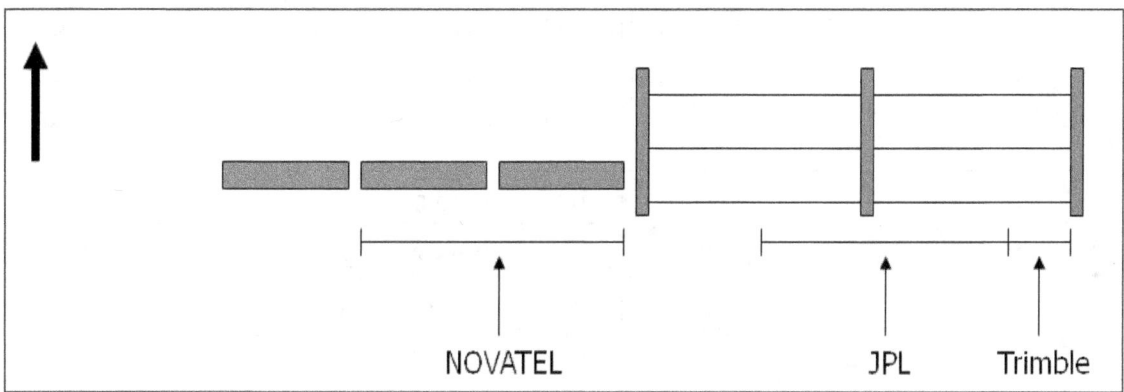

Figure 5-27. Equipment Areas on West Side of Chamber

Table 5-6. Anechoic Chamber Test Events

TE	Days	Short Description	Signals
1	1, 2	5H	5 MHz, F_c=1552.7, -45 (LP)
2	1, 2	10H	10 MHz, F_c=1550.2, -45 (LP)
3	1, 2	5L	5 MHz, F_c=1528.5, -45 (LP)
4	1, 2	10L	10 MHz, F_c=1531.0, -45 (LP)
5	1, 2	5H	5 MHz, F_c=1552.7, +45 (RP)
6	1, 2	10H	10 MHz, F_c=1550.2, +45 (RP)
7	1, 2	5L	5 MHz, F_c=1528.5, +45 (RP)

5-21

8	1, 2	10L	10 MHz, F_c=1531.0, +45 (RP)
9	3	5H	5 MHz, Fc=1552.7 MHz, -45 (LP)
10	3	10H	10 MHz, Fc=1550.2 MHz, -45 (LP)
11	3	5L	5 MHz, Fc=1528.5 MHz, -45 (LP)
12	3	10L	10 MHz, Fc=1531.0 MHz, -45 (LP)
13	3	5H	5 MHz, Fc=1552.7 MHz, +45 (RP)
14	3	10H	10 MHz, Fc=1550.2 MHz, +45 (RP)
15	3	5L	5 MHz, Fc=1528.5 MHz, +45 (RP)
16	3	10L	10 MHz, Fc=1531.0 MHz, +45 (RP)
17	4	5L, 5H	5 MHz, Fc=1552.7 MHz, Fc=1528.8MHz, Both
18	4	5L, 5H	5 MHz, Fc=1552.7 MHz, Fc=1528.8MHz, Both
19	4	10L, 10H	10 MHz, Fc=1531.0 MHz, Fc=1550.2 MHz, Both
20	4	5L, 10L	10 MHz, Fc=1531.0 MHz, Fc=1550.2 MHz, Both
21	4	5H Tone	5 MHz, F=1552.7 MHz
22	4	5L Tone	5 MHz, F=1528.8 MHz
23	4	10H Tone	10 MHz, F=1550.2 MHz
24	4	10L Tone	10 MHz, F=1531.0 MHz
25	4	5L, 5H Tone	5 MHz, F=1552.7 MHz, F=1528.8MHz
26	4	10 H, 10L	10 MHz, F=1531.0 MHz, F=1550.2

GPS signals were generated by an Advanced Global Navigation Simulator (AGNS) produced by the US Navy SPAWAR Systems Center. This unit can generate the full range of GPS signals to simulate over 32 satellites. These signals were sent to 8 antennas which were hung from the ceiling in the chamber, to provide spatial diversity to the RF environment.

Test signals were calibrated beforehand, using the simulator and a specialized receiver in a closed loop. Calibration removed errors in the signals and provided a measurement of signal power losses for each antenna location. Special care was taken to insure that the antennas were not in the near field of the LSQ transmit antenna.

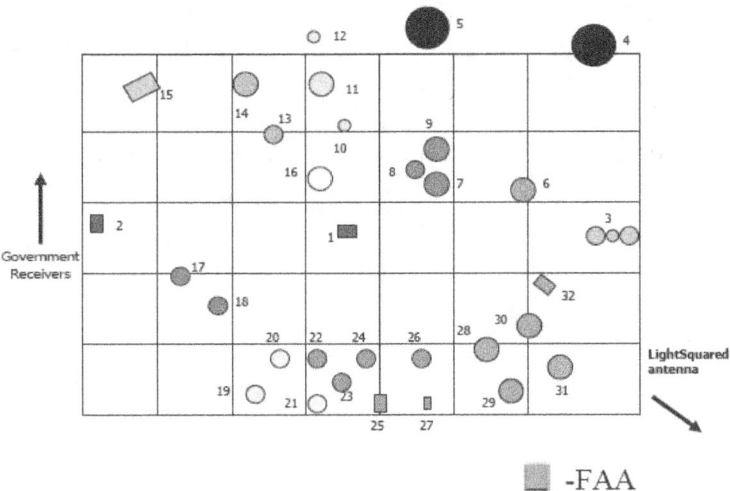

Figure 5-28. Anechoic Chamber Antenna Locations

Anechoic Chamber Test Results

Data Processing

Data were processed and analyzed at the FAA Technical Center. Initial analysis focused only on outage periods – those times when a receiver was unable to track enough GPS signals to produce a position solution. Some limited analysis of carrier-to-noise density was also conducted. The goal was to estimate the effective distance from the LSQ antenna at which signal loss would occur in the operational environment.

The raw or partly processed data were converted to a text format and organized by test event. Using logs of the transmitted power as it changed during the test, the receiver effects were observed and documented. Calculations were then performed to estimate real-world performance based on the test configuration. Using the transmit power level and free-space loss to the antenna, the received power at the antenna was calculated. Using free-space loss and the maximum transmit power level to be used in operations the corresponding effective distance in the operational environment was estimated based on the previous calculation of received power at the antenna.

Results

Table 5-7 through

Table **5-10** present a summary of all outages during the chamber testing, one Table for each day. They show the test event (as defined in Table 5-6), the receiver type, start and stop time with duration of the outage, the EIRP as recorded in the time vs. power logs, and the effective distance at the beginning and end of the outage, calculated as described above.

Table 5-11 shows which receivers were affected during each test condition. In some cases the entry is "NA," which means not analyzed. This can occur for several reasons. In the case of

Receivers #3, 4 and 20, they were removed from the chamber on the last day (Day 4) for installation in an aircraft to support the succeeding LSQ flight test. For Receiver #24, the primary data recording system failed, and extraction of the backup recording has not been completed. This data will be available at a later date. For Receiver #23 on Day 4, a recording problem prevented any data from being collected. This is an unrecoverable error. All of the Receiver #25 data is unrecoverable because the receiver apparently rejected the simulator signal and would not compute a position, even though it was tracking all the satellite signals.

Table 5-7. Outage Summary for Chamber Day 1

Test Event	Receiver	Start of Outage (GPS Seconds of Week)	End of Outage (GPS Seconds of Week)	Duration (Seconds)	Onset EIRP (dBm)	Effective Distance (meters)	Recovery Distance (meters)
6	#23	148145	149223	1078	21.2	1152	2580
7	#23	152945	153390	445	33.2	409	12928
8	#23	159909	160018	109	40.2	182	82
8	#23	160435	163893	3458	41.2	163	364
4	#23	163961	164643	682	38.2	230	52
2	#23	170734	172052	1318	18.2	2299	5775
1	#23	174154	174218	64	18.2	2299	1451
6	#3	148250	149299	1049	31.2	465	4144
4	#3	164103	164588	485	48.2	66	262
2	#3	170843	172310	1467	25.2	928	36938
1	#3	174258	175790	1532	25.2	928	3694
4	#4	164078	164532	454	46.2	83	183
2	#4	170858	171924	1066	26.2	827	1851
1	#4	174352	175415	1063	31.2	514	3644
4	#20	164080	164093	13	46.2	83	74
4	#20	164108	164488	380	48.2	66	117
2	#20	170915	170944	29	30.2	522	414
2	#20	171823	171839	16	25.2	928	928
1	#20	174408	175186	778	35.2	293	585
6	#1	148292	149032	740	34.2	329	522
4	#1	164103	164477	374	48.2	66	117
2	#1	170898	171838	940	29.2	585	928
1	#1	174364	175265	901	32.2	414	1041

Table 5-8. Outage Summary for Chamber Day 2

Test Event	Receiver	Start of Outage (GPS Seconds of Week)	End of Outage (GPS Seconds of Week)	Duration (Seconds)	Onset EIRP (dBm)	Effective Distance (meters)	Recovery Distance (meters)
1	#20	229930	230619	689	34.2	329.2	465
2	#20	233448	234271	823	33.2	369.4	737
4	#20	239785	239808	23	45.2	92.8	73.7
4	#20	240012	240163	151	47.2	73.7	116.8
5	#20	256408	256935	527	41.2	147.1	261.5
6	#20	252735	253374	639	44	261.5	329.2
1*	#3	229151	229175	24	-15.8	104104.5	82692
1*	#3	229411	231305	1894	2.2	13105.9	92782
2	#3	233345	234755	1410	24.2	1041	29340
4	#3	239809	240245	436	47.2	73.7	233.1
6	#3	252637	253793	1156	30.2	521.8	8269.3
5	#3	256235	257489	1254	30.2	521.8	16499
1*	#4	229153	229175	22	-15.8	104104	82693
1*	#4	229413	229523	110	2.2	13105.9	5845
1	#4	229851	230693	842	31.2	465	826.9
2	#4	233376	234494	1118	26.2	826.9	3693.8
4	#4	239803	240180	377	46.2	82.7	116.8
6	#4	252667	253465	798	32.2	414.4	656.9
5	#4	256354	256991	637	38.2	207.7	369.4
2	#2	233346	234369	1023	24.2	1041	1470.5
4	#2	239796	240166	370	46.2	82.7	104.1
1	#24	229777	230853	1076	26.2	915.3	3247.5
2	#24	233239	234519	1280	17.2	2579.5	5146.9
4	#24	239607	240399	792	33.2	408.8	815.7
8	#24	246493	247047	554	40.2	182.6	289.4
6	#24	252537	253617	1080	23.2	1292.8	2299
5	#24	256283	257115	832	33.2	408.8	1152.2
1	#23	229656	230891	1235	18.2	2299	4088.34

4	#23	239726	240289	563	41.2	162.8	364.4
1	#21	229558	229572	14	11.2	5146.9	4587.2
1	#21	229641	231177	1536	17.2	2579.5	36437.1
2	#21	233204	234657	1453	14.2	3643.7	14505.9
4	#21	239614	240441	827	34.2	364.4	1152.2

* - see Specific results below

Table 5-9. Outage Summary for Day 3

Test Event	Receiver	Start of Outage (GPS Seconds of Week)	End of Outage (GPS Seconds of Week)	Duration (Seconds)	Onset EIRP (dBm)	Effective Distance (meters)	Recovery Distance (meters)
13A	#19	318611	319335	724	33.2	418.9	1324.7
13A	#20	318840	318906	66	33.2	418.9	418.9
9	#20	349727	349735	8	13.2	4189	4189
13A	#3	318601	320654	2053	33.2	418.9	13246.9
11	#3	336102	338300	2198	43.2	132.5	418.9
13A	#4	318811	318927	116	33.2	418.9	418.9
16	#4	333111	333260	149	43.2	132.5	132.5
13A	#2	318811	319337	526	33.2	418.9	1324.7
13A	#1	318808	318920	112	33.2	418.9	418.9
13A	#23	318690	318728	38	33.2	418.9	418.9
13A	#23	318754	319346	592	33.2	418.9	418.9
13A	#21	318601	320469	1868	33.2	418.9	418.9

Table 5-10. Outage Summary for Day 4

Test Event	Receiver	Start of Outage (GPS Seconds of Week)	End of Outage (GPS Seconds of Week)	Duration (seconds)	Onset EIRP (dBm)	Effective Distance (meters)	Recovery Distance (meters)
17	#19	401341	402759	1418	12.2	4587	11522
20	#19	404293	405693	1400	12.2	4700	11806
19	#19	410881	412305	1424	12.2	4700	13247
18	#19	413553	415035	1482	10.2	5917	14863
25*	#19	421861	423495	1634	4.2	11806	26431
26	#19	425027	426351	1324	15.2	3328	8358
17	#1	401463	402566	1103	22.2	1826	2580
20	#1	404432	405504	1072	22.2	1486	2330
19	#1	411077	412015	938	25.2	1052	1324
18	#1	413762	414757	995	24.2	1181	1871
26	#1	425207	426086	879	27.2	836	1052
20	#22	404420	405497	1077	21.2	1668	2643
19	#22	411080	412062	982	25.2	1052	1871
18	#22	413765	414786	1021	24.2	1181	2356
25	#22	422181	423183	1002	25.2	1052	2356
26	#22	425302	426144	842	33.2	419	1668
17	#21	401315	402902	1587	10.2	5775	36437
20	#21	404235	405801	1566	9.2	6639	26431
19	#21	410844	412353	1509	9.2	6639	18712
18	#21	413524	415137	1613	8.2	7449	33275
21	#21	417004	417783	779	40.2	187	2356
25	#21	421962	423675	1713	10.2	5917	105224
26	#21	424967	426651	1684	11.2	5274	83583

* - see Specific results below

Table 5-11. Receivers Affected by Each Test Condition

TE	#1	#19	#20	#3	#4	#21	#22	#23	#24
1	X		X	X	X	X		X	X
2	X		X	X	X	X	X	X	X
3									
4	X		X	X	X	X	X	X	X
5			X	X	X				X
6	X		X	X	X			X	X
7								X	
8								X	X
9									NA
10									NA
11				X					NA
12									NA
13	X	X	X	X	X	X	X	X	NA
14									NA
15									NA
16					X				NA
17	X	X	NA	NA	NA	X		NA	NA
18	X	X	NA	NA	NA	X	X	NA	NA
19	X	X	NA	NA	NA	X	X	NA	NA
20	X	X	NA	NA	NA	X	X	NA	NA
21			NA	NA	NA	X		NA	NA
22			NA	NA	NA			NA	NA
23			NA	NA	NA			NA	NA
24			NA	NA	NA			NA	NA
25		X	NA	NA	NA	X	X	NA	NA
26	X	X	NA	NA	NA	X	X	NA	NA

Analysis

Interpretation of Results

The initial analysis is quite limited and is focused solely on the receivers' ability to determine position under the test conditions. In most cases, degradation in receiver performance occurs well before this point. Also note that, although the effective distance at the end of the outage is provided, it is not necessarily indicative of the power level required to permit reacquisition. Future work will attempt to better quantify degradation in performance, which is expected to be significantly more severe than the outage numbers presented.

The analysis also does not consider operational use of the receivers. The receiver antenna gain patterns have not been considered, and the variation in power levels from each satellite was not simulated during the test. While the transmit antennas were all placed at least 15 degrees above the horizon, the geometry was not representative of the real world. For example, an aircraft in flight will typically be above the LSQ antenna, rather than below it. This will cause the antenna gain to be lower, and there will be additional effects due to blockage by the fuselage.

Specific Results

Results are fairly consistent across receiver types, although some are obviously more susceptible than others. Aviation certified receivers typically perform better than their non-certified counterparts. However, this may be due as much to the antenna as the receiver. The antenna used for the certified receivers has a much higher rejection outside the GPS band, while the other antenna used for the non-aviation receivers has a wide bandwidth.

Although it did not have the greatest effective range, the only test configuration which caused all receivers to lose lock was TE 13. Loss of lock for aircraft receivers, when it occurred, typically happened between 1 and 2 thousand meters for the dual channel cases, and at less than 1 thousand meters for the single channel cases. Non-certified receivers showed much more variation, as would be expected. These receivers are not designed to a single standard and represent a wide variety of designs.

In the Tables several entries have been marked with an asterisk (*). These numbers appear to be anomalous but initial analysis does not reveal any basis for excluding them. They have been included because they may represent receiver behavior that could occur in the live environment. In that case, they represent by far the worst-case performance. Those data points have been presented again in Table 5-12.

Table 5-12. List of Possibly Anomalous Data

1*	#3	229151	229175	24	-15.8	104104.5	82692
1*	#3	229411	231305	1894	2.2	13105.9	92782
1*	#4	229153	229175	22	-15.8	104104	82693
1*	#4	229413	229523	110	2.2	13105.9	5845
25*	#19	421861	423495	1634	4.2	11806	26431

Table 5-13 contains the worst case performance when the data from Table 5-12 are excluded for aviation and non-aviation receivers. This represents the greatest effective distance at which these receivers lost the ability to navigate.

Table 5-13. Worst Case Performance

Type	Receiver	Description	Effective Range
Aviation	#22 & #3	Single Channel Ramp – TE 2	1041 m
Aviation	#1	Dual Channel Ramp – TE 17	1826 m
Non-Aviation	#21	Single Channel Ramp – TE 1	5147 m
Non-Aviation	#21	Dual Channel Ramp – TE 18	7449 m

It is expected that further analysis will be conducted to examine the more detailed behavior of receivers in the LSQ signal environment.

Live Sky Testing

(The GPS LightSquared Live Sky Test Plan Draft -- 7 April 2011, is an FOUO document and not releasable)

FAA

Summary

FAA participated in Live Sky Tests at Holloman AFB on 14-17 April 2011. There were two components to FAA tests; 1) flight tests with various aviation receivers, and, 2) ground tests with WAAS reference and CMC aviation receivers. This report focuses on quick look observations from ground test receiver analysis. Summary observations:

- Receiver #5 tracked through *all* LSQ test signals generated with no loss of signal tracking for satellites above 5 degrees elevation. While signal tracking was not impacted, there were anomalies observed with LSQ signal generation that resulted in questions on the validity of this testing. For example, LSQ 5 MHz High (designated 5H) signal generation was the only signal that resulted in significant C/No degradation (approximately 9 dB) but this degradation was not observed consistently since other 5H test periods resulted in negligible degradation. The only other LSQ test configuration that resulted in C/No degradation was the 5 MHz Low/5 MHz High test (5L/5H). The C/No degradation was 1 dB for this LSQ test configuration.

- Receiver #1 tracked through *most* LSQ test signals generated but lost lock on a significant number of satellites with the 5L/5H Phase 1 configuration. C/No data have yet to be processed for this receiver so observations quantifying potential degradations cannot be provided. It is also important to note that results from the 10 MHz Low/10 MHz High Phase 2 dual channel configuration for this receiver are *not* considered representative. The antenna used during this period of testing is not suitable for use in aviation applications.

The physical distance from FAA antennas to the LSQ transmit tower for these tests was approximately 451 meters but the effective distance was much greater. This effective distance takes into a 3 dB reduction based on Balloon pad calibration data and the maximum EIRP reported for LSQ signals of 57.4 dBm which is almost 6 dB less than the stated level by LSQ. Balloon pad calibration indicated significant variation across the pad which along with fundamental LSQ signal generation mentioned above is of concern for validity of these tests. The effective distance for FAA equipment considering this lower radiated power and pad calibration correction was therefore approximately 1.2 km.

Discussion

FAA testing conducted on the Balloon Pad at Holloman AFB included Receiver #5 and Receiver #1. (Other receivers were tested but those units are not pertinent to the FAA aviation focus). Receiver #5 was connected to a WAAS-125 antenna for both days while Receiver #1 was connected to a aviation antenna for 15 April and a survey antenna for 16 April. The survey antenna filtering and gain are not appropriate for use with an aviation receiver and therefore Receiver #1 results from the 16th are not considered valid or representative. In addition to these GPS receivers, instrumentation for time domain sampling (a Zeta 'Snapshot System') of the RF environment was included in the test configuration and connected to the WAAS-125 antenna.

The LSQ transmit tower was located approximately 451 meters from the FAA data collection location on the Balloon pad. Free space loss for this distance for a signal at 1552.7 MHz is 89.3 dB. However, calibration of the signal strength at the balloon pad conducted at the start of testing on 15 April indicated signal loss at the FAA data location was approximately 3dB greater than free space loss would predict. This equates to an effective distance for LSQ testing of approximately 631 meters. In addition, the LSQ EIRP reported for these tests was approximately 5.7 dB lower than stated by LSQ. Taking this lower power into consideration indicates that the effective distance was approximately 1.2 km or greater. LSQ signals generated during these tests were 5 MHz High, 5 MHz Low, 5 MHz High and Low simultaneously, 10 MHz High, 10 MHz Low, and 10 MHz High and Low simultaneously. 5 MHz was centered at 1552.7, 5 MHz low at 1528.8 MHz, 10 MHz High at 1550.2, and 10 MHz low at 1531.0 MHz.

The signal level present at the WAAS antenna LNA input was an important consideration given the LNAs high gain of approximately 48 dB and 1 dB compression point of 10 dBm. Table 5-14 uses estimates for the reported 5H signal LSQ EIRP for this configuration, effective signal loss and WAAS antenna performance to provide a signal level at the LNA input of approximately -45 dBm. An estimate was also generated using spectral data collected during two 5H tests. These results are provided in Table 5-15 and suggest a range of values from -42 to -48 dBm. This range is related to variation observed with the 5H signal during testing and is discussed in greater detail in a later section of this report.

Table 5-14. LSQ Power at WAAS Antenna LNA Input from Reported LSQ EIRP

Description of Link Budget Parameters	Estimates
GPSD Reported EIRP of LSQ Signal (5H 20W)	+57.3 dBm
Free Space Loss for Distance between WAAS Antenna and Tower (~451m)	-89.3 dB
Adjustment based on Pad Calibration (26.3 – (-66)) – Free Space Loss	3.0 dB
Effective Loss--Free Space Loss plus Adjustment (effective distance ~631m)	-92.3 dB
LSQ Signal Power at FAA Van	-35.0 dBm
WAAS Antenna Pattern Gain at ~5 Degrees -7 dBic or -10 dBil	-10 dB
LSQ Power at Input to WAAS Antenna LNA	-45.0 dBm

Table 5-15. LSQ Power at WAAS Antenna LNA Input from Snapshot Measurements

Description of Link Budget Parameters	Estimates
Snapshot Power Level (5H Distorted/5H Not Distorted)	+12 dBm/+6 dBm
Attenuation Set in SnapApp (no Gain)	-17 dB
Gain of Snapshot External Amplifier	+33 dB
Loss from Cables/Splitter from WAAS Antenna Output	-10 dB
WAAS antenna amplifier Gain	+48 dB
LSQ Power at Input to WAAS Antenna LNA	-42 dBm/-48 dBm

Tower Location: 32.8658N, -106.1265E, 1245m (altitude assumed 30m higher than WAAS antenna)
WAAS Antenna Location: 32.86935N, -106.1288.2E, 1215m
Distance between tower and WAAS antenna = 450.7m

Analysis of Receiver #5 data focused primarily on L1 C/A signal tracking and C/No observations. For Receiver #1, only L1 C/A signal tracking was available for this quick look analysis. Figure 5-29 shows a representation of Receiver #5 L1 C/No computed for all GPS satellites tracked. This C/No data is computed by correcting each satellite for nominal antenna gain and satellite power and then averaging all these corrected values for each time step. (If the receiver were operating as expected with no RFI present, this metric would indicate zero dB).

Figure 5-29 shows this C/No metric for the entire April 15th test period and highlights each specific test conducted. The large C/No degradation is associated with the 5H Ramp test and there is a question concerning the validity of this signal since the 5H test configuration did show consistent performance throughout the testing (more detail in a later section). The only other period where noticeable C/No degradation was observed occurred with the 5L/5H Ramp and Full Power (20W) tests conducted at the end of this test period. The C/No degradation was approximately 1 dB for this LSQ configuration. Figure 5-30 shows the number of GPS L1 signals tracked by both Receivers #1 and #5. Receiver #5 only shows GPS L1 signals while Receiver #1 shows GPS plus SBAS. For comparison purposes, the number of L1 signals tracked for Receiver #5 was increased by two to represent SBAS tracking. This Figure shows that Receiver #5 tracking was not impacted by any of the LSQ signals and Receiver #1 tracking was impacted only when 5L/5H was generated. The Receiver #1 tracking degradation for this LSQ configuration is rather dramatic with only four L1 signals being tracked.

Figure 5-31 and Figure 5-32 show the same observations for 16 April testing. As noted previously, Receiver #1 used a non-aviation antenna for this test period so its results are not shown. With the brief exception of a 5H test transmission that was aborted, Receiver #5 C/No degradation for this entire test period is considered negligible. The 5L/5H LSQ configuration impact appeared to be only 0.5 dB for this test sequence. Lastly, L1 signal tracking was not impacted for Receiver #5 throughout the 16 April test period.

Finally, Table 5-16 provides a summary of Receiver #5 and Receiver #1 observations from 15 and 16 April 2011 LSQ testing.

Table 5-16. Tracking and C/No Observations for Various LSQ Signals Tested

Signal Tested	Receiver #1	Receiver #5
5H	Lost tracking on one SV	Negligible to 9 dB C/No Degradation; *LSQ Signal Validity Questioned*
5L	No Impact	No Impact
5L/5H	Loss of Tracking on all but Four Satellites	1 dB C/No Degradation
10H	No Impact	No Impact
10L	No Impact	No Impact
10L/10H	Receiver #1 Observations Not Considered Valid	No Impact

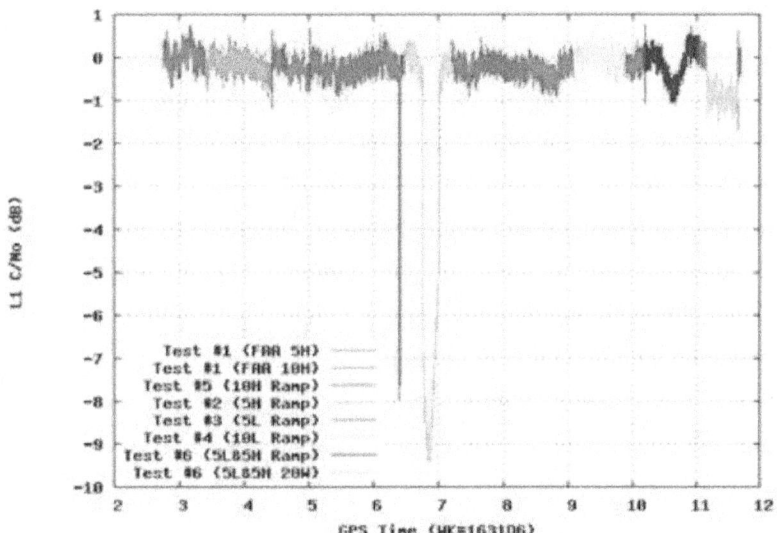

Figure 5-29. Receiver #5 L1 C/No Corrected for Nominal Antenna Gain and GPS Signal Strength for 15 April 2011. Large C/No Degradation Associated with 5H Signal Generation Anomaly.

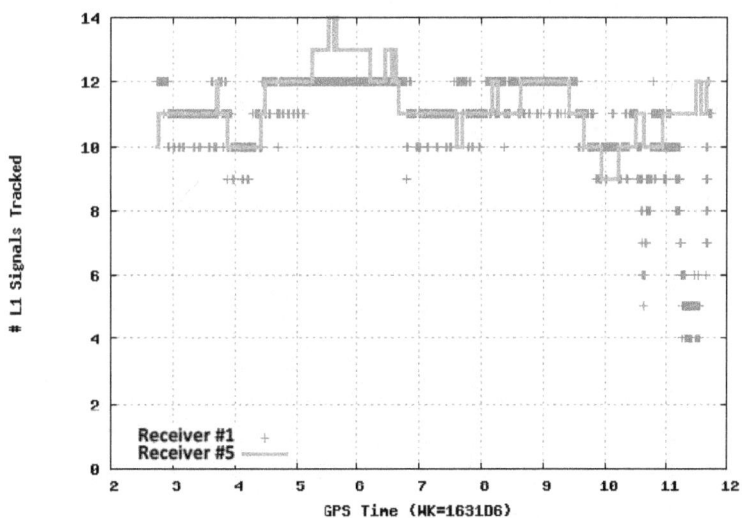

Figure 5-30. Number of Receiver #1 and Receiver #5 L1 Signals Tracked during 15 April 2011 LSQ Testing

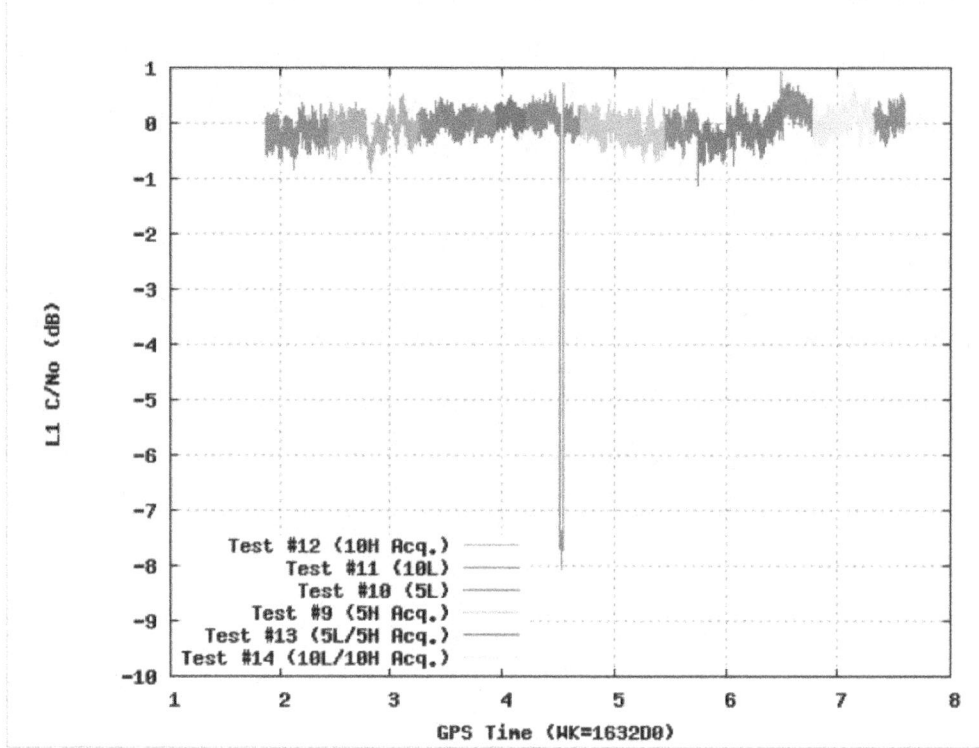

Figure 5-31. Receiver #5 L1 C/No Corrected for Nominal Antenna Gain and GPS Signal Strength for 16 April 2011. Large C/No Degradation Associated with 5H Signal Generation Anomaly.

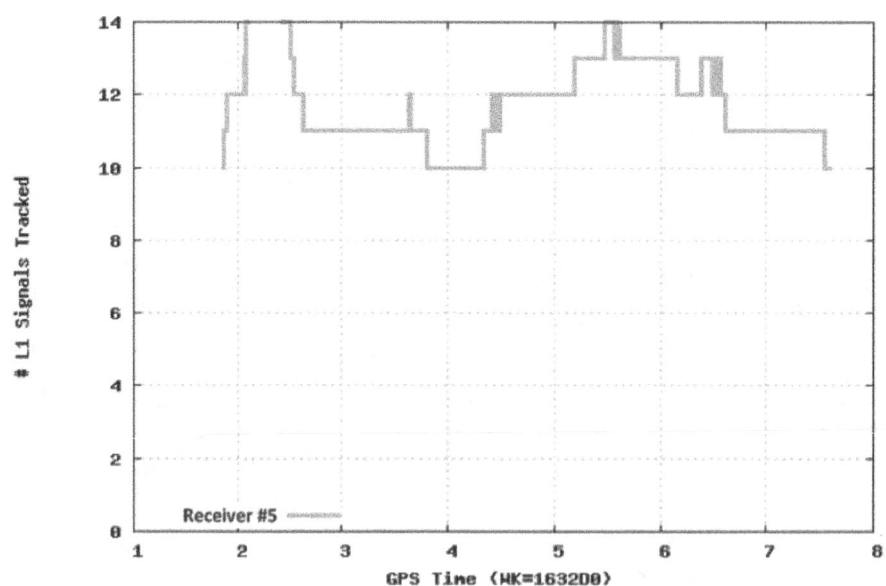

Figure 5-32. Number of Receiver #5 L1 Signals Tracked for 16 April 2011 LSQ Testing

LSQ Signal Generation Anomaly

Quick look analysis was performed using FAA data collected from the balloon pad for 15 April and 16 April tests. GPS receiver data utilized for this quick analysis was obtained from Receivers #5, 23, 25 and 19. Receiver #5 was connected to a WAAS-125 antenna (2225NW) for both test days while Receivers #23, 25, and 19 were connected to a aviation antenna on Day 1 and a survey antenna on Day 2. In addition to GPS receiver observations, the RF environment was sampled during critical test points with instrumentation capable of time domain sampling. This instrumentation was connected to a WAAS-125 antenna for both test days.

Figure 5-33 shows L1 AGC response from Receiver #5 for 15 April testing with various LSQ test configurations highlighted in different colors. Figure 5-34 shows the number of satellites tracked for Receivers #23, 25 and 19 for the same time period as Figure 5-33 (Receiver #5 did not experience any loss of tracking so its data is not shown). LSQ test configurations are highlighted at the bottom of Figure 5-34. Figure 5-35 and Figure 5-36 show the same information for 16 April testing. Figure 5-37 and Figure 5-38 show spectral plots comparing specific LSQ test configurations.

One significant concern from these initial observations is the validity of the LSQ signals generated during these tests. This concern was highlighted during 16 April testing when the 1st attempt at 5H step testing (Test #9) was halted because it was reported the waveform was distorted. This "distorted" signal resulted in the Receiver #5 AGC algorithm becoming fixed (AGC jump to ~6000 count level—possibly saturated) which is indicative of significant power present at the receiver's input. The LSQ signal generator was reportedly reset after this distortion was observed and the power indicated by the Receiver #5 AGC response in subsequent conduct of Test #9 was relatively benign (this performance can be seen in Figure 5-31). Receiver #5 AGC response indicating the presence of lower power was further confirmed with spectral plots shown in Figure 5-37 and Figure 5-38. Figure 5-37 compares spectrums of LSQ 5H from Test #9 (20W Step) of the "distorted" waveform and after LSQ equipment was reset (again, 20W Step). The signal power after reset is much lower, consistent with Receiver #5 AGC observations. Figure 5-38 provides a further comparison showing the LSQ 5H signal from Test #9 (20W Step) with the LSQ 5H signal from Test #13 (20W Step). Test #13 used simultaneous 5L/5H signals and the power observed for the High signal is again greater than observed with Test #9 after LSQ equipment was reset. This is also confirmed in Figure 5-35 with Receiver #5 AGC response and generally consistent with satellites tracked from Receivers #23, 25 and 19.

These observations and observations from 15 April call into question the validity of the 5 MHz High LSQ signal generated during these tests. The validity of this signal is particularly important to FAA since it appears the LSQ signal generated during the FAATC flyovers on 15 April may *not* have been conducted with a representative signal.

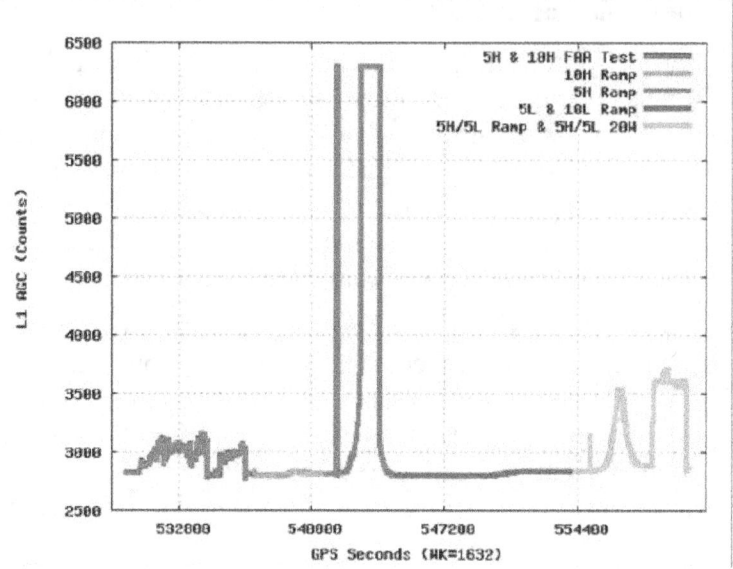

Figure 5-33. AGC Response for Receiver #5 from Day 1 Testing

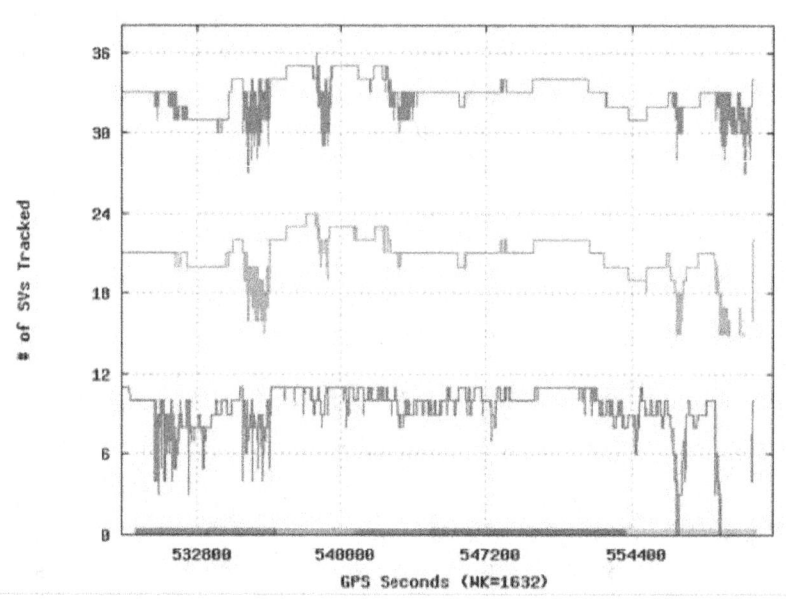

Figure 5-34. Number of Satellites Tracked for Receivers #23, 25 and 19 from Day 1 Testing

5-38

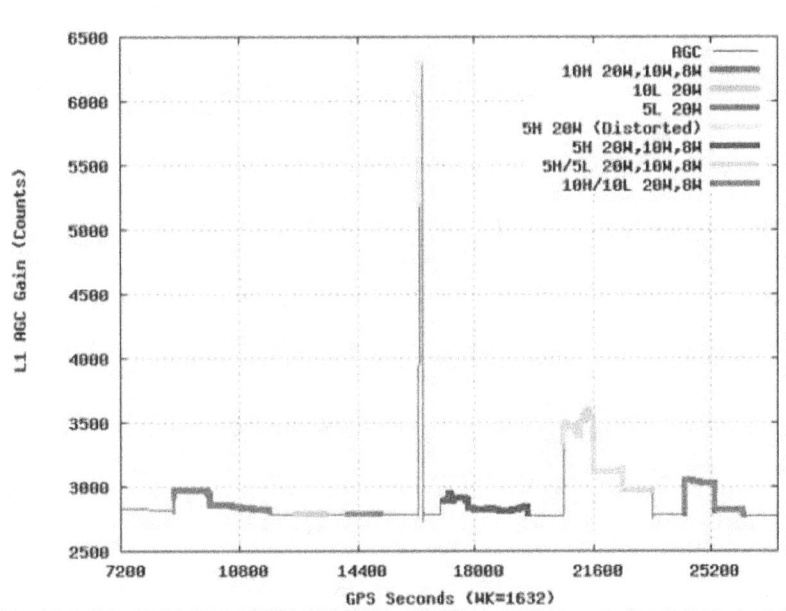

Figure 5-35. AGC Response for Receiver #5 from Day 2 Testing

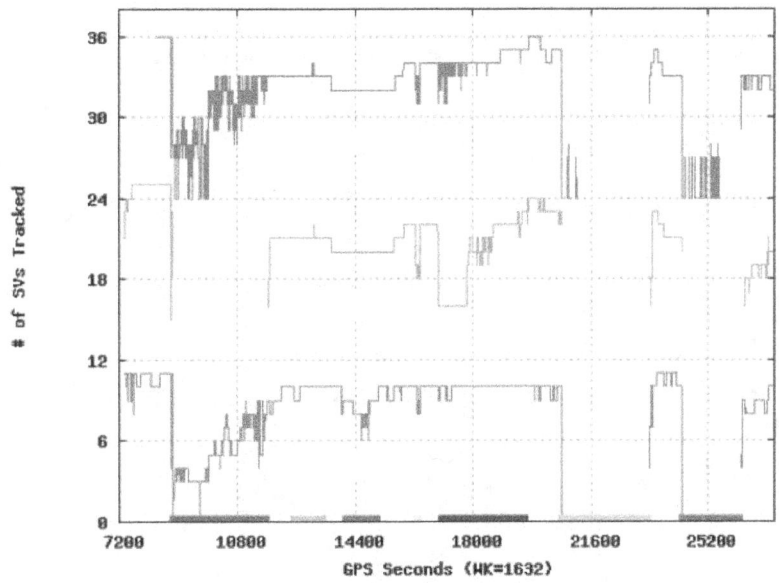

Figure 5-36. Number of Satellites Tracked for Receivers #23, 25 and 19 from Day 2 Testing

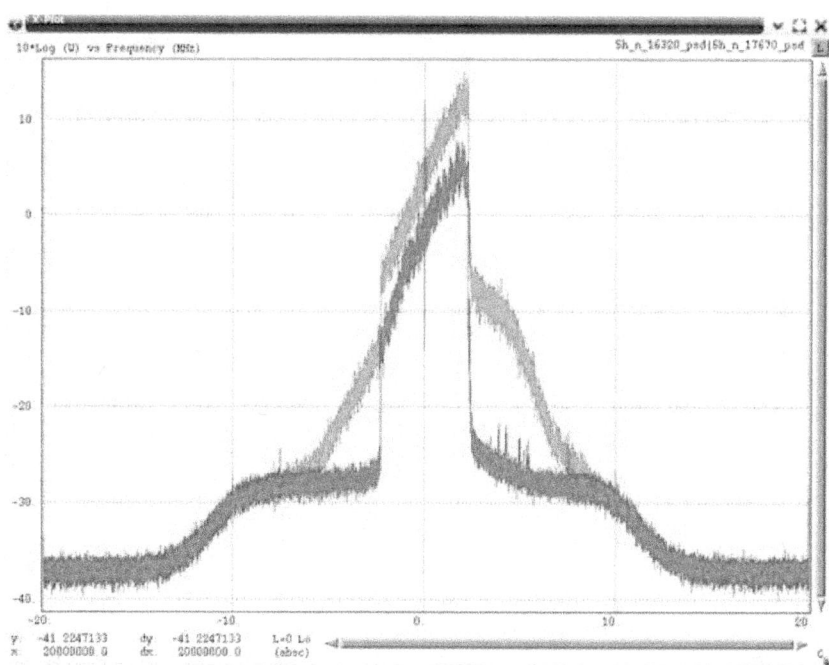

Figure 5-37. Comparison of 5 High Step Test from Day 2 (Test #9) of "Distorted" Waveform (Green) and Waveform Generated after Reset of LSQ Equipment (Magenta). Distorted Waveform is approximately 6 dB Higher in Power when both were reported at 20W.

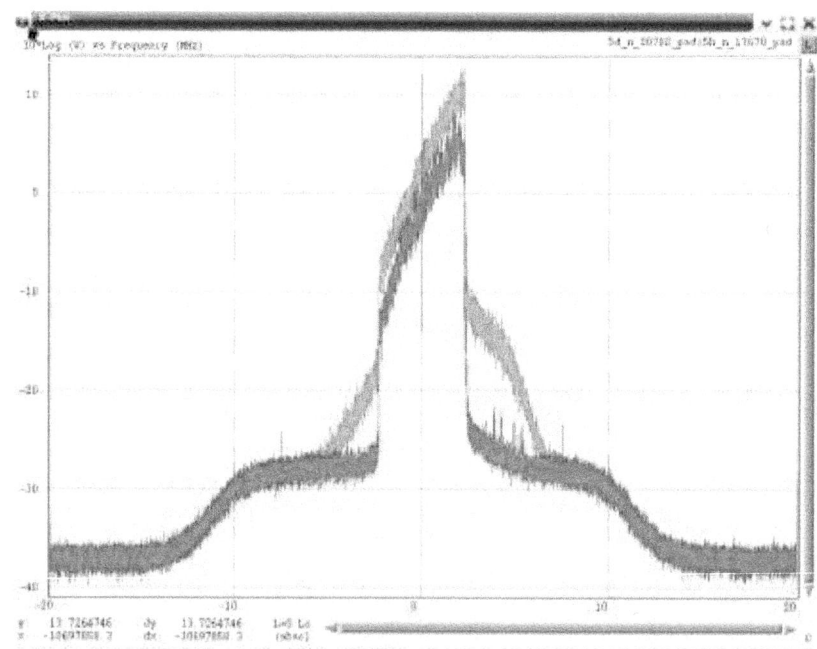

Figure 5-38. Comparison of 5 MHz Step Test from Day 2 (Test 9) after Reset of LSQ Equipment (Magenta) with Simultaneous 5MHz High/Low (Green) Waveform (Test 13) (High/Low Waveform is approximately 4 dB Higher in Power when both were Reported at 20W)

5-40

References

Capt. Diefel (GPSD) and Tom Powell (Aerospace) Emails on 25 April 2011 providing LSQ Test Sequence, LSQ power levels, and Balloon Pad Calibration data.

DOI

The Bureau of Land Management (BLM) arranged to have a number mapping and survey level receivers collect data during the LightSquared open sky testing at Holloman AFB. These receivers are a representative cross section of mapping and survey receivers that are currently in use within the BLM, other DOI agencies, and the U.S. Forest Service.

All of the mapping receivers that tested encountered problems with the exception of Receiver #26. Initial checking of the files showed that the collected data on the mapping receivers was only 70 to 75% of the possible yield. Receivers #27 and #28 had the worst point yields on both days of testing. When the data was further checked and compared to the test broadcast times two behaviors were noted. In the first case five or more satellites were tracked but the signal to noise (SNR) strengths of the satellites were below the usable software thresholds and positions were not computed. The second behavior was that the receivers lost lock on all satellites for a portion or the whole test. When the test signal was turned off the receivers would resume normal operation. The major issues with Receiver #29 occurred during the Test #1 full power testing on the Holloman Day 2 schedule and on the Test #5 test with a combination of signal strength decreases or no tracking. Interestingly the only receiver that did not have any tracking problems was Receiver #26. It should be noted that data was only collected during Day 2 of the Holloman AFB testing. Data was not collected on the third day due to the receiver being out of memory.

Receiver #30 and Receiver #31 both exhibited major problems in tracking with all tests. The typical behavior is that when a test signal was broadcast the receivers would lose total lock on the satellites and not track until the signal was turned off. This matches the behaviors seen by other government and industry testers of GPS and GNSS receivers.

Conclusions

GPS and GNSS technology is a major field data collection tool used by all resource management agencies. If the LightSquared implementation plan goes forward as proposed it will have a severe negative impact on the agencies' ability to efficiently and effectively collect data to manage our nation's resources. We will be severely limited in our use of GPS / GNSS real time survey receivers. We could potentially be forced to go back to total station surveys which will add costs in terms of operation and personnel. In addition the LightSquared plan could result in the Continually Operating Reference Station (CORS) GPS/GNSS network not being able to collect data and providing access to the National Spatial Reference System (NSRS). This will hamper our ability to collect or reference accurate geospatial data.

NOAA

NOAA / National Geodetic Survey participated in the NPEF sponsored LightSquared Live Sky testing at Holloman AFB on April 15, 2011. The NOAA vehicle was configured with four high precision geodetic / survey GPS receivers connected through an eight way splitter to a geodetic antenna using magnetic mounts on the vehicle roof. Another antenna similarly mounted was connected to a single survey receiver with the manufacturer recommended geodetic antenna. To maintain receiver anonymity in presenting the results random codes were assigned to the geodetic/ survey receivers tested. These codes were obtained from the LightSquared / United States GPS Industry Council (USGIC) Working Group Facilitator and will also be used in reporting NOAA results from the LightSquared Live Sky testing in Las Vegas May 18 - 22.

Due to high wind conditions on April 15th, the LightSquared Ancillary Terrestrial Component (ATC) reference station could only be raised to 32 ft. (9.8 m.) instead of the 100 ft. (30.48 m.) specified operational height. The NOAA vehicle was approximately positioned 315 m. (32 51 57.0N, 106 7 35.1W - ATC coordinate location) from the LightSquared transmitter for Tests #2, Test #3, and Test #4. After Test #4 the test director requested that the NOAA vehicle move about 100 m. closer to the LightSquared transmitter for the remainder of the testing that day. The NOAA vehicle was repositioned approximately 230 m. from the transmitter for Test #5, Test #9 (Ramp) and Test #7. The test conditions for all tests are noted in Table 5-17. The NOAA vehicle position on April 15th is shown in Figure 5-39.

Table 5-17. Live Sky Test Results, 15 April 2011

Test #2 – 5 MHz – High Band- Full Power	Event time (GPS)	Transmitted Power EIRP –Total (dBm)
Start Test	2:39:00	54.1
Added + 3dB to each port	2:42:00	57.1
End Test	3:09:00	57.1
Test #3 – 5 MHz – Low Band – Full Power		
Start Test	3:25:00	57.2
End Test	3:40:00	57.2
Test #4 – 10 MHz – Low Band – Full Power		
Start Test	3:54:00	57.2
End Test	4:09:00	57.2

Test #5 – 10 MHz – High Band – Full Power		
Start Test	4:22:00	57.2
End Test	4:37:00	57.2
Test #9 – Ramp - 5 MHz – High Band – Variable Power		
Start Test	5:08:00	Variable
End Test	5:50:00	Variable
Test # 7 - 10 MHz – High Band and 10 MHz Low Band – Full Power		
Start Test	6:05:00	54.2 dBm – One Channel
Added Second Channel	6:05:37	54.2 dBm – Each Channel
End Test	6:20:00	54.2 dBm – Each Channel

Figure 5-39. Live Sky Test Locations, 15 April 2011

The Test #2 results for receiver H07007A connected to geodetic antenna B through the splitter are shown in Figure 5-40. Receiver H07007A lost tracking at the start of the 5 MHz high band test and did not recover until the test was completed. The LightSquared transmitter was adjusted to output more power at GPS time 2:42:00 to 57.1 dBm, but receiver H07007A had already lost track at 54.1 dBm at the start of Test #2. The LightSquared transmitter at Holloman was not able to generate the maximum specified power of 62 dBm but could only achieve 57.1 dBm (approximately 5 dBm less than allowed). The test results in Figure 5-31 show the L1 C/A Signal to Noise Ratio as a function of time for each PRN tracked during Test #2.

Near the completion of Test #3 receiver H07007A was disconnected from the 8 position splitter and connected to a separate geodetic antenna (Antenna C) to provide a broader range of test data. Test #3 and Test #4 results for Receiver H07007A/C-antenna are shown in Figure 5-41. During Test #3 (5 MHz- Lower Band – Full Power) the Signal to Noise Ratio for all PRNs tracked by receiver-A dropped by about 5 dB. At the beginning of Test #4 the Signal to Noise Ratio dropped about 11 dB for all tracked PRNs. During the remainder of Test #4, the Signal to Noise Ratio dropped an additional 4 dB ending Test #4 with a net decrease of 15 dB for PRNs 7, 8, 17, 26 and 28. PRN 11 had a net decrease of 17 dB.

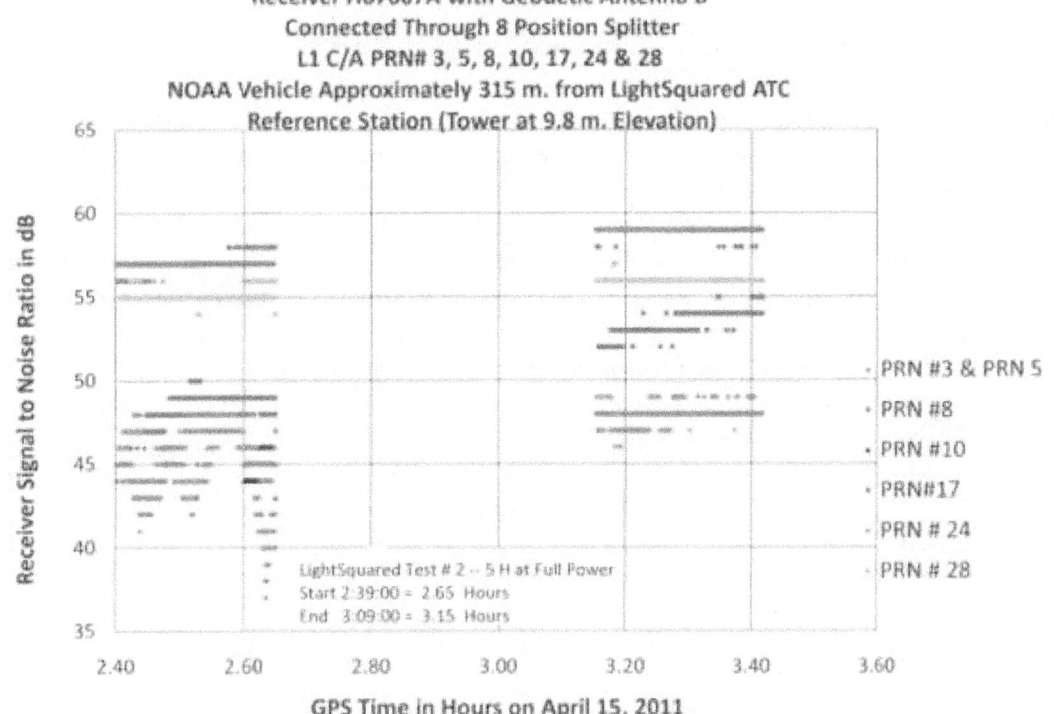

Figure 5-40. Results for Receiver H07007A with Antenna B

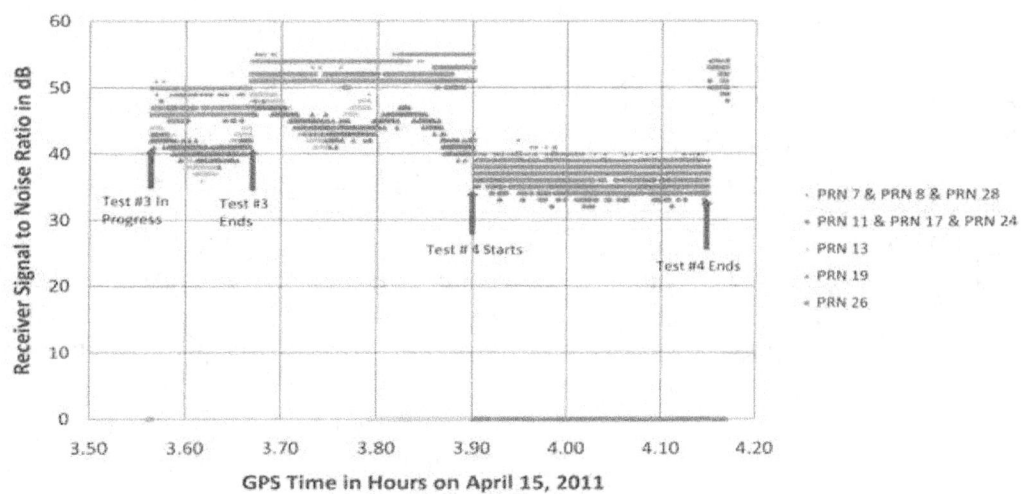

Figure 5-41. Results for Receiver H07007A with Antenna C

In addition to the 8 splitter receiver configuration at NOAA Test Site #1 another geodetic receiver (Receiver B/A-ant.) was also tested. The antenna connected to this receiver was a manufacturer recommended antenna. This receiver data acquisition was started after the 8 splitter receivers were set to take data and as a result Test # 2 was already over before the data acquisition was started for this receiver. However, no SNR degradation or loss of tracking was observed for Receiver B/A-ant during Tests # 3 and #4. The SNR degradation or loss of track for all receivers tested is summarized in Table 5-18 for NOAA Test Site #1 (315 m.). For receivers H92053, H80708 and H33451, the RINEX file conversion software were earlier versions of v2.11 and did not output the receiver Signal to Noise Ratios except in a compressed form which is not useful. The receiver performance for these receivers for the tests in Table 5-17 are summarized by noting positioning performance in Table 5-18 and Table 5-19.

Table 5-18. Summary of Receiver SNR Degradation or Loss of Tracking @ 315m from LightSquared ATC Transmitter

	Test #2	Test #3	Test #4
Receiver H07007A/B-ant.	All PRNs lose track and do not recover until Test # 2 is completed		
Receiver H07007A/C-ant.		Partial Data Acquisition – SNR ratios of all PRNs decreased by about 5 dB	SNRs for all PRNs tracked decreased 11 dB at beginning of test and dropped another 4 dB at the end of test
Receiver H07007B/A-ant.	No Data – Data acquisition started too late	No SNR degradation or tracking loss	No SNR degradation or tracking loss
Receiver H91389/B-ant.	5 PRNs lose track 4 seconds into test – all remaining PRNs lose track @2:54:48	3 PRNs lose track 3 seconds into test-the SNRs of the 6 remaining PRNs decrease between 17 to 19 dB – all remaining PRNs lose tracking @3:35:30 with 4:30 min. remaining in test	5 PRNs lose track 5 seconds into test-the SNRs of the 4 remaining PRNs decrease 14 to 25 dB - all remaining PRNs lose tracking @3:54:22- 22 seconds into test

Receiver H92053/B-ant.	15 minutes into test @2:54:13 less than 4 PRNs tracked – no position solution for remainder of test	3 seconds into test @3:25:03 less than 4 PRNs tracked – no position solution for remainder of test	6 seconds into test @3:54:06 less than 4 PRNs tracked – no position solution for remainder of test
Receiver H80708/B-ant.	13 seconds into test @2:42:13 less than 4 PRNs tracked – no position solution for remainder of test	4 seconds into test @3:25:04 less than 4 PRNs tracked – no position solution for remainder of test	4 seconds into test @3:54:04 less than 4 PRNs tracked – no position solution for remainder of test

The NOAA vehicle was moved after Test #4 from 315m to approximately 230m from the LightSquared ATC transmitter at the request of the Test Director. The SNR degradation or loss of track for all receivers tested in summarized in Table 5-19 for Test Site # 2.

Table 5-19. Summary of Receiver SNR Degradation or Loss of Tracking @ 230m from LightSquared ATC Transmitter

	Test #5	Test #9 (Ramp)	Test #7
Receiver H07007A/C-ant.	All PRNs lose track and do not recover until Test # 5 is completed	Tracking until 5:12:03 @42.4 dBm - then less than 4 PRNs tracked – no position solution for remainder of test	One second into test all PRNs lose track for the duration
Receiver H07007B/A-ant.	All PRN SNRs drop 1-5 dB at start of test; all PRN SNRs drop an additional 3 dB (3-8 dB) by end of test	Tracking until 5:26:37 @57.5 dBm - Max Power then less than 4 PRNs tracked – no position solution until 5:35:13 @51.5 dBm when tracking resumes with 4 PRNs	No SNR degradation for 2 PRNs and 1-4 dB degradation for remaining PRNs at start-30 seconds into the test 7 PRNs lose tracking and remaining 3 PRNs SNRs decrease an additional 14 dB

Receiver H91389/B-ant.	5 PRNs lose track 4 seconds into test – all remaining PRNs lose track @2:54:48	Tracking until 5:16:54 @47.5 dBm - less than 4 PRNs tracked – no data until 5:40:37 @45.4 dBm when tracking resumes with 4 PRNs	3 seconds into test @6:05:03 less than 4 PRNs tracked – no position solution for remainder of test
Receiver H92053/B-ant	29 seconds into test @4:22:29 less than 4 PRNs tracked – no position solution for remainder of test	Tracking until 5:25:46 @56.5 dBm - then less than 4 PRNs tracked – no position solution until 5:41:26 @45.4 dBm when tracking resumes	30 seconds into test @6:05:30 less than 4 PRNs tracked – no position solution for remainder of test
Receiver H80708/B-ant.	4 seconds into test @4:22:04 no PRNs tracked – no position solution for remainder of test	Tracking until 5:14:09 @44.4 dBm - then no PRNs tracked – no position solution for remainder of test	RINEX file ends @5:14:09 – No data for Test #7

The GPS accuracy of Receiver H07007 A/ C-antenna was determined using NOAA / NGS post processed software during the time interval between the end of Test #3 and the beginning of Test #4 (Figure 5-41). The application computes differential position coordinates using the closest CORS reference station to the NOAA vehicle. The Receiver H07007A/ C-antenna accuracy relative to the average vehicle coordinate when the LightSquared reference station was not transmitting is shown in Figure 5-42. The NGS post processed 95% accuracy is three meters or less with CORS reference stations up to 200 km. from a rover position. The receiver H07007A/ C-antenna accuracy during LightSquared transmitter Test#4 is shown in Figure 5-43. The 95% position accuracy of Receiver A/ C-antenna degraded from 2.6m to 3.1m and more outliers occurred during Test #4. The GPS accuracy of Receiver B/A-antenna was measured during Test # 5 and no degradation was noted as the PRN SNRs decreased 3-8 dB (Table 5-19).

The carrier phase accuracy was determined using NOAA / NGS product OPUS-RS. OPUS (Online Positioning User Service) is a free Web-based utility enabling its users to submit GPS data to NOAA's National Geodetic Survey where it will be automatically processed to obtain precise coordinates for the location associated with this data. The biggest difference between OPUS and OPUS-RS is the occupation time. OPUS requires a minimum occupation time of at least two hours and OPUS-RS requires a minimum occupation time of fifteen minutes. The LightSquared ATC transmissions in different phases during the testing on April 15 were 15 minutes in duration for all tests except for the ramp test (Test # 9) which lasted about an hour.

OPUS-RS also has the capability to estimate the accuracy and availability at a given coordinate for 15 minute and one hour data sets. Table 5-20 lists the predicted and measured carrier phase accuracy for Receiver H07007A/C-antenna. This is the only receiver to maintain tracking and experience SNR degradation during a LightSquared ATC test without losing tracking. Carrier phase accuracy was not measured for Receiver H07007A/B-antenna as this receiver did not experience any SNR degradation or lost tracking during Test #4.

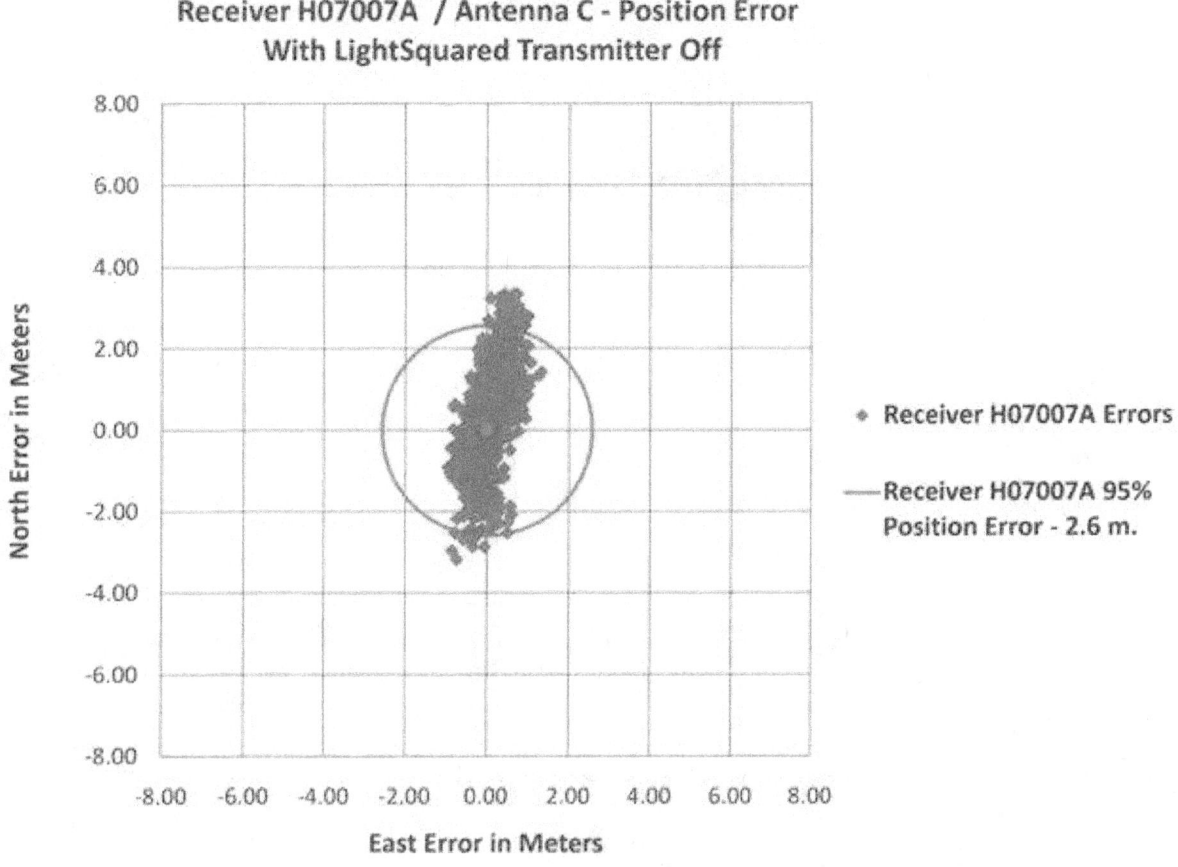

Figure 5-42. Receiver H07007A/Antenna C Position Error with LightSquared Transmitter OFF

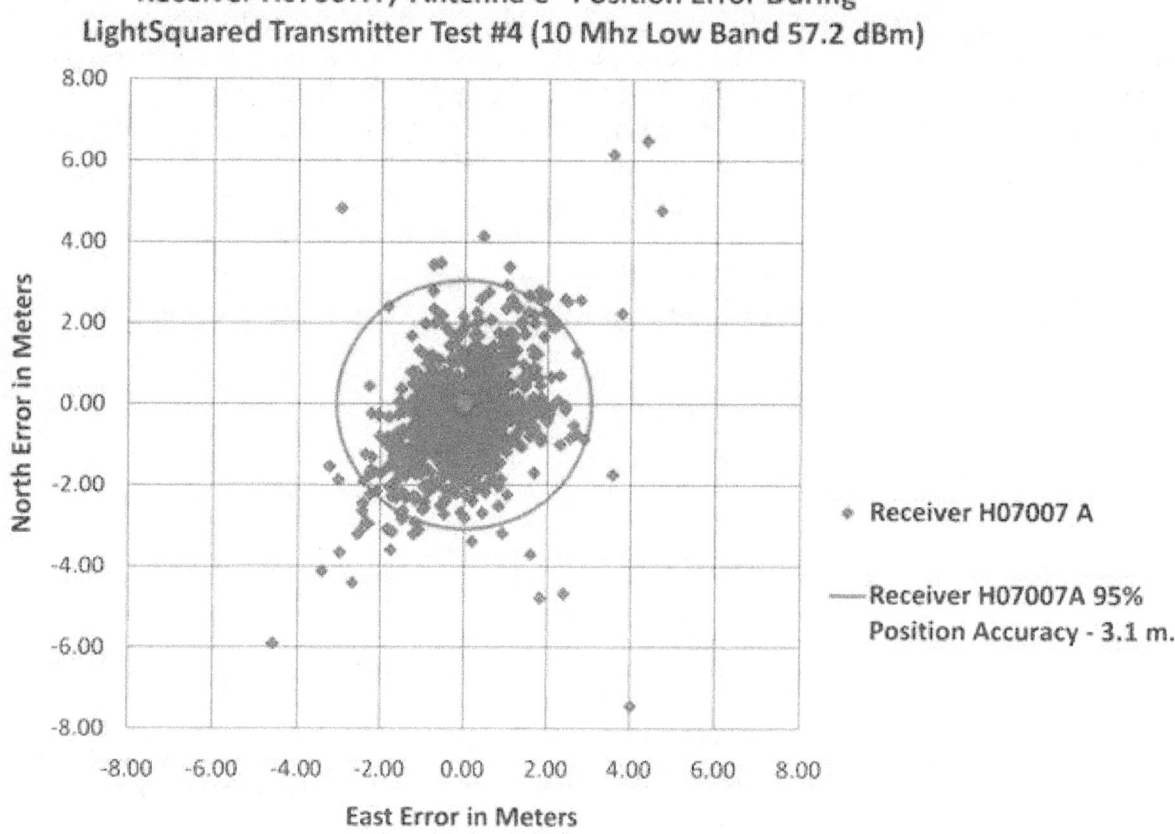

Figure 5-43. Reciever H07007A Position Error with LightSquared Transmitter ON (10MHz Low Band 57.2 dBm)

Table 5-20. OPUS-RS Carrier Phase Accuracy During Test #4

	95% Predicted Position Accuracy	95% Measured Position Accuracy
Receiver H07007A/C-ant. Test site #1	2 cm.	1.2 cm Test # 4 (898 Data Points)

Summary Analysis and Conclusions

Most geodetic survey receivers lost tracking at 315 meters or less from the LightSquared ATC reference transmitter station. The better performance was provided by Receiver H07007B/A-ant. (connected to the manufacturer recommended antenna). No SNR degradation or tracking loss was observed for this receiver during Test #3 (5 MHz – Low band – Full Power) or Test #4 (10 MHz – Low Band – Full Power). During Test #5 (10 MHz – High Band – Full Power) this receiver experienced 3-8 dB SNR degradation but no degradation in pseudorange or carrier phase accuracy. Receiver H07007B/C-antenna (connected to a separate geodetic antenna instead of the common antenna in the splitter) experienced about 15 dB SNR degradation and also had a 0.5m.decrease in pseudorange accuracy during Test #4. There was no degradation in carrier phase accuracy (Table 5-20) for this receiver. The remaining three GPS receivers (H91389, H92053 and H80708) connected to common antenna B through the splitter all lost tracking during Test #2, Test #3, and Test #4. All receivers lost track during Test #5 and Test #7 except as noted above for Receiver H07007B/A-antenna. All receivers lost tracking during the Ramp test and either resumed tracking as the power was decreased or were not able to reacquire the GPS satellites for the remainder of the ramp test. Test# 5, Test #9, and Test #7 may also be more severe as the 5 and 10MHz high bands were transmitted at full power which are closer to the GPS band.

This data set may not qualify as official data for the Holloman AFB Live Sky testing as the LightSquared ATC tower height was only at 32 feet instead of the operational height of 100 feet for the subsequent days of testing. However, this data set may be a preview of what can be expected during the LightSquared Live Sky testing in Las Vegas. Three of the four LightSquared ATC reference stations will have antenna heights between 15.2 – 18.3 meters compared to the NOAA data set logged at the 9.8 meter antenna height.

National Continuously Operating Reference Station (CORS) System

The National Geodetic Survey has established a national CORS system to support non-navigation post-processing applications of GPS. More recently, the CORS network has also served a troposphere and ionosphere monitoring network by those two scientific communities. Additionally, the national CORS is being modernized to serve as the foundation for future applications that support near- and real-time positioning (differing from navigation applications by the lack of a safety-of-life component). The national CORS system provides code range and carrier phase data from a nationwide network of GPS stations for access by the Internet. As of March 2005, data were being provided from more than 650 stations.

The NGS manages and coordinates data contributions from GPS stations established by other groups rather than by building an independent network of reference stations. In particular, use is being made of data from stations operated by components of DOT and DHS that support real-time navigation requirements (mostly WAAS and NDGPS). These real-time stations make up approximately 26 percent of all national CORS stations. Other stations currently contributing data to the national CORS system include stations operated by the NOAA and NASA in support of crustal motion activities, stations operated by state and local governments in support of surveying applications, and stations operated by NOAA's Forecast Systems Laboratory in support of meteorological applications.

The national CORS is a GPS augmentation system managed by NOAA that archives and distributes GPS data for precision positioning and atmospheric modeling applications. It serves as the basis for the National Spatial Reference System, defining high accuracy coordinates for all CONUS-based Federal radionavigation systems. Historically, CORS served post-processing users of GPS, but is being modernized to support real-time users at a similar level of accuracy.

State of New Mexico Emergency Services

SUSANA MARTINEZ
GOVERNOR

RICHARD E. MAY
CABINET SECRETARY

SAMUEL L. OJINAGA
ACTING DIRECTOR

STATE OF NEW MEXICO
DEPARTMENT OF FINANCE AND ADMINISTRATION
LOCAL GOVERNMENT DIVISION
Bataan Memorial Building, Suite 201 ♦ Santa Fe, New Mexico 87501
(505) 827-4950 ♦ FAX No. (505) 827-4943

May 11, 2011

Bernard J. Gruber, Col, USAF
Director
Global Positioning Systems Directorate
Front Office
483 N. Aviation Blvd.
Los Angeles AFB, CA 90245-2808

Karen Van Dyke
Director, Positioning, Navigation, and Timing (Acting)
DOT/Research and Innovative Technology Administration (RITA)
1200 New Jersey Avenue, SE
Washington, DC 20590

Thomas J. Nagle, SMC/GPC
Program Manager, Civil Applications
GPS Directorate, Los Angeles AFB
Building 271, Room B2-548
483 North Aviation Blvd.
El Segundo, CA 90245-2808

Dear Colonel Gruber, Ms. Van Dyke and Mr. Nagle:

In March 2011 I was informed of a company called LightSquared that is asking for FCC approval to build a nationwide 4G wireless network. There is concern from major GPS providers that LightSquared's frequency interferes with GPS signals necessary for routine 911 caller location.

I was asked by the Federal Aviation Agency (FAA) to coordinate first responder representatives from fire, EMS and law enforcement for testing of the LightSquared network in a live sky testing environment at Holloman AFB, New Mexico on April 15 – 16, 2011. The objective of the test was to determine if any level of interference to GPS signals were a result of LightSquared testing.

The attached reports are provided by law enforcement, EMS and fire first responders who participated in the field test. Law enforcement was represented by New Mexico State Police personnel Mike De Fausell and Officer Daniel Vaughan of New Mexico State Police District 4 office in Las Cruces. Mike is a subject matter expert in communications technology with an emphasis on radio. The attached reports verify there was a negative effect on the GPS equipment.

EMS and Fire reports are from local government first responders from Otero County. They represent typical fire and EMS field equipment. See the attached report from Otero County Emergency Manager Paul Quairoli detailing anomalies in GPS reception.

In conclusion the attached reports substantiate concerns that the LightSquared network will cause interference to GPS signals and jeopardize 911 and public safety nationwide.

If you have any questions, please feel free to contact me at 505-827-4804 or bill.range@state.nm.us.

Sincerely,

Bill Range, ENP, PMP
New Mexico E-911 Program Director
Department of Finance and Administration, Local Government Division

LightSquared Test

On April 15, 2011, at approximately 2354, we experienced system failure when we parked under the LightSquared tower. Once the power was shut off at the tower, we left the tower site. When we got to the turn off for the dirt road, the system came back up and the Alamogordo office was able to see us moving again.

Our system has cell phone connectivity, radio connectivity, and satellite connectivity. Our mobile data terminal will automatically select and connect to the strongest signal. The GPS is only over the satellite transceiver.

When the tests were started again our GPS positions were skewed. When the LightSquared tower was turned off the system would normal out.

I believe it was approximately 0400 when they began the high dual five test, the GPS positions were skewed and remained skewed even after power was turned off. As they began the next tests, we started getting GPS reading from the Alamogordo office every ten minutes. These GPS readings continued to be incorrect the rest of the test period. We asked the Alamogordo office to send the GPS readings with the time via the MDC so there would be a record of the information.

We were unable to get the system to normal out until we were leaving Holloman AFB on April 16, 2011 at approximately 0700; we did another reset of the equipment. At that point the system began to function correctly.

My times and GPS reading were given to Captain Justin Deifel, USAF at the closing briefing.

Submitted by:

Mike De Fausell
New Mexico State Police
District Four Communications

6. Subtask 6 - Simulation Activities

Task Statement

Coordinate simulation activities to further assess effects on GPS usage under various scenarios.

NASA Simulations

Overview

This report describes analysis of LightSquared base station interference to four high-precision GPS receivers used in NASA spaceborne and terrestrial applications. All four receivers are capable of processing the L1 C/A-code and L1/L2 P(Y) code GPS signals. The P(Y) code signals are processed using various semi-codeless techniques to obtain the L2 carrier phase. Interference assessment is based on estimating the interference levels expected in various spaceborne and terrestrial scenarios and comparing them against interference limits/thresholds obtained through conduction measurements on the four receivers by JPL. This testing was performed at JPL on March 22, 2011 using a simulated LightSquared Phase 1 signal (i.e., two 5 MHz channels centered at 1528.8 MHz and 1552.7 MHz) and is described in the previously distributed report, "A Preliminary Report on the Effects of Conducted LightSquared Emissions on Four High-Precision GPS Receivers." LightSquared provided filters for this conducted testing and a LightSquared representative participated in the testing. The spaceborne analysis includes both an atmospheric radio occultation (RO) application where the GPS receiver antenna is directed towards the Earth limb in order to measure properties of the atmosphere and the more typical navigation application where the GPS receiver antenna is pointed upwards to obtain spacecraft position, velocity, time and/or attitude. Two precision terrestrial receivers used in the IGS (International GNSS Service) and SCIGN (Southern California Integrated GPS Network) are also examined.

Analysis Assumptions

Table 6-1 shows the GPS characteristics and LightSquared base station characteristics used in the various analyses. Three types of analysis were performed: (1) aggregate base station interference into spaceborne GPS receiver; (2) interference from single base station into terrestrial receiver; and (3) aggregate base station interference into terrestrial receiver. For the space receiver analysis, 3 cases were considered: (a) radio occultation (RO) receiver onboard COSMIC-2 satellite in 800 km/72° inclined orbit (see Figure 6-1); (b) RO receiver onboard COSMIC-2 satellite in 520 km/24° inclined orbit; and (c) navigation receiver onboard typical LEO in 400 km altitude orbit.

GPS Receiver Characteristics

Spaceborne Receiver Analysis

For the spaceborne receiver analysis a MATLAB simulation program was developed to model the receiver onboard a satellite in various orbits and interference statistics calculated for a LightSquared base station deployment of base stations distributed among certain cities in the US. This city data was provided by LightSquared but has been redacted in this report for proprietary reasons. Two types of space receiver applications were considered: (1) the RO application which involves pointing the GPS receiver antenna towards the earth limb in order to receive GPS signals traversing the atmosphere; and (2) the more typical navigation application in which the antenna is pointed in the zenith direction towards the GPS constellation. In both cases interference thresholds for the TRIG and IGOR space receivers (as determined by the JPL conduction testing) are considered.

The TRIG and IGOR receivers are designed for RO measurements but can also be used for navigation/Precision Orbit Determination (POD). In the RO technique a GPS receiver in LEO observes the propagation delay of GPS signals which travel through the atmosphere. Occultations occur as each GPS satellite rises or sets on the horizon as viewed by the space receiver. From the changing delay, the (altitude) variation in the atmosphere's index of refraction can be measured and altitude profiles of ionosphere electron density, atmospheric density, pressure, temperature, and water vapor can be derived. Consequently, the receiver antenna main-beam is directed towards the earth limb (and also, in this case, the main-beams of the interfering base stations). JPL is planning the next generation of RO measurements with receivers onboard the COSMIC-2 constellation, which will have initial launch in 2014 and consist of six satellites in a 520 km orbit at 24 degrees inclination and six more at 800 km orbit and 72 degrees inclination. Each satellite will have actively steered array antennas with approximately +15 dBic gain directed along the limb of the earth in the forward (for rising GPS satellites) and aft (for setting GPS satellites) directions. Figure 6-2 shows the gain pattern for the forward antenna with the main-beam directed 26.2° below the satellite velocity vector towards earth limb. The 12 elements of the array are on a 60 cm tall x 40 cm wide mounting plate and mounted on the front of the spacecraft so that the plate is vertical and the outward normal to the plate is parallel to the spacecraft's velocity vector (assuming circular orbit).

The TRIG is the next generation NASA/JPL RO receiver designed to work with new signals from GPS and other GNSS satellites. It can also be used for POD. It has a very wide RF pre-select filter (i.e. 3 dB bandwidth from 1100 MHz to 1660 MHz) to allow the receiver to be reprogrammed in flight to different frequencies over the full range of GNSS signals. The wide bandwidth also results in lower insertion loss, less variation of signal delay and phase with temperature, and allows newer processing techniques by using a signal bandwidth much greater than the conventional 20 MHz.

The IGOR is the current generation RO receiver based on the NASA/JPL Black Jack space receiver. These receivers have been deployed as primary science payloads on the COSMIC mission, TerraSAR-X, Tandem-X, and TACSAT-2 missions. IGOR has a wideband pre-select filter and narrowband L1 and L2 filters. IGOR can also function as a POD GPS receiver.

For the usual space navigation application, the TRIG/IGOR receivers are assumed to use a zenith pointed choke ring antenna with 6.8 dBic gain with gain pattern shown in Figure 6-3. For this analysis a typical LEO altitude of 400 km is assumed and again a 72° inclination is considered which causes the satellite to pass over the entire CONUS numerous times.

The interference thresholds used in the analysis are shown in Table 6-2 and are based on the conduction testing by JPL last March. Although anechoic chamber testing and live-sky testing have also been performed with these receivers, the conduction testing offers the best accuracy since signal, noise, and interference levels can be carefully controlled and calibrated. In the conduction testing, the primary observable was the degradation in C/No due to simulated LightSquared Phase 1 signal interference (two 5 MHz channels) measured during steady state tracking. (It should be noted, however, that JPL also collected pseudorange, carrier phase, and position solution data. They also collected data for the TRIG using a Phase 0 simulated LightSquared signal.) Table 6-2 shows the interference levels (sum of interference powers in both 5 MHz channels) at the output of the GPS receiver antenna that result in 1 dB, 3 dB, and 5 dB C/No degradation for the four NASA receivers along with the interference level that causes loss of GPS signal tracking. It's apparent that the next-generation TRIG space receiver is the most sensitive of the four receivers.

Terrestrial Receiver Analysis (single base station)

This analysis considers the impact of interference from a single LightSquared base station on the four receivers assuming they are located at fixed positions on the ground. The TRIG/IGOR space receivers are tested on the ground prior to launch and during "burn-in" operations. Receivers #15 & #16 are commonly used in surveying and high precision ground networks such as the IGS (Figure 6-6 and Figure 6-6) and SCIGN (Figure 6-8 and Figure 6-9). Receiver #16 is a standard dual frequency (L1/L2) phase and pseudorange measuring instrument that can track up to 12 GPS satellites. Receiver #15 is a newer 36-channel receiver capable of tracking GPS L1/L2/L2C/L5 and GLONASS L1/L2. Since the closest base station will dominate the aggregate interference, it's useful to estimate the required separation distance between GPS receiver and base station in order that certain interference threshold levels are not exceeded. For this analysis the GPS receiver is assumed to be 1 meter above the ground (e.g. tripod mounted) with a zenith pointed choke ring antenna with gain pattern shown in Figure 6-3. This antenna is designed specifically to reduce multipath effects and consists of vertically aligned concentric rings centered about the antenna element (usually a crossed dipole) connected to a ground plane. The vertical rings shape the antenna pattern such that multipath signals incident on the antenna at the horizon and negative elevation angles are attenuated. The separation distance contours were calculated with MathCAD software for different interference thresholds given in Table 6-2.

Terrestrial Receiver Analysis (multiple base stations)

This analysis considered aggregate interference from the LightSquared deployment in one of LightSquared's planned initial markets. LightSquared provided the locations and height above ground for base stations that it is planning to deploy in one of its initial market areas. The objective is to determine the interference impact to a high precision ground network GPS receiver if it were to be located at different positions in the area (or a similar LightSquared market area). Again the receivers are assumed to use zenith pointed choke ring antennas at 1 meter above ground. For this analysis a MATLAB program was developed which sub-divides

6-3

the geographic area into a large number of quadrangles or cells (i.e. 878,628 cells each approx 100 square meters in size) and the aggregate interference calculated at the centroid of each map cell from the base stations within radio LOS of the map cell location. The result is an interference matrix map that shows the aggregate interference over the geographic area. By applying different interference thresholds (Table 6-2) to the matrix map, the % area where interference exceeds the threshold can be determined.

LightSquared Base Station Characteristics

As shown in Table 6-1, for all three analysis types, base station sector main-beam EIRP levels and antenna patterns are the same and based on data provided by LightSquared. The main-beam EIRP per channel is 62 dBm (32 dBW) per (5 MHz) OFDM channel and assuming two 5 MHz channels per sector (i.e. Phase 1 spectrum) this is 65 dBm (35 dBW) per sector.

Spaceborne Receiver Analysis

For the spaceborne receiver analysis the aggregate interference power at the output of the GPS receiver antenna is calculated at one second time steps in the satellite orbit from base stations distributed among certain US cities. Since specific lat/lon locations for the base stations in each city were not available and the GPS receiver in this case is onboard a satellite, it was assumed for the interference calculations that all base stations for a particular city are co-located at the city center. For example, two base stations separated by 10 km will have an angular separation of only 0.7° at 800 km satellite altitude so that the difference in receive antenna gain between the two will be very small. Sector antenna gain towards the satellite is calculated by first determining the appropriate AZ/EL angles from the base-station/satellite geometry; then summing the AZ plane discrimination with the EL plane discrimination; and then subtracting this total discrimination from the max sector gain to get the net sector gain towards the satellite. The maximum interference from a base station will occur when it sees the satellite at low elevation angles. Free-space loss is assumed, but because of uncertainty in the path loss due to blockage and shadowing of base stations on the satellite horizon from terrain or man-made structures, analysis results were generated for two base station mask angles: (1) a 0° elevation mask on the base stations so that all base stations which see the satellite above 0° elevation angle are included in the aggregate interference calculation; and (2) a 5° mask angle so that only base stations which see the satellite above 5° elevation angle contribute to the aggregate interference. For the space receiver analysis, results were also generated for the case when the base station EIRP is increased from 32 dBW to 42 dBW, which is the maximum authorized power under the FCC rules. LightSquared, however, has stated that they plan to operate at a maximum EIRP level of 32 dBW per channel.

Terrestrial Receiver Analysis (single base station)

For this analysis of interference from single base station, a base station height of 18.3 meters (60 feet) above ground is assumed. GPS receiver height is assumed to be 1 meter. Separation distance results were calculated for a number of different propagation models besides free-space loss (i.e. Hata, Extended Hata, Walfisch-Ikegami, NTIA/ITM). These models are based on extensive measurements of radio propagation losses and used in cellular systems planning. Figure 6-5 shows that there is a significant spread in path loss among these models. For example, for a 10 km distance path loss varies from 115 dB (free-space) to 180 dB (extended HATA in urban area). This leads to a significant difference in separation distances. The issue of which propagation model is appropriate in various terrestrial interference scenarios requires further discussion.

Terrestrial Receiver Analysis (multiple base stations)

As noted previously, this analysis considers aggregate interference from base stations in one of LightSquared's initial market deployments. Again results were generated for different propagation models shown in Figure 6-5.

Analysis Results

(*Editor's Note:* The results presented in the following sections are intended to draw no conclusions or make any recommendations as to what level of interference may be tolerated by the various GPS receivers based on the scenarios for those receivers.)

Spaceborne Receiver Analysis Results

Interference results for the RO GPS RX onboard a COSMIC-2 satellite (800 km/72° orbit) are shown in Table 6-3 and Table 6-4. Table 6-3 assumes a 0° elevation mask on the base stations while Table 6-4 assumes a 5° elevation mask on the base stations. The entries in these tables are interpreted as follows. Consider, for example, Table 6-3 and an aggregate interference threshold of -82 dBm (2nd column). For this row in the Table, the first column indicates that an interference power level of -82 dBm at the output of the GPS receiver antenna will cause a 1 dB drop in the C/No for the TRIG receiver (for both the L1 C/A-code and L1 P-code channels of the receiver). Column 3 indicates that over the 10-day simulation period, the aggregate interference at the GPS antenna output actually exceeds this level about 9% of the time (i.e. since 10 days = 240 hours, the interference exceeds -82 dBm for 0.09 x 240 = 21.6 hours total over the 10-day period). In other words, for 9% of the time, the receiver C/No degradation is at least 1 dB. In the table header, the peak interference level is shown to reach -55.1 dBm (enough for the TRIG to lose lock). Column 4 indicates that over the 10-day period, there are 268 interference events (i.e. 268 separate time intervals during which interference exceeds -82 dBm). Note that these time intervals may be very short or fairly long depending on how many interfering base stations the satellite sees on the particular orbit pass over the US. The sum duration of all 268 interference events is the 21.6 hours. Also, there can be multiple interference events for a single orbit pass as different numbers of base stations pass through the FOV of the receiver antenna. Column 5 indicates that the average duration of an interference event is about 4.9 minutes and the maximum duration from column 6 is 16.9 minutes. Table 6-3 also shows that for a threshold of -67 dBm (where TRIG loses lock), interference exceeds this level about 3% of the time with 152 interference events of average duration 2.9 min and max duration 10.6 min. It should be noted that the duration of an atmospheric occultation (as the signal path moves from skimming the Earth's surface to an altitude of about 100 km) is only one to two minutes. Table 6-4 with the 5° elevation mask ignores interference from the low elevation angle base stations, but still shows average interference event duration of 3.8 min at the -67 dBm TRIG loss of lock threshold. (Compared to Table 6-3 there are fewer events, 57 vs 152, but the average duration is longer.)

The impact to the IGOR space receiver is seen to be much less. Note, however, that these results are only for the forward looking RO antenna. There will also be an aft pointing RO antenna, so interference will occur both when the CONUS is coming into the forward looking antenna FOV and when it is leaving the aft looking antenna FOV. Further analysis is required to determine the interference statistics when both antennas are included.

For the case of RO receiver onboard COSMIC-2 satellite in the 520 km/24° inclined orbit, the peak interference was found to be -88.2 dBm. This is much lower than for the 800 km/72° inclined orbit since the satellite does not pass over the US, but only sees a few base stations on the southern border. This level of interference is expected to cause less than 1 dB of degradation to the TRIG receiver.

Interference results for the navigation mode GPS RX with zenith pointed antenna onboard a LEOSAT (400 km/72° orbit) are shown in Table 6-5 (0° base station elevation mask) and Table 6-6 (5° base station elevation mask). The majority of GPS receivers used in space are small, lightweight, low-power devices providing spacecraft 3-dimensional position and velocity as well as timing and possibly 3-axis attitude determination. Table 6-5 and Table 6-6 show that compared to the RO case, interference effects are much less due to the backlobes and sidelobes of the receiving antenna facing towards the earth (and interfering base stations). Note also that no satellite body masking is included in this case which will likely further reduce the interference.

Although LightSquared is planning to operate the base stations at a maximum EIRP of 32 dBW per channel, the current FCC rules allow them to operate up to 42 dBW EIRP. Table 6-7, Table 6-8, Table 6-9, and Table 6-10 show the interference results if the base stations were to operate at 42 dBW EIRP.

Terrestrial Receiver (single base station) Analysis Results

Separation distance contours for the four receivers are shown in Figure 6-10 through Figure 6-13. In these polar plots, the base station is assumed to be at the center of the plot with the 3 sector antennas oriented in the 0°, 120°, and 240° azimuth directions. The radial rings show distance from the center (base station) in km. Contours are shown for several different propagation models. The least conservative models are shown on the left side and the most conservative on the right side. Note the different distance scales on the plots. In each case, the contours are associated with the receiver interference threshold that causes 1 dB C/No drop in the C/A-code channel. Referring to Table 6-2, these thresholds are -82 dBm (TRIG); -57 dBm (IGOR); -54 dBm (Receiver #15); and -68 dBm (Receiver #16). Base station height is 18.3 meters and GPS rx height is 1 meter. For these heights the radio LOS distance is 22 km so a receiver beyond 22 km is assumed not to receive interference. There is large variation in required separation distance depending on the assumed propagation model. Free-space loss yields the largest (most protective) separation distances: 22 km (TRIG); 4 km (IGOR); 3 km (Receiver #15); and 14 km (Receiver #16).

Terrestrial Receiver (multiple base station) Analysis Results

The results of this analysis are shown in Table 6-11 (redacted due to competitive sensitive data).

Table 6-1. NASA GPS Receiver Analysis Assumptions

		SPACEBORNE RECEIVER ANALYSIS	TERRESTRIAL RECEIVER ANALYSIS (SINGLE LSQ BASE STATION)	TERRESTRIAL RECEIVER ANALYSIS (MULTIPLE LSQ BASE STATIONS)
GPS CHARACTERISTICS	COMPUTATION METHOD	MATLAB TIME SIMULATION TO COMPUTE AGG INTERFERENCE FROM CONUS BASE STATIONS INTO ORBITING GPS RX (10-DAY SIM PERIOD @ 1-SEC TIME STEP)	MATHCAD CALCULATION USED TO COMPUTE REQUIRED SEPARATION DISTANCE CONTOURS FROM SINGLE BASE STATION	MATLAB INTERFERENCE MATRIX MAP COMPUTATION TO DETERMINE AGG LEVEL OF INTERFERENCE FROM MULTIPLE BASE STATIONS IN LAS VEGAS DEPLOYMENT
	GPS RX TYPE (all dual-frequency semi-codeless)	TRIG (next-gen space/occulation rx); IGOR (current gen space/occulation rx)	TRIG; IGOR; JAVAD; ASHTECH	JAVAD; ASHTECH
	ORBIT	COSMIC 2 HI ALT (800 km/72°) (FIG 1) COSMIC 2 LO ALT (520 km/24°) GENERIC LEO (400 km/72°)	N/A	N/A
	GPS RX ANTENNA TYPE	OCCULT 12-ELEMENT ARRAY (15.2 dBic for COSMIC-2 ORBITS) (FIG 2); CHOKE RING (6.8 dBic for GENERIC LEO) (FIG 3)	CHOKE RING (6.8 dBic) (FIG 3)	CHOKE RING (6.8 dBic) (FIG 3)
	GPS RX ANTENNA POINTING	TOWARDS EARTH LIMB (COSMIC-2 OCCULT ORBITS); ZENITH (GENERIC LEO)	ZENITH POINTED	ZENITH POINTED
	GPS RX ANTENNA PATTERN	OCCULT 12-ELEMENT ARRAY; CHOKE RING	CHOKE RING	CHOKE RING
	INTERFERENCE THRESHOLD	THRESHOLDS AS MEASURED DURING JPL CONDUCTED TESTING (TABLE 2)	THRESHOLDS AS MEASURED DURING JPL CONDUCTED TESTING (TABLE 2)	THRESHOLDS AS MEASURED DURING JPL CONDUCTED TESTING (TABLE 2)
	POLARIZATION LOSS	3 DB	3 DB	3 DB
LIGHTSQUARED BASE STATION CHARACTERISTICS	DEPLOYMENT	Redacted for Commercial Sensitivity Reasons		
	SPECTRUM PHASE	PHASE 1: TWO (5 MHz) CHANNELS	PHASE 1: TWO (5 MHz) CHANNELS	PHASE 1: TWO (5 MHz) CHANNELS
	CHANNEL FREQS	1526.3 - 1531.3 MHz/ 1550.2 - 1555.2 MHz	1526.3 - 1531.3 MHz/ 1550.2 - 1555.2 MHz	1526.3 - 1531.3 MHz/ 1550.2 - 1555.2 MHz
	EIRP/CHANNEL STRUCTURE	62 dBm per (5 MHz) channel	62 dBm per (5 MHz) channel	62 dBm per (5 MHz) channel
	CHANNELS PER SECTOR	2 (PHASE 1)	2 (PHASE 1)	2 (PHASE 1)
	EIRP per SECTOR	65 dBm	65 dBm	65 dBm
	SECTORS per BASE STATION	Redacted for Commercial Sensitivity Reasons		
	SECTOR ANTENNA PATTERN			
	PROPAGATION MODEL	Redacted	RESULTS GENERATED FOR VARIOUS PROP MODELS (FREE-SPACE, HATA, EXTENDED HATA, Walfisch-Ikegami, NTIA/ITM) (FIG 6)	RESULTS GENERATED FOR VARIOUS PROP MODELS (FREE-SPACE, HATA, EXTENDED HATA, Walfisch-Ikegami, NTIA/ITM) (FIG 6)

Table 6-2. Summary of JPL Conduction Testing Interference Thresholds

LSQ Signal Spectrum	Interference Criterion	NASA GPS RECEIVER SUSCEPTIBILITY TO LSQ INTERFERENCE (BASED ON JPL CONDUCTED TESTING) NOTE: POWER LEVEL SHOWN IS TOTAL POWER AT OUTPUT OF GPS RX PASSIVE ANTENNA (dBm)											
		TRIG			IGOR			JAVAD Delta G3T			Ashtech Z-12		
		L1 C/A	L1 P	L2 P	L1 C/A	L1 P	L2 P	L1 C/A	L1 P	L2 P	L1 C/A	L1 P	L2 P
LSQ Phase 1 (two 5 MHz channels @ 1526.3-1531.3 and 1550.2-1555.2)	1 dB C/No degradation	C: -82	C: -82	C: -78	C: -57	C: -59	C: -51	C: -54	C: -56	C: -43	C: -68		
	3 dB C/No degradation	C: -78	C: -80	C: -77	C: -53	C: -54	C: -49	C: -51	C: -52	C: -43	C: -65		
	5 dB C/No degradation	C: -75	C: -73	C: -74	C: -49	C: -51	C: -48	C: -49	C: -50	C: -43	C: -62		
	Loss of Lock	C: -67	C: -67	C: -67	C: -45	C: -45	C: -45	C: -43	C: -43	C: -43	C: -38	C: -38	C: -38

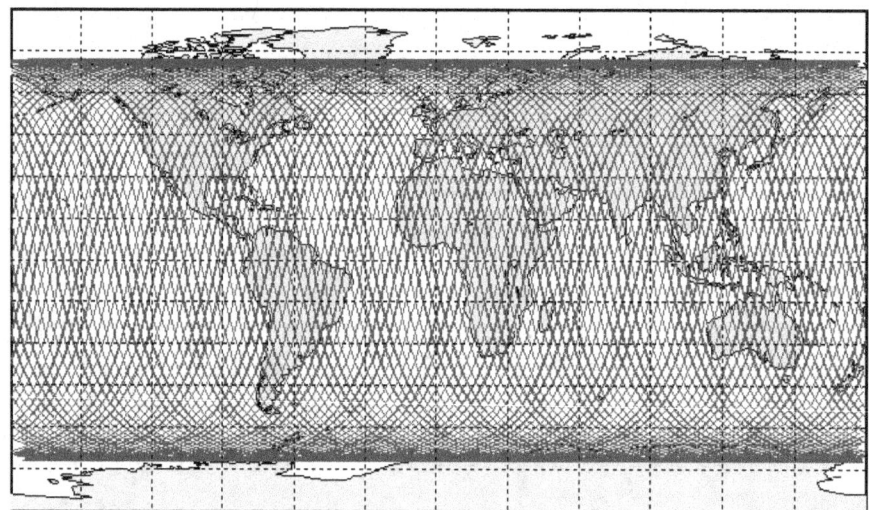

Figure 6-1. Ground Track of COSMIC-2 Satellite in 800 km/72° Orbit over 10-Day Sim Period

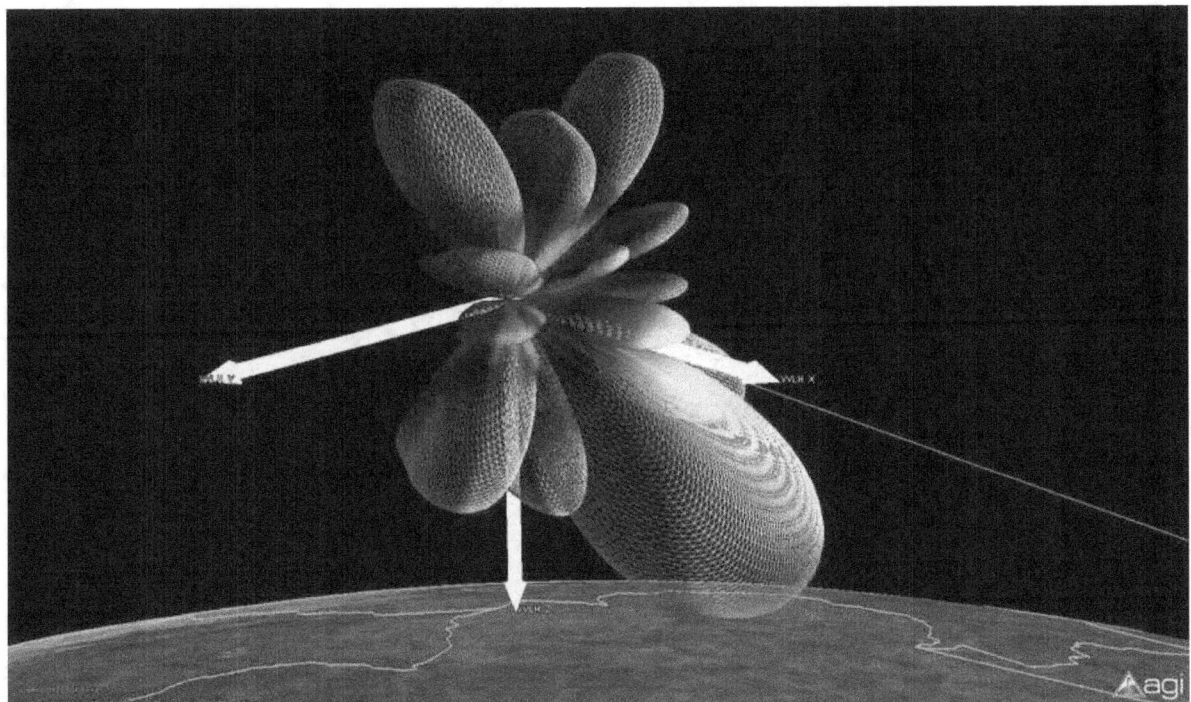

Figure 6-2. Gain Pattern of JPL GPS RX Occultation Antenna (12-element array with 15.2 dBic main beam pointed towards Earth limb)

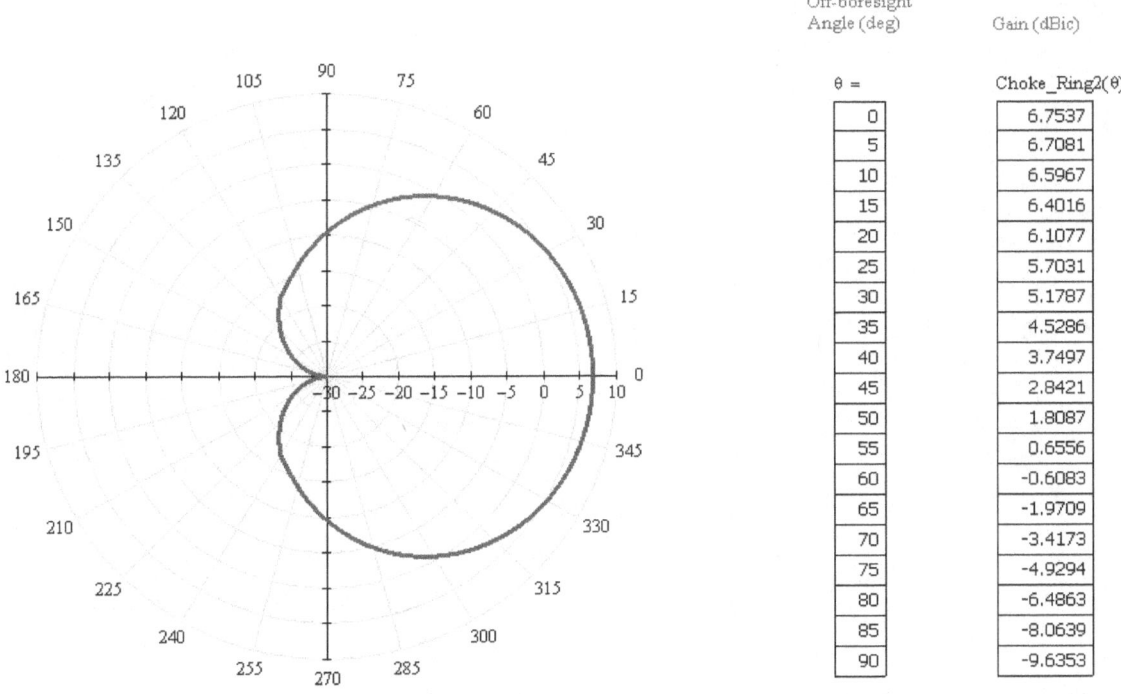

Off-boresight Angle (deg)	Gain (dBic)
$\theta =$	$Choke\_Ring2(\theta)$
0	6.7537
5	6.7081
10	6.5967
15	6.4016
20	6.1077
25	5.7031
30	5.1787
35	4.5286
40	3.7497
45	2.8421
50	1.8087
55	0.6556
60	-0.6083
65	-1.9709
70	-3.4173
75	-4.9294
80	-6.4863
85	-8.0639
90	-9.6353

Figure 6-3. GPS Receiver Choke Ring Gain Pattern (6.75 dBic gain)

Figure 6-4. Spaceborne GPS RX Occultation Scenario (Main beam of Array Antenna is Pointed 26.2° Below the Satellite Local Horizontal Towards the Earth Limb)

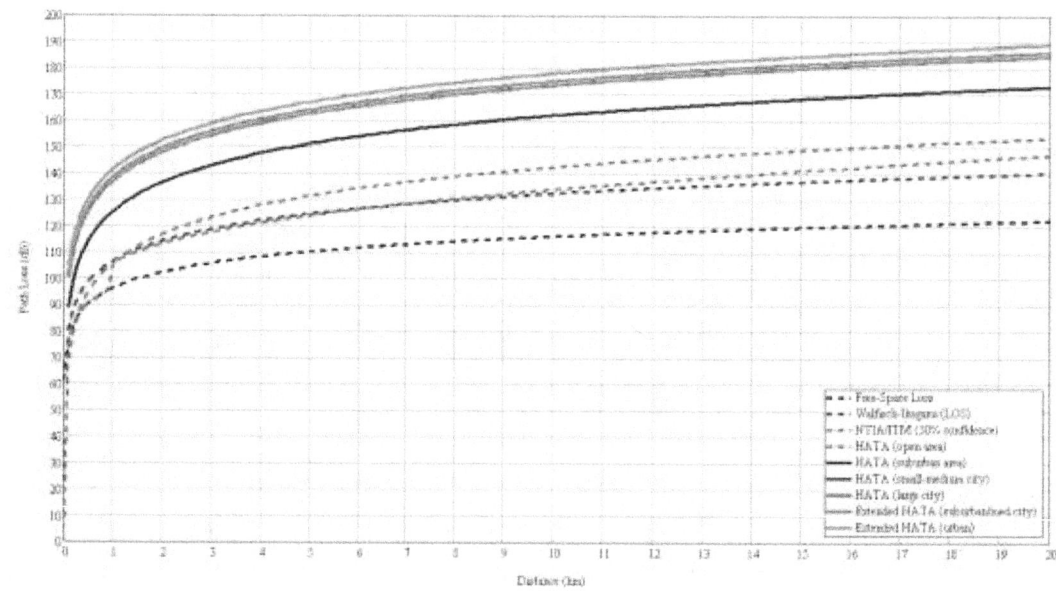

Figure 6-5. Comparison of Various Terrestrial Propagation Models

6-10

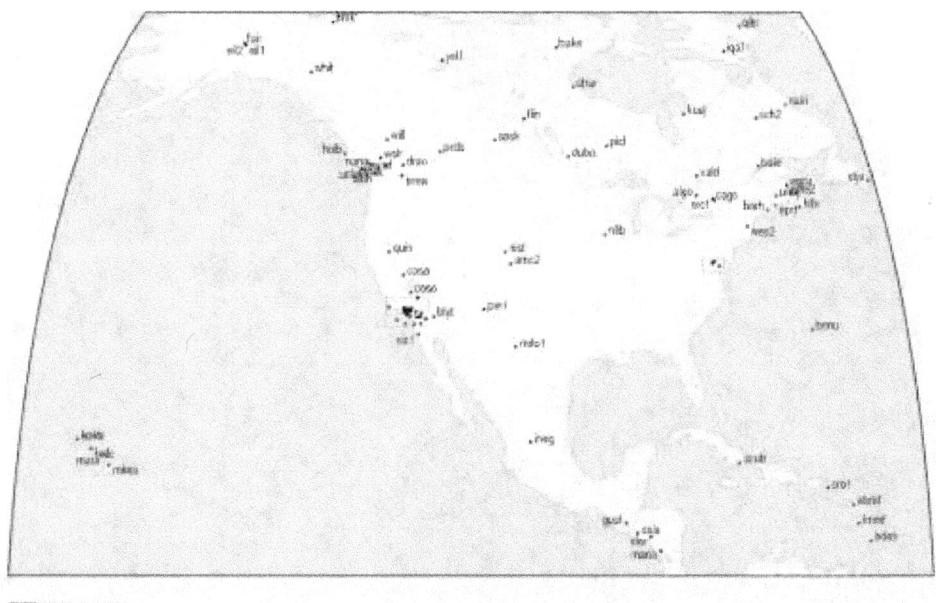

Figure 6-6. Locations of GPS Receivers of the International GNSS Service (IGS). There are 58 receivers in CONUS. The IGS collects, archives, and distributes GPS data for a wide range of applications and experiments (e.g. earth rotation, ionospheric maps, GPS/GLONASS ephemeris).

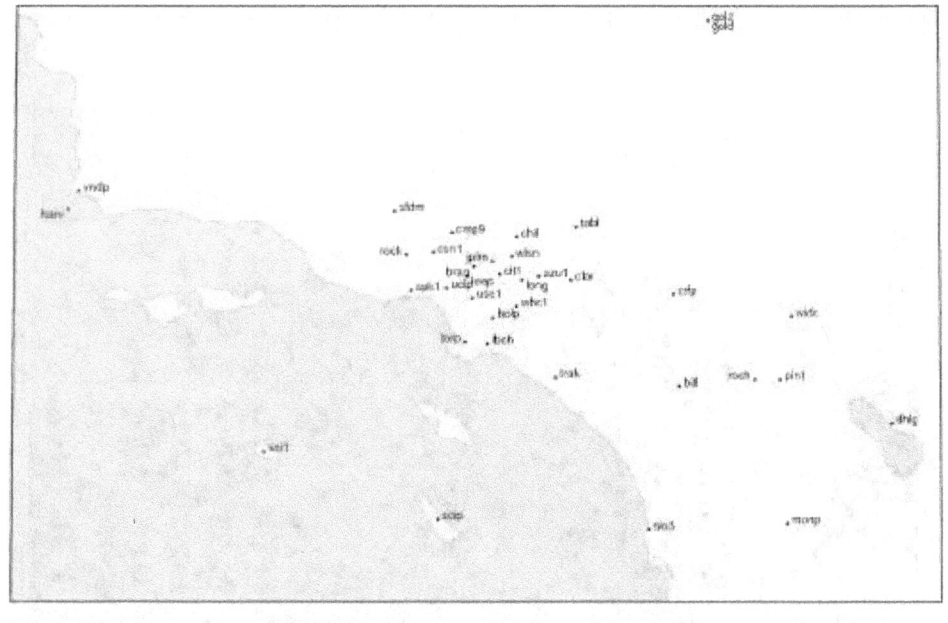

Figure 6-7. IGS Receivers in Sothern California Area

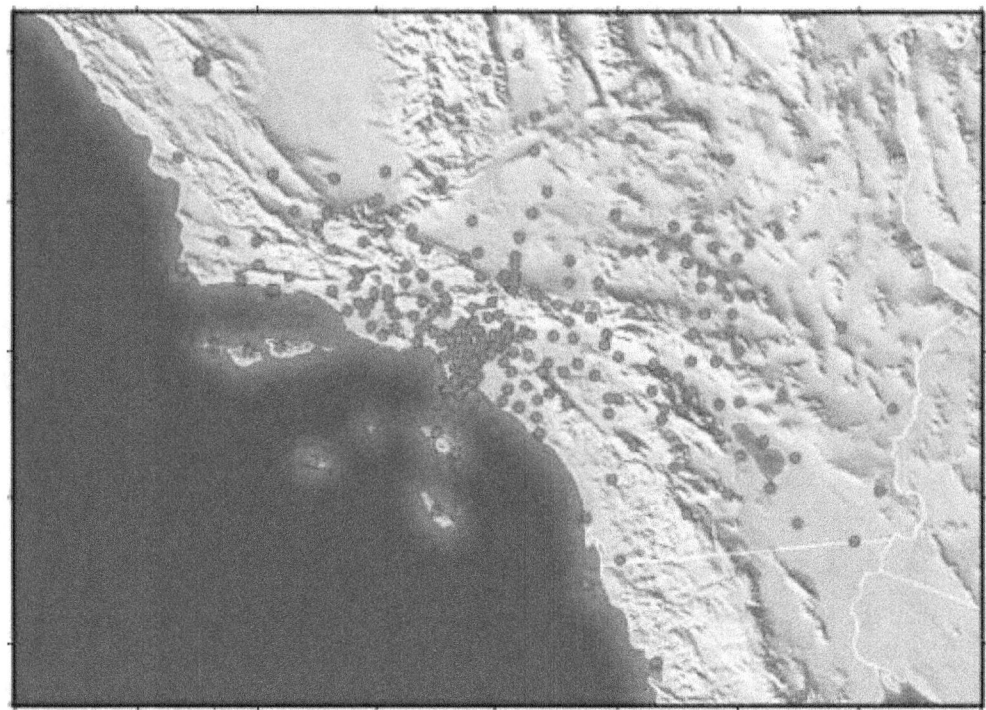

Figure 6-8. Locations of the 123 GPS Receivers of the SCIGN (Southern California Integrated GPS Network. The network continuously records mm-scale movements of the Earth's crust to estimate earthquake hazard)

Figure 6-9. Packard SCIGN Station (located in Elysian Park above downtown L.A.)

Table 6-3. Interference Results for JPL Occultation GPS RX Onboard COSMIC-2 Satellite (800 km/72° orbit) With Earth Limb Pointed Array Antenna (0° elevation mask on base stations)

LSQ Interference Results for JPL Occultation GPS Receiver					
GPS RX Onboard COSMIC-2 Satellite in 800 km/72° Orbit					
Two LSQ channels per sector @ 32 dBW max EIRP per channel					
0° Elevation Mask on LSQ Base Stations					
Peak Interference Level = -55.1 dBm					
RX C/No Degradation (based on JPL conduction testing)	Agg Interference Threshold **(dBm)** (int power at output of GPS RX antenna)	% Time (over 10-day period) that Interference Exceeds Threshold	# of Interference Events over 10-day sim period	Avg Duration of Interference Event (min)	Max Interference Event Duration (min)
	-56.000	0.009	11.000	0.112	0.367
IGOR (1 dB; C/A)	-57.000	0.074	59.000	0.180	0.800
	-58.000	0.217	80.000	0.390	2.167
IGOR (1 dB; P1)	-59.000	0.384	93.000	0.595	3.533
	-60.000	0.595	86.000	0.996	5.550
	-61.000	0.829	105.000	1.137	5.767
	-62.000	1.154	136.000	1.222	6.033
	-63.000	1.531	156.000	1.413	7.617
	-64.000	1.918	157.000	1.760	8.233
	-65.000	2.297	158.000	2.094	8.900
	-66.000	2.652	165.000	2.314	9.783
TRIG (Lost Lock; C/A & P1 & P2)	-67.000	3.033	152.000	2.873	10.600
	-68.000	3.414	157.000	3.131	10.750
	-69.000	3.787	185.000	2.948	11.483
	-70.000	4.150	153.000	3.906	11.683
	-71.000	4.477	139.000	4.638	12.017
	-72.000	4.800	145.000	4.767	12.433
TRIG (5 dB; P1)	-73.000	5.131	147.000	5.027	12.683
TRIG (5 dB; P2)	-74.000	5.452	163.000	4.817	13.350
TRIG (5 dB; C/A)	-75.000	5.851	193.000	4.366	13.700
	-76.000	6.262	205.000	4.399	13.917
TRIG (3 dB; P2)	-77.000	6.696	225.000	4.285	14.167
TRIG (3 dB; C/A) ; TRIG (1 dB; P2)	-78.000	7.135	240.000	4.281	15.167
	-79.000	7.601	257.000	4.259	16.117
TRIG (3 dB; P1)	-80.000	8.084	264.000	4.409	16.717
	-81.000	8.554	279.000	4.415	16.950
TRIG (1 dB; C/A & P1)	-82.000	9.059	268.000	4.867	16.983
	-83.000	9.491	258.000	5.297	17.083
	-84.000	9.878	254.000	5.600	17.150
	-85.000	10.252	266.000	5.550	17.283
	-300.000	15.749	175.000	12.960	25.300

Table 6-4. Interference Results for JPL Occultation GPS RX Onboard COSMIC-2 Satellite (800 km/72° orbit) With Earth Limb Pointed Array Antenna (5° elevation mask on base stations)

LSQ Interference Results for JPL Occultation GPS Receiver
GPS RX Onboard COSMIC Satellite in 800 km/72° Orbit

Two LSQ channels per sector @ 32 dBW max EIRP per channel

5° Elevation Mask on LSQ Base Stations

Peak Interference Level = -60.2 dBm

RX C/No Degradation (based on JPL conduction testing)	Agg Interference Threshold (dBm) (int power at output of GPS RX antenna)	% Time (over 10-day period) that Interference Exceeds Threshold	# of Interference Events over 10-day sim period	Avg Duration of Interference Event (min)	Max Interference Event Duration (min)
	-56.000	0.000	0.000	0.000	0.000
IGOR (1 dB; C/A)	-57.000	0.000	0.000	0.000	0.000
	-58.000	0.000	0.000	0.000	0.000
IGOR (1 dB; P1)	-59.000	0.000	0.000	0.000	0.000
	-60.000	0.000	0.000	0.000	0.000
	-61.000	0.082	18.000	0.653	1.733
	-62.000	0.236	23.000	1.478	2.983
	-63.000	0.429	41.000	1.506	3.717
	-64.000	0.684	57.000	1.727	5.933
	-65.000	0.918	52.000	2.542	6.433
	-66.000	1.210	56.000	3.111	7.033
TRIG (Lost Lock; C/A & P1 & P2)	-67.000	1.502	57.000	3.795	7.983
	-68.000	1.817	81.000	3.230	8.150
	-69.000	2.069	76.000	3.921	8.433
	-70.000	2.355	79.000	4.292	8.917
	-71.000	2.655	75.000	5.097	9.583
	-72.000	2.994	94.000	4.586	9.850
TRIG (5 dB; P1)	-73.000	3.328	95.000	5.044	10.467
TRIG (5 dB; P2)	-74.000	3.578	94.000	5.481	11.067
TRIG (5 dB; C/A)	-75.000	3.844	110.000	5.032	11.450
	-76.000	4.113	111.000	5.335	11.533
TRIG (3 dB; P2)	-77.000	4.420	107.000	5.948	11.533
TRIG (3 dB; C/A) TRIG (1 dB; P2)	-78.000	4.697	121.000	5.589	11.750
	-79.000	4.982	127.000	5.649	12.750
TRIG (3 dB; P1)	-80.000	5.275	128.000	5.934	13.217
	-81.000	5.562	121.000	6.619	13.717
TRIG (1 dB; C/A & P1)	-82.000	5.853	134.000	6.290	14.083
	-83.000	6.116	132.000	6.672	14.350
	-84.000	6.410	143.000	6.455	14.350
	-85.000	6.703	165.000	5.850	14.433
	-300.000	12.180	189.000	9.280	21.683

Table 6-5. Interference Results for JPL GPS RX Onboard LEOSAT (400 km/72° orbit) With Zenith Pointed Choke Ring Antenna (0° elevation mask on base stations)

LSQ Interference Results for JPL GPS Receiver with Zenith Pointed 7 dBic Choke Ring Antenna
GPS RX Onboard LEO Satellite in 400 km/72° Orbit

Two LSQ channels per sector @ 32 dBW max EIRP per channel

0° Elevation Mask on LSQ Base Stations
Peak Interference Level = -78.1 dBm

RX C/No Degradation (based on JPL conduction testing)	Agg Interference Threshold (dBm) (int power at output of GPS RX antenna)	% Time (over 10-day period) that Interference Exceeds Threshold	# of Interference Events over 10-day sim period	Avg Duration of Interference Event (min)	Max Interference Event Duration (min)
	-56.000	0.000	0.000	0.000	0.000
IGOR (1 dB; C/A)	-57.000	0.000	0.000	0.000	0.000
	-58.000	0.000	0.000	0.000	0.000
IGOR (1 dB; P1)	-59.000	0.000	0.000	0.000	0.000
	-60.000	0.000	0.000	0.000	0.000
	-61.000	0.000	0.000	0.000	0.000
	-62.000	0.000	0.000	0.000	0.000
	-63.000	0.000	0.000	0.000	0.000
	-64.000	0.000	0.000	0.000	0.000
	-65.000	0.000	0.000	0.000	0.000
	-66.000	0.000	0.000	0.000	0.000
TRIG (Lost Lock; C/A & P1 & P2)	-67.000	0.000	0.000	0.000	0.000
	-68.000	0.000	0.000	0.000	0.000
	-69.000	0.000	0.000	0.000	0.000
	-70.000	0.000	0.000	0.000	0.000
	-71.000	0.000	0.000	0.000	0.000
	-72.000	0.000	0.000	0.000	0.000
TRIG (5 dB; P1)	-73.000	0.000	0.000	0.000	0.000
TRIG (5 dB; P2)	-74.000	0.000	0.000	0.000	0.000
TRIG (5 dB; C/A)	-75.000	0.000	0.000	0.000	0.000
	-76.000	0.000	0.000	0.000	0.000
TRIG (3 dB; P2)	-77.000	0.000	0.000	0.000	0.000
TRIG (3 dB; C/A) TRIG (1 dB; P2)	-78.000	0.000	0.000	0.000	0.000
	-79.000	0.161	80.000	0.290	1.467
TRIG (3 dB; P1)	-80.000	0.601	183.000	0.473	4.717
	-81.000	1.517	364.000	0.600	8.300
TRIG (1 dB; C/A & P1)	-82.000	2.980	322.000	1.332	11.533
	-83.000	3.915	257.000	2.193	13.067
	-84.000	4.651	290.000	2.309	13.133
	-85.000	5.387	264.000	2.938	13.983
	-300.000	15.327	165.000	13.377	25.167

Table 6-6. Interference Results for JPL GPS RX Onboard LEOSAT (400 km/72° orbit) With Zenith Pointed Choke Ring Antenna (5° elevation mask on base stations)

LSQ Interference Results for JPL GPS Receiver with Zenith Pointed 7 dBic Choke Ring Antenna
GPS RX Onboard LEO Satellite in 400 km/72° Orbit

Two LSQ channels per sector @ 32 dBW max EIRP per channel

5° Elevation Mask on LSQ Base Stations
Peak Interference Level = -81.3 dBm

RX C/No Degradation (based on JPL conduction testing)	Agg Interference Threshold (dBm) (int power at output of GPS RX antenna)	% Time (over 10-day period) that Interference Exceeds Threshold	# of Interference Events over 10-day sim period	Avg Duration of Interference Event (min)	Max Interference Event Duration (min)
	-56.000	0.000	0.000	0.000	0.000
IGOR (1 dB; C/A)	-57.000	0.000	0.000	0.000	0.000
	-58.000	0.000	0.000	0.000	0.000
IGOR (1 dB; P1)	-59.000	0.000	0.000	0.000	0.000
	-60.000	0.000	0.000	0.000	0.000
	-61.000	0.000	0.000	0.000	0.000
	-62.000	0.000	0.000	0.000	0.000
	-63.000	0.000	0.000	0.000	0.000
	-64.000	0.000	0.000	0.000	0.000
	-65.000	0.000	0.000	0.000	0.000
	-66.000	0.000	0.000	0.000	0.000
TRIG (Lost Lock; C/A & P1 & P2)	-67.000	0.000	0.000	0.000	0.000
	-68.000	0.000	0.000	0.000	0.000
	-69.000	0.000	0.000	0.000	0.000
	-70.000	0.000	0.000	0.000	0.000
	-71.000	0.000	0.000	0.000	0.000
	-72.000	0.000	0.000	0.000	0.000
TRIG (5 dB; P1)	-73.000	0.000	0.000	0.000	0.000
TRIG (5 dB; P2)	-74.000	0.000	0.000	0.000	0.000
TRIG (5 dB; C/A)	-75.000	0.000	0.000	0.000	0.000
	-76.000	0.000	0.000	0.000	0.000
TRIG (3 dB; P2)	-77.000	0.000	0.000	0.000	0.000
TRIG (3 dB; C/A) TRIG (1 dB; P2)	-78.000	0.000	0.000	0.000	0.000
	-79.000	0.000	0.000	0.000	0.000
TRIG (3 dB; P1)	-80.000	0.000	0.000	0.000	0.000
	-81.000	0.000	0.000	0.000	0.000
TRIG (1 dB; C/A & P1)	-82.000	0.147	15.000	1.407	2.383
	-83.000	0.493	60.000	1.184	3.867
	-84.000	1.107	55.000	2.899	7.283
	-85.000	1.793	103.000	2.507	8.083
	-300.000	11.515	167.000	9.929	21.450

Table 6-7. Interference Results for RO GPS RX Onboard COSMIC-2 Satellite (800 km/72° orbit) With Earth Limb Pointed Array Antenna (0° elevation mask on base stations/42 dBW EIRP)

LSQ Interference Results for JPL Occultation GPS Receiver
GPS RX Onboard COSMIC Satellite in 800 km/72° Orbit

Two LSQ channels per sector @ 42 dBW max EIRP per channel

0° Elevation Mask on LSQ Base Stations

Peak Interference Level = -45.1 dBm

RX C/No Degradation (based on JPL conduction testing)	Agg Interference Threshold (dBm) (int power at output of GPS RX antenna)	% Time (over 10-day period) that Interference Exceeds Threshold	# of Interference Events over 10-day sim period	Avg Duration of Interference Event (min)	Max Interference Event Duration (min)
IGOR (Lost Lock)	-46.000	0.009	11.000	0.112	0.367
	-47.000	0.074	59.000	0.180	0.800
IGOR (5dB;P2)	-48.000	0.217	80.000	0.390	2.167
IGOR (5 dB; C/A)	-49.000	0.384	93.000	0.595	3.533
	-50.000	0.595	86.000	0.996	5.550
IGOR (1 dB; P2) IGOR(5dB;P1)	-51.000	0.829	105.000	1.137	5.767
	-52.000	1.154	136.000	1.222	6.033
IGOR (3 dB; C/A)	-53.000	1.531	156.000	1.413	7.617
IGOR (3dB; P1)	-54.000	1.918	157.000	1.760	8.233
	-55.000	2.297	158.000	2.094	8.900
	-56.000	2.652	165.000	2.314	9.783
IGOR (1 dB; C/Λ)	-57.000	3.033	152.000	2.873	10.600
	-58.000	3.414	157.000	3.131	10.750
IGOR (1 dB; P1)	-59.000	3.787	185.000	2.948	11.483
	-60.000	4.150	153.000	3.906	11.683
	-61.000	4.477	139.000	4.638	12.017
	-62.000	4.800	145.000	4.767	12.433
	-63.000	5.131	147.000	5.027	12.683
	-64.000	5.452	163.000	4.817	13.350
	-65.000	5.851	193.000	4.366	13.700
	-66.000	6.262	205.000	4.399	13.917
TRIG (Lost Lock; C/A & P1 & P2)	-67.000	6.696	225.000	4.285	14.167
	-68.000	7.135	240.000	4.281	15.167
	-69.000	7.601	257.000	4.259	16.117
	-70.000	8.084	264.000	4.409	16.717
	-71.000	8.554	279.000	4.415	16.950
	-72.000	9.059	268.000	4.867	16.983
TRIG (5 dB; P1)	-73.000	9.491	258.000	5.297	17.083
TRIG (5 dB; P2)	-74.000	9.878	254.000	5.600	17.150
TRIG (5 dB; C/A)	-75.000	10.252	266.000	5.550	17.283
	-76.000	10.624	247.000	6.194	17.600
TRIG (3 dB; P2)	-77.000	10.978	243.000	6.506	17.733
TRIG (3 dB; C/A) TRIG (1 dB; P2)	-78.000	11.325	244.000	6.683	17.733
	-79.000	11.647	244.000	6.874	17.750
TRIG (3 dB; P1)	-80.000	11.912	239.000	7.177	17.783
	-81.000	12.170	258.000	6.793	17.983
TRIG (1 dB; C/A & P1)	-82.000	12.459	257.000	6.981	19.033
	-83.000	12.712	258.000	7.095	19.033
	-84.000	12.985	259.000	7.219	20.067
	-85.000	13.269	255.000	7.493	20.067
	-300.000	15.749	175.000	12.960	25.300

Table 6-8. Interference Results for RO GPS RX Onboard COSMIC-2 Satellite (800 km/72° orbit) With Earth Limb Pointed Array Antenna (5° elevation mask on base stations/42 dBW EIRP)

LSQ Interference Results for JPL Occultation GPS Receiver
GPS RX Onboard COSMIC Satellite in 800 km/72° Orbit

Two LSQ channels per sector @ 42 dBW max EIRP per channel

5° Elevation Mask on LSQ Base Stations
Peak Interference Level = -50.2 dBm

RX C/No Degradation (based on JPL conduction testing)	Agg Interference Threshold (dBm) (int power at output of GPS RX antenna)	% Time (over 10-day period) that Interference Exceeds Threshold	# of Interference Events over 10-day sim period	Avg Duration of Interference Event (min)	Max Interference Event Duration (min)
IGOR (Lost Lock)	-46.000	0.000	0.000	0.000	0.000
	-47.000	0.000	0.000	0.000	0.000
IGOR (5dB;P2)	-48.000	0.000	0.000	0.000	0.000
IGOR (5 dB; C/A)	-49.000	0.000	0.000	0.000	0.000
	-50.000	0.000	0.000	0.000	0.000
IGOR (1 dB; P2) IGOR(5dB;P1)	-51.000	0.082	18.000	0.653	1.733
	-52.000	0.236	23.000	1.478	2.983
IGOR (3 dB; C/A)	-53.000	0.429	41.000	1.506	3.717
IGOR (3dB; P1)	-54.000	0.684	57.000	1.727	5.933
	-55.000	0.918	52.000	2.542	6.433
	-56.000	1.210	56.000	3.111	7.033
IGOR (1 dB; C/A)	-57.000	1.502	57.000	3.795	7.983
	-58.000	1.817	81.000	3.230	8.150
IGOR (1 dB; P1)	-59.000	2.069	76.000	3.921	8.433
	-60.000	2.355	79.000	4.292	8.917
	-61.000	2.655	75.000	5.097	9.583
	-62.000	2.994	94.000	4.586	9.850
	-63.000	3.328	95.000	5.044	10.467
	-64.000	3.578	94.000	5.481	11.067
	-65.000	3.844	110.000	5.032	11.450
	-66.000	4.113	111.000	5.335	11.533
TRIG (Lost Lock; C/A & P1 & P2)	-67.000	4.420	107.000	5.948	11.533
	-68.000	4.697	121.000	5.589	11.750
	-69.000	4.982	127.000	5.649	12.750
	-70.000	5.275	128.000	5.934	13.217
	-71.000	5.562	121.000	6.619	13.717
	-72.000	5.853	134.000	6.290	14.083
TRIG (5 dB; P1)	-73.000	6.116	132.000	6.672	14.350
TRIG (5 dB; P2)	-74.000	6.410	143.000	6.455	14.350
TRIG (5 dB; C/A)	-75.000	6.703	165.000	5.850	14.433
	-76.000	7.024	174.000	5.813	14.733
TRIG (3 dB; P2)	-77.000	7.293	186.000	5.646	15.267
TRIG (3 dB; C/A) TRIG (1 dB; P2)	-78.000	7.615	208.000	5.272	15.267
	-79.000	7.936	192.000	5.952	15.267
TRIG (3 dB; P1)	-80.000	8.217	192.000	6.163	15.433
	-81.000	8.473	200.000	6.101	15.517
TRIG (1 dB; C/A & P1)	-82.000	8.743	205.000	6.141	15.583
	-83.000	8.984	211.000	6.131	15.583
	-84.000	9.212	212.000	6.257	15.583
	-85.000	9.474	218.000	6.258	15.600
	-300.000	12.180	189.000	9.280	21.683

Table 6-9. Interference Results for GPS RX Onboard LEOSAT (400 km/72° orbit) With Zenith Pointed Choke Ring Antenna (0° elevation mask on base stations/42 dBW EIRP)

LSQ Interference Results for JPL GPS Receiver with Zenith Pointed 7 dBic Choke Ring Antenna
GPS RX Onboard LEO Satellite in 400 km/72° Orbit

Two LSQ channels per sector @ 42 dBW max EIRP per channel

0° Elevation Mask on LSQ Base Stations
Peak Interference Level = -68.1 dBm

RX C/No Degradation (based on JPL conduction testing)	Agg Interference Threshold (dBm) (int power at output of GPS RX antenna)	% Time (over 10-day period) that Interference Exceeds Threshold	# of Interference Events over 10-day sim period	Avg Duration of Interference Event (min)	Max Interference Event Duration (min)
TRIG (Lost Lock; C/A & P1 & P2)	-67.000	0.000	0.000	0.000	0.000
	-68.000	0.000	0.000	0.000	0.000
	-69.000	0.161	80.000	0.290	1.467
	-70.000	0.601	183.000	0.473	4.717
	-71.000	1.517	364.000	0.600	8.300
	-72.000	2.980	322.000	1.332	11.533
TRIG (5 dB; P1)	-73.000	3.915	257.000	2.193	13.067
TRIG (5 dB; P2)	-74.000	4.651	290.000	2.309	13.133
TRIG (5 dB; C/A)	-75.000	5.387	264.000	2.938	13.983
	-76.000	6.160	297.000	2.986	14.083
TRIG (3 dB; P2)	-77.000	6.820	200.000	4.911	14.667
TRIG (3 dB; C/A) TRIG (1 dB; P2)	-78.000	7.177	211.000	4.898	14.750
	-79.000	7.551	225.000	4.832	14.967
TRIG (3 dB; P1)	-80.000	7.974	240.000	4.785	15.650
	-81.000	8.319	210.000	5.704	17.267
TRIG (1 dB; C/A & P1)	-82.000	8.620	179.000	6.935	17.733
	-83.000	8.896	197.000	6.503	17.933
	-84.000	9.103	151.000	8.681	18.083
	-85.000	9.186	122.000	10.842	18.083
	-300.000	15.327	165.000	13.377	25.167

Table 6-10. Interference Results for GPS RX Onboard LEOSAT (400 km/72° orbit) With Zenith Pointed Choke Ring Antenna (5° elevation mask on base stations/42 dBW EIRP)

LSQ Interference Results for JPL GPS Receiver with Zenith Pointed 7 dBic Choke Ring Antenna
GPS RX Onboard LEO Satellite in 400 km/72° Orbit

Two LSQ channels per sector @ 42 dBW max EIRP per channel

5° Elevation Mask on LSQ Base Stations
Peak Interference Level = -71.3 dBm

RX C/No Degradation (based on JPL conduction testing)	Agg Interference Threshold (dBm) (int power at output of GPS RX antenna)	% Time (over 10-day period) that Interference Exceeds Threshold	# of Interference Events over 10-day sim period	Avg Duration of Interference Event (min)	Max Interference Event Duration (min)
TRIG (Lost Lock; C/A & P1 & P2)	-67.000	0.000	0.000	0.000	0.000
	-68.000	0.000	0.000	0.000	0.000
	-69.000	0.000	0.000	0.000	0.000
	-70.000	0.000	0.000	0.000	0.000
	-71.000	0.000	0.000	0.000	0.000
	-72.000	0.147	15.000	1.407	2.383
TRIG (5 dB; P1)	-73.000	0.493	60.000	1.184	3.867
TRIG (5 dB; P2)	-74.000	1.107	55.000	2.899	7.283
TRIG (5 dB; C/A)	-75.000	1.793	103.000	2.507	8.083
	-76.000	2.389	105.000	3.276	9.217
TRIG (3 dB; P2)	-77.000	3.050	122.000	3.600	9.617
TRIG (3 dB; C/A) TRIG (1 dB; P2)	-78.000	3.529	89.000	5.710	10.633
	-79.000	3.927	100.000	5.655	10.850
TRIG (3 dB; P1)	-80.000	4.247	94.000	6.506	11.100
	-81.000	4.539	96.000	6.809	11.367
TRIG (1 dB; C/A & P1)	-82.000	4.790	92.000	7.497	11.633
	-83.000	5.062	118.000	6.177	11.967
	-84.000	5.361	104.000	7.423	12.183
	-85.000	5.609	104.000	7.767	13.000
	-300.000	11.515	167.000	9.929	21.450

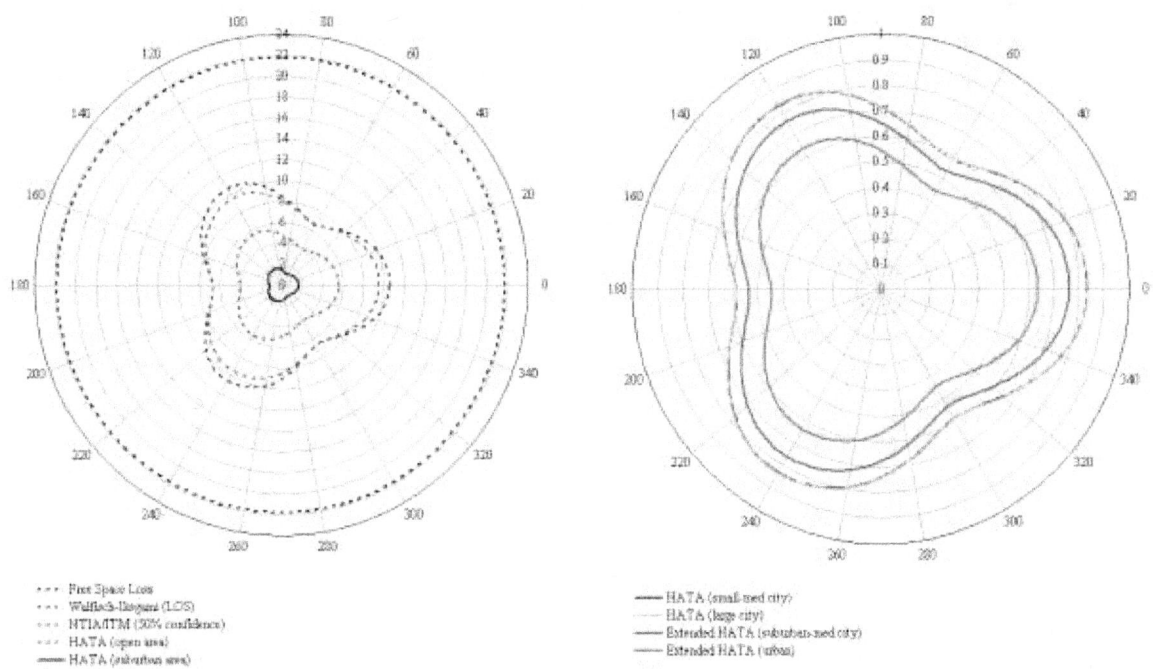

Figure 6-10. Separation Distance Contours for TRIG and Interference Threshold = -82 dBm (1 dB C/No degradation)

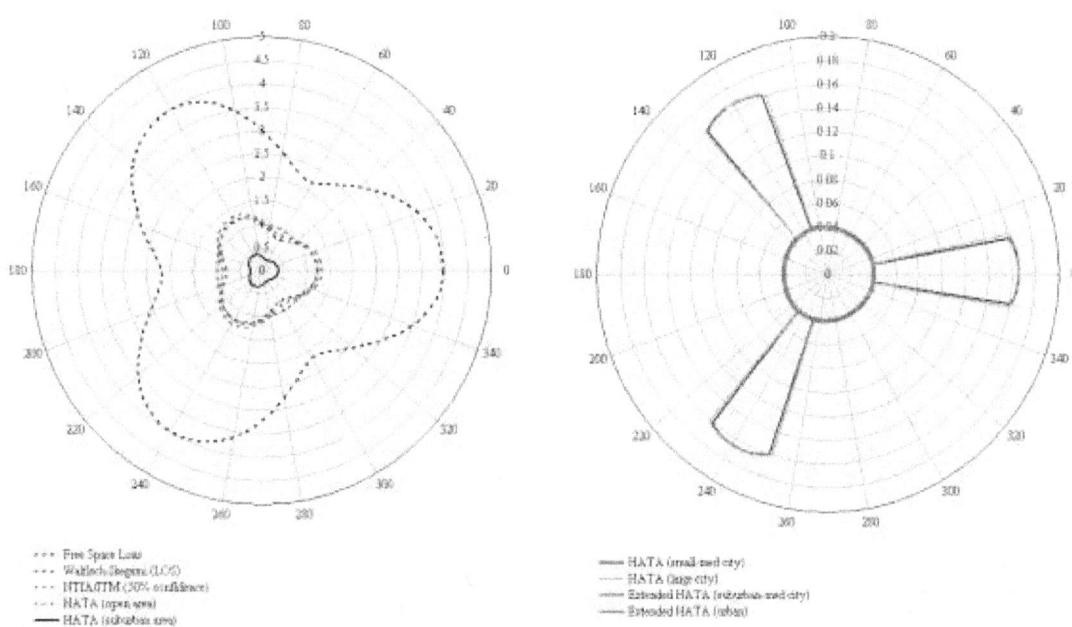

Figure 6-11. Separation Distance Contours for IGOR and Interference Threshold = -57 dBm (1 dB C/No degradation)

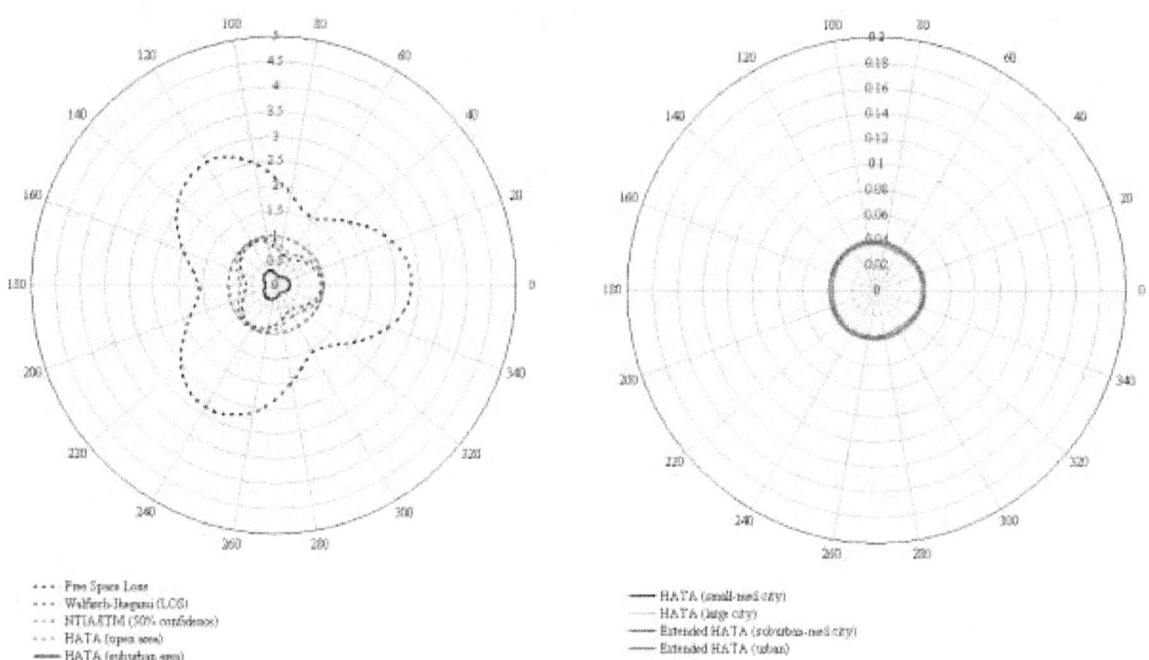

Figure 6-12. Separation Distance Contours for Receiver #15 and Interference Threshold = -54 dBm (1 dB C/No degradation)

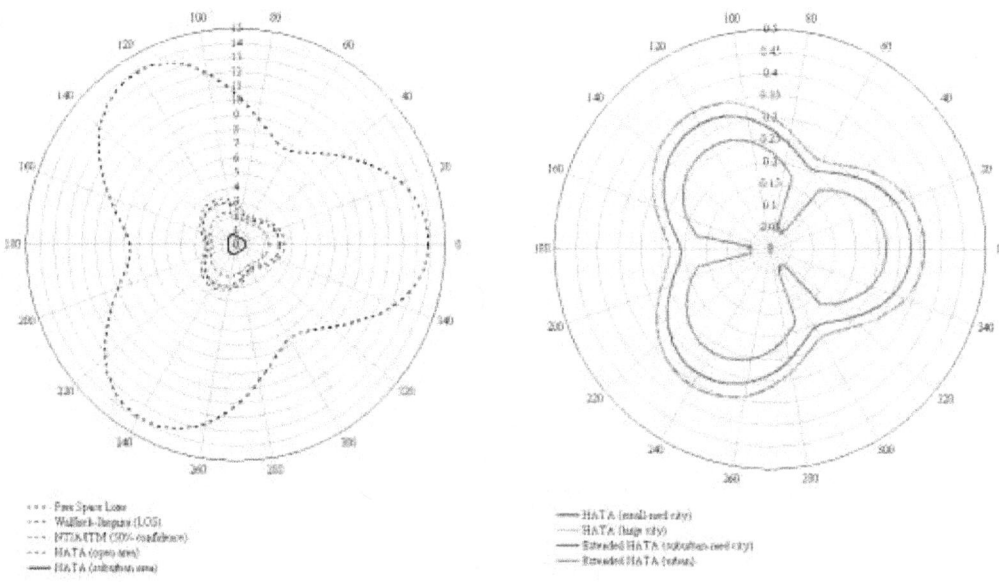

Figure 6-13. Separation Distance Contours for Receiver #16 and Interference Threshold = -68 dBm (1 dB C/No degradation)

Table 6-11. Exclusion Areas for LightSquared Las Vegas Deployment for Different Propagation Models

Note: Values are total area in which interference exceeds the 1 dB C/No degradation thresholds (-56/-68 dBm) for Receivers #15 & #16

Propagation Model	Rx #15 1 dB C/No degradation threshold	Rx #16 1 dB C/No degradation threshold
	-56 dBm	-68 dBm
Free-Space Loss	2008 km^2	3529 km^2
Walfisch-Ikegami (LOS)	532.1 km^2	1478 km^2
NTIA/ITM (50% confidence)	632 km^2	1420 km^2
Hata (open area)	424 km^2	1123 km^2
Hata (suburban)	32.4 km^2	154.8 km^2
Hata (small-med city)	5.3 km^2	34.9 km^2
Hata (large city)	5.3 km^2	34 km^2
Extended Hata (suburban-med city)	4 km^2	28.1 km^2
Extended Hata (urban)	2.6 km^2	18.3 km^2

FAA Simulation

Impact of LightSquared Emissions on Aviation

Following charts show impact for the LightSquared planned initial deployment of terrestrial base stations.

Assumptions

- Effective isotropic radiated power (EIRP) of 62 dBm/sector
  - Based upon LightSquared's stated plans
  - Importantly, the FCC has authorized 10× higher EIRPs
- Base station antenna gain patterns provided by LightSquared
- Free-space propagation modeling

What LightSquared Received Power Levels are Harmful?

FAA TSOs and ICAO SARPs both require that avionics meet all performance requirements for interference levels less than -86.4 dBm* at the LightSquared upper frequency of 1552.7 MHz

- Only require that avionics do not output hazardously misleading information with interference beyond this level

Avionics tests

- Initial testing conducted, more rigorous testing underway

- Small sample size: ~half-dozen certified receiver models owned by FAA (vs many dozen models fielded)

- Least robust receiver to LightSquared emissions based upon initial tests was Receiver #2 – significant degradation at -64 dBm and failure to produce a position output at -47 dBm

- The popular Receiver #3 began to degrade at -54 dBm and failed to produce a position output at -37 dBm

*All power levels mentioned in this subtask report are referenced to the output port of the passive airborne antenna element

Analysis Approach

For a grid of latitude/longitudes at each stated altitude, the total power received from all visible LightSquared base stations was computed:

- Base station patterns on following chart

- Airborne GPS antenna gain pattern shown on subsequent chart

- Free space path loss

- 4/3-Earth radius model used to determine visibility

- 0.5 degree grid used for CONUS-level charts

Contours depict where total received interference exceeds either maximum tolerable level from avionics standards or a level determined to cause degradation from initial characterization testing.

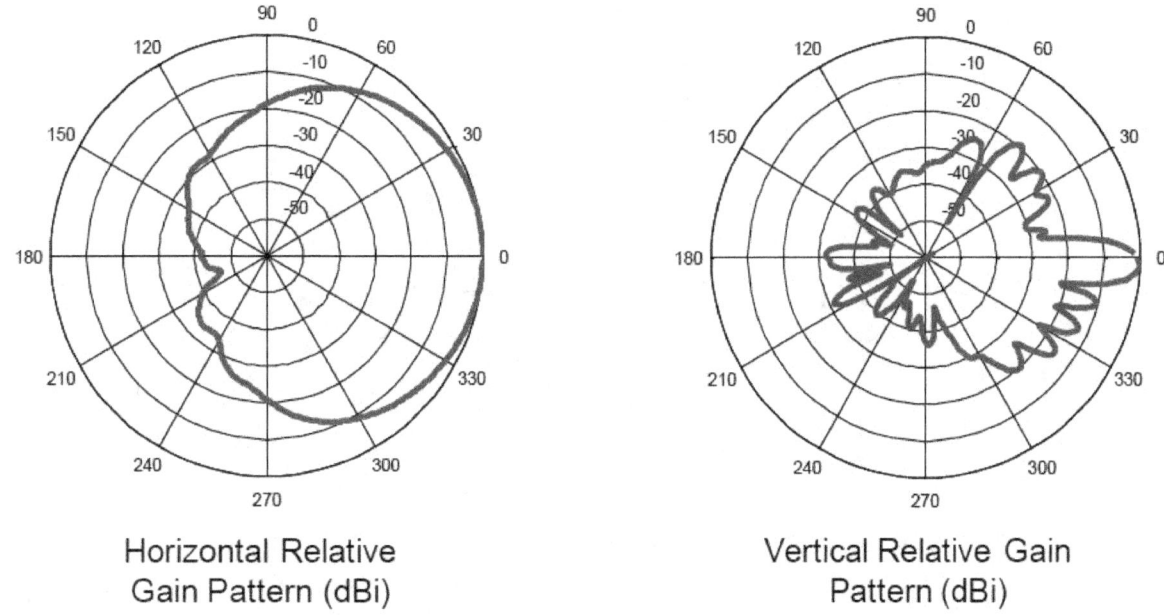

Horizontal Relative
Gain Pattern (dBi)

Vertical Relative Gain
Pattern (dBi)

Tongyu TDJ-151717DE-65F with 2
degree electrical downtilt

Maximum gain = 16.51 dBi

Figure 6-14. Base Station Gain Patterns

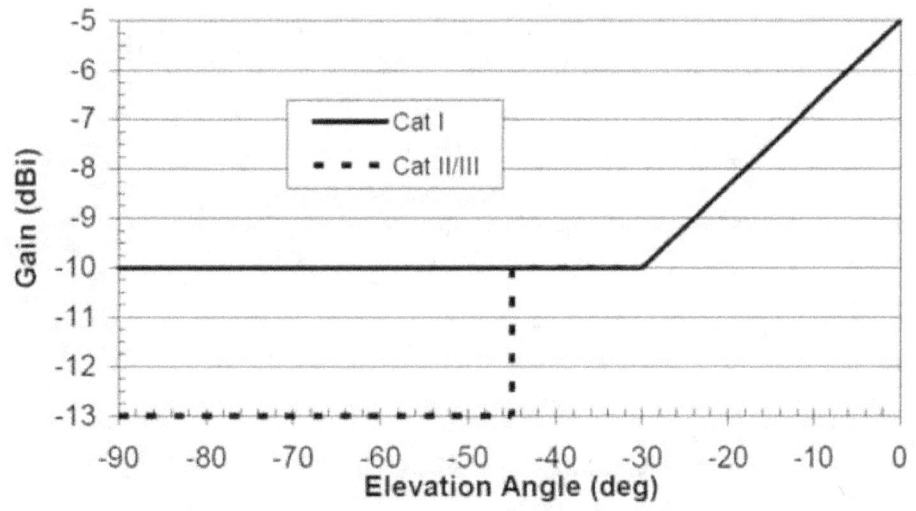

Analysis utilized "CAT I" pattern shown above from RTCA DO-235B

Figure 6-15. Airborne Antenna Gain Pattern

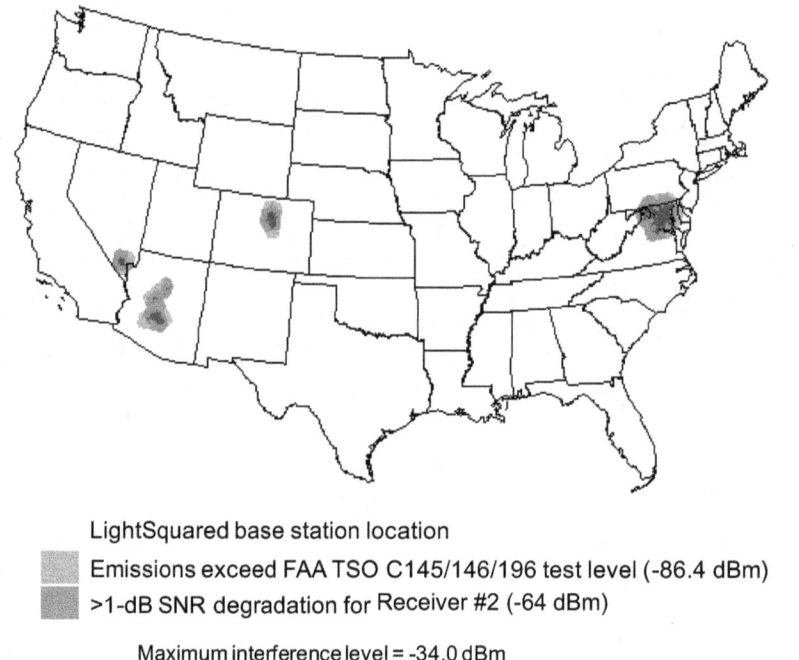

LightSquared base station location

Emissions exceed FAA TSO C145/146/196 test level (-86.4 dBm)

>1-dB SNR degradation for Receiver #2 (-64 dBm)

Maximum interference level = -34.0 dBm

Figure 6-16. Initial LightSquared Deployment (2391 of 40000+ Towers) Aircraft at 200'

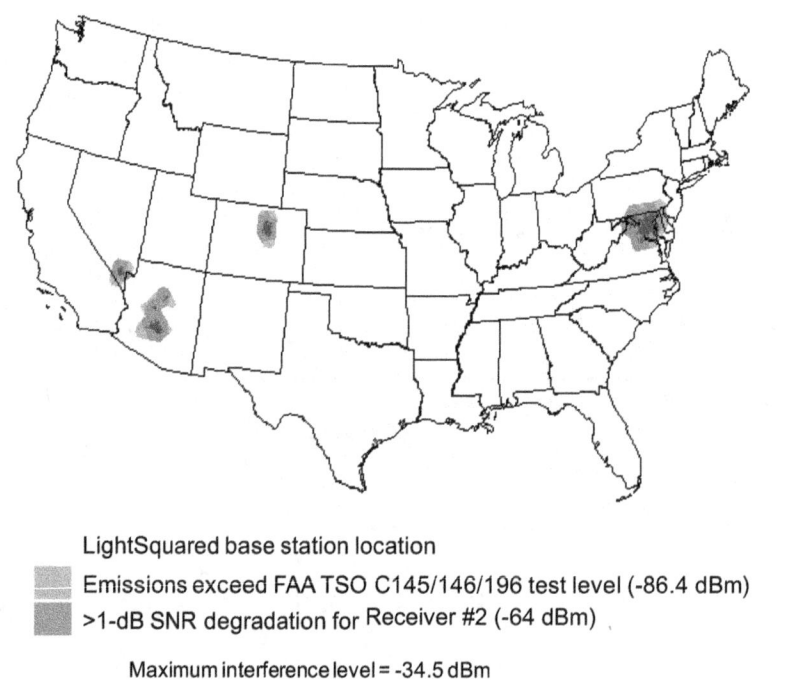

LightSquared base station location

Emissions exceed FAA TSO C145/146/196 test level (-86.4 dBm)

>1-dB SNR degradation for Receiver #2 (-64 dBm)

Maximum interference level = -34.5 dBm

Figure 6-17. Initial LightSquared Deployment (2391 of 40000+ Towers) Aircraft at 250'

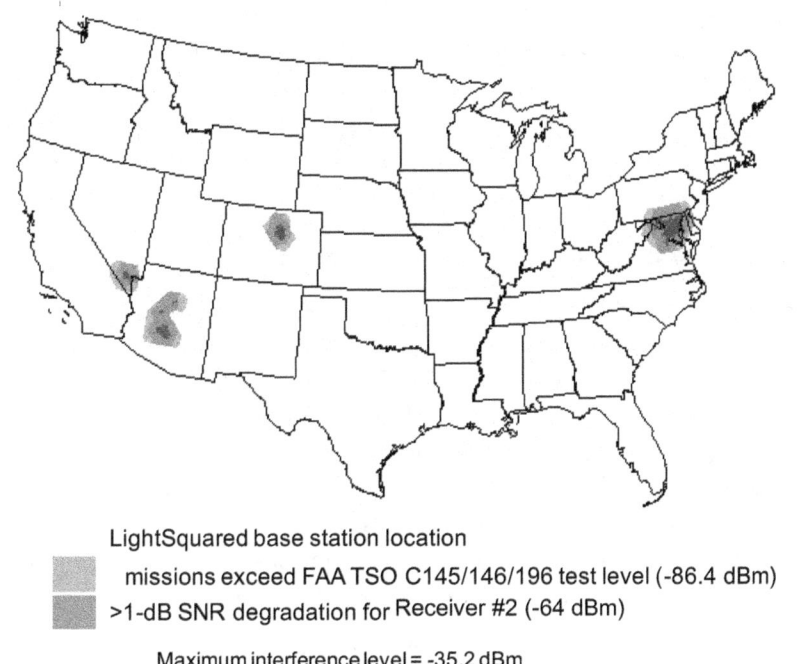

LightSquared base station location

missions exceed FAA TSO C145/146/196 test level (-86.4 dBm)

>1-dB SNR degradation for Receiver #2 (-64 dBm)

Maximum interference level = -35.2 dBm

Figure 6-18. Initial LightSquared Deployment (2391 of 40000+ Towers)
Aircraft at 350'

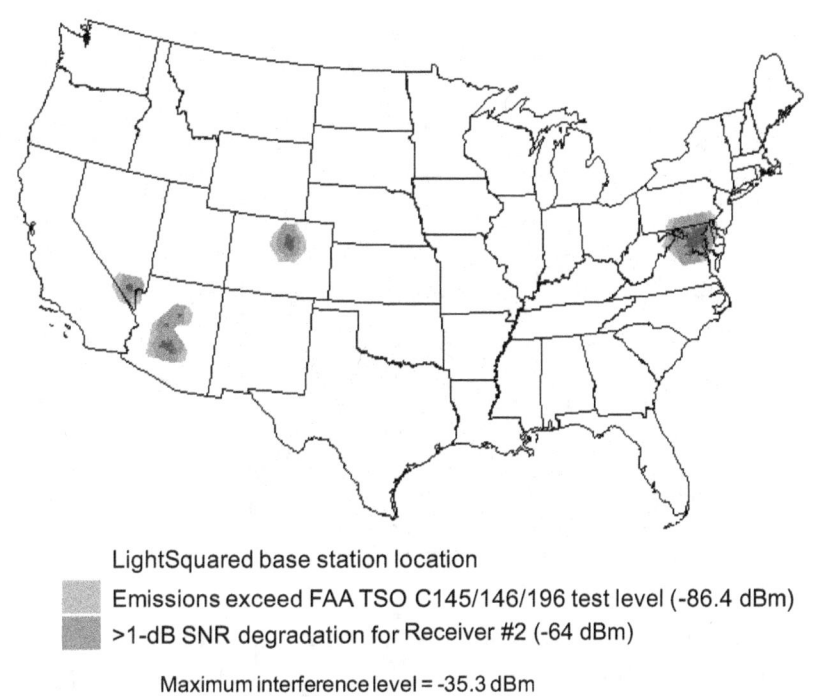

LightSquared base station location

Emissions exceed FAA TSO C145/146/196 test level (-86.4 dBm)

>1-dB SNR degradation for Receiver #2 (-64 dBm)

Maximum interference level = -35.3 dBm

Figure 6-19. Initial LightSquared Deployment (2391 of 40000+ Towers)
Aircraft at 400'

6-27

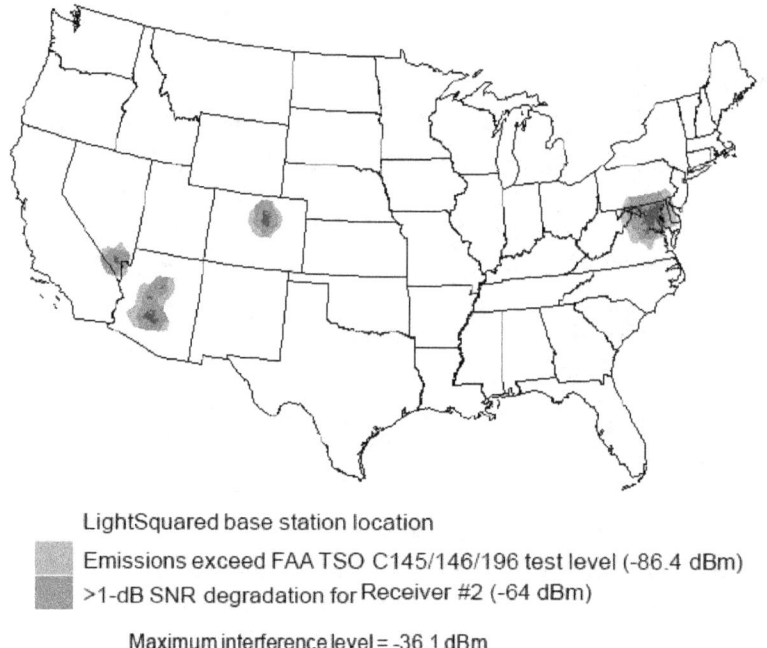

LightSquared base station location

Emissions exceed FAA TSO C145/146/196 test level (-86.4 dBm)

>1-dB SNR degradation for Receiver #2 (-64 dBm)

Maximum interference level = -36.1 dBm

Figure 6-20. Initial LightSquared Deployment (2391 of 40000+ Towers) Aircraft at 500'

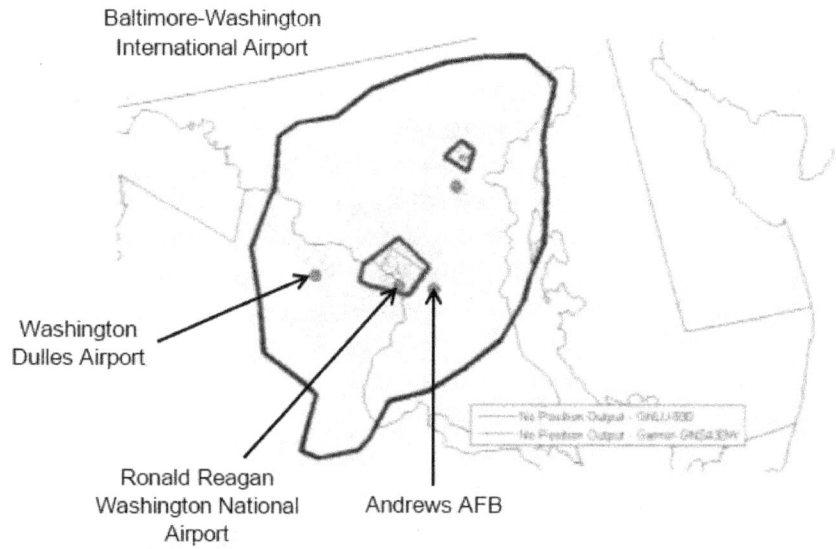

Figure 6-21. Initial LightSquared Deployment (2391 of 40000+ Towers) Aircraft at 500' (Zoom View above Baltimore-Washington)

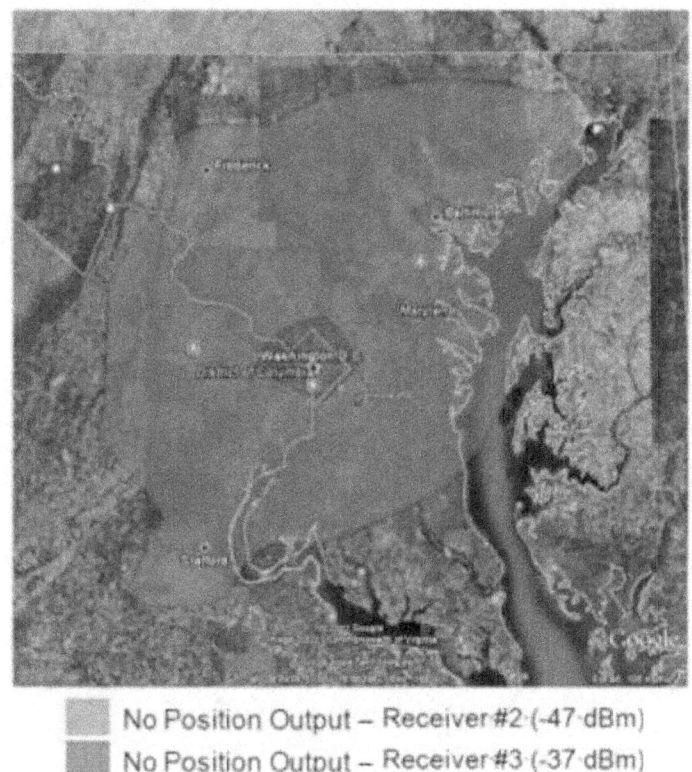

No Position Output – Receiver #2 (-47 dBm)
No Position Output – Receiver #3 (-37 dBm)

Figure 6-22. Initial LightSquared Deployment Aircraft at 500'

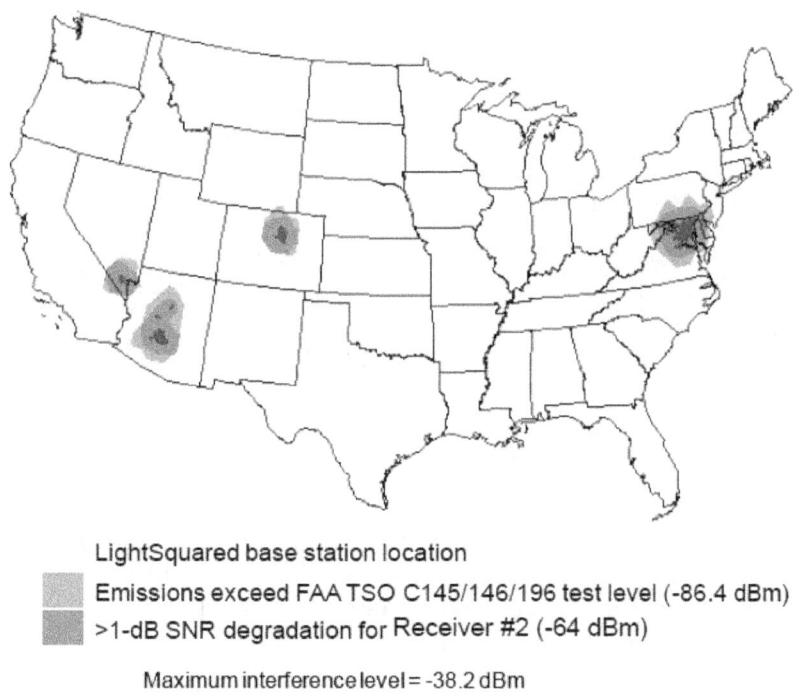

LightSquared base station location
Emissions exceed FAA TSO C145/146/196 test level (-86.4 dBm)
>1-dB SNR degradation for Receiver #2 (-64 dBm)

Maximum interference level = -38.2 dBm

Figure 6-23. Initial LightSquared Deployment Aircraft at 1,000'

6-29

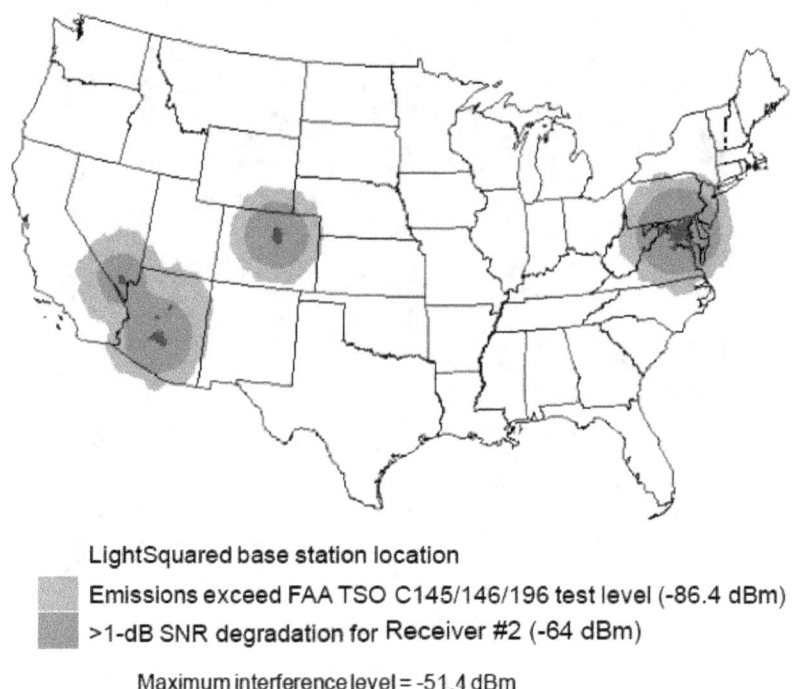

LightSquared base station location

Emissions exceed FAA TSO C145/146/196 test level (-86.4 dBm)

>1-dB SNR degradation for Receiver #2 (-64 dBm)

Maximum interference level = -51.4 dBm

Figure 6-24. Initial LightSquared Deployment Aircraft at 10,000'

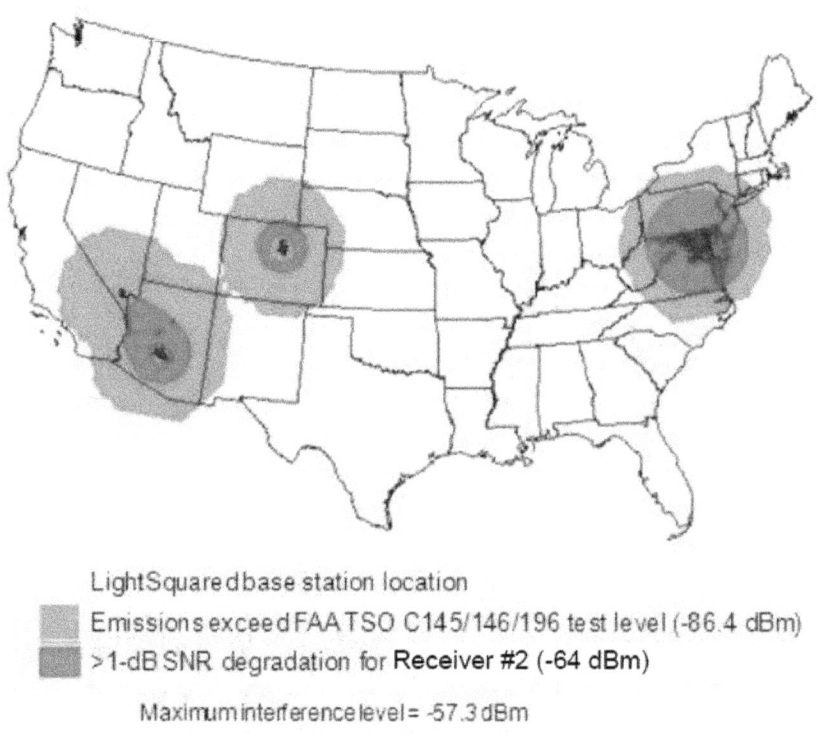

LightSquared base station location

Emissions exceed FAA TSO C145/146/196 test level (-86.4 dBm)

>1-dB SNR degradation for Receiver #2 (-64 dBm)

Maximum interference level = -57.3 dBm

Figure 6-25. Initial LightSquared Deployment Aircraft at 20,000'

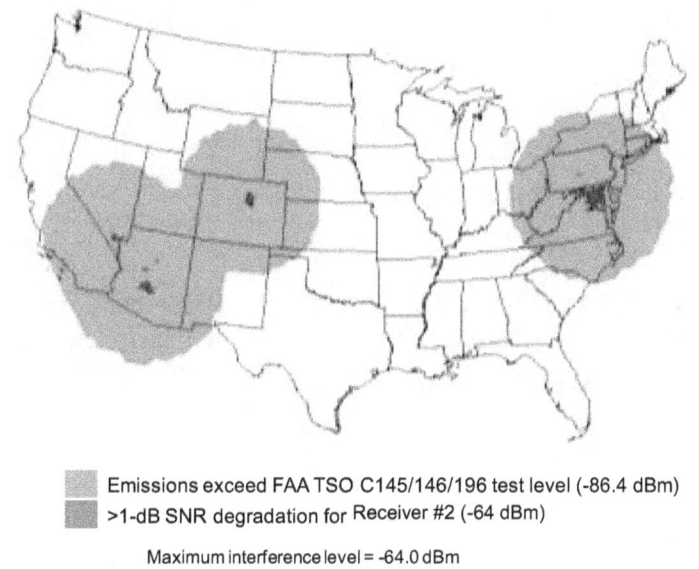

Emissions exceed FAA TSO C145/146/196 test level (-86.4 dBm)

>1-dB SNR degradation for Receiver #2 (-64 dBm)

Maximum interference level = -64.0 dBm

Figure 6-26. Initial LightSquared Deployment Aircraft at 40,000'

Intermodulation Product Simulation

Overview

This report provides an assessment of intermodulation products that may arise in some GPS receivers due to high-powered LightSquared ancillary terrestrial component (ATC) base station emissions driving low noise amplifiers (LNAs) within the receiver into saturation.

LNA Model

Consider the simple LNA system model shown in Figure 6-27. The LNA takes an input voltage, $x(t)$, which is typically the filtered output of a passive antenna element, and provides an output voltage, $y(t)$, with a nominal power gain of G. This note focuses on a typical airborne active antenna LNA that provides a nominal power gain of 34.5 dB[2].

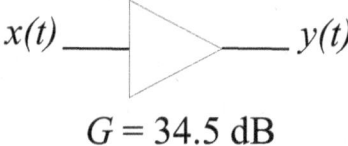

$$G = 34.5 \text{ dB}$$

Figure 6-27. Low Noise Amplifier System Model

---

[2] Per RTCA DO-301, the overall active antenna amplifier subassembly must provide a minimum gain of 26.5 dB and a nominal gain of 29.5 dB. The nominal gain of 34.5 dB, used here for the LNA subcomponent, presumes 5 dB of losses for, e.g., pre-/post-selection filters and burnout protection circuitry.

For an ideal LNA, the input-output voltage characteristics may be described as:

$$y = a_1 x \qquad (1)$$

where $a_1 = \sqrt{G}$ with G being the nominal power gain .

As is well-known, actual LNAs are only well-modeled by (1) for small input voltages. For larger input voltages, the output voltage saturates. A truncated Taylor series expansion is often used (see, e.g., [1]) as a more accurate model:

$$y = \sum_{i=1}^{N} a_i x^i \qquad (2)$$

For example, Figure 6-28 shows the voltage input-output characteristics of an LNA modeled using equation (2) with $N = 5$ and the following coefficients:

$$a_1 = 53.088 \ (\text{unitless})$$
$$a_2 = 0$$
$$a_3 = -997490 / R \ (\text{volts}^{-2}) \qquad (3)$$
$$a_4 = 0$$
$$a_5 = 6.5e9 / R^2 \ (\text{volts}^{-4})$$

Where $R = 50 \ \Omega$ is the resistance assumed to relate voltage to power. The a_1 coefficient was selected as $a_1 = \sqrt{G}$ to provide a nominal gain of 34.5 dB. The a_2 and a_4 coefficients were selected as zero to provide an odd-symmetric input-output voltage characteristic.

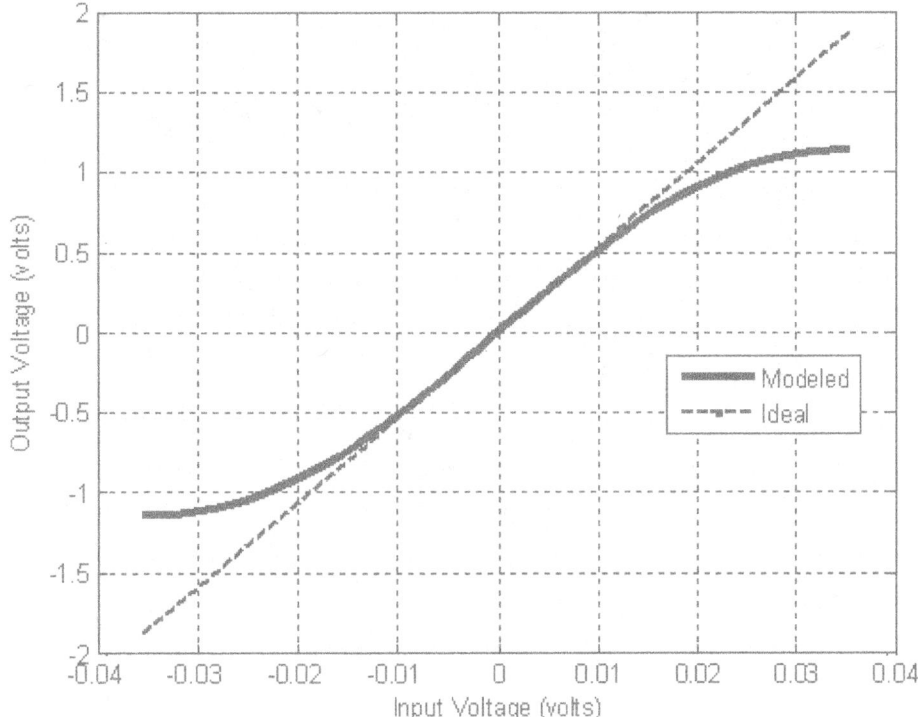

Figure 6-28. Input-Output Voltage Characteristic for Modeled Airborne Active Antenna LNA

a_3 was selected to achieve a representative *1-dB compression point* and *third-order intercept point*. The 1-dB compression point, P_1, is either the input (*input 1-dB compression point*) or output (*output 1-dB compression point*) power level at which the LNA provides 1-dB less gain than an ideal LNA with the same nominal gain value. Figure 6-29 shows the input-output power characteristics of the modeled LNA. Airborne antenna active subassemblies are required to have an input 1-dB compression point above -25 dBm within the passband. These subassemblies are defined to include protection circuitry and a preselector filter between the passive antenna output port and LNA input port. The modeled LNA is consistent with this requirement, providing an input 1-dB compression point of -22.2 dBm (see Figure 6-29), which would provide an input 1-dB compression point above -20 dBm for the overall active subassembly presuming combined insertion losses of greater than 2.2 dB for the preselector filter and protection circuit.

The concept of the third-order intercept point is explained, e.g., in [1]. A typical LNA has a third-order intercept point, P_3, which is 10 – 15 dB above its 1-dB compression points (provided that both are consistently referenced to either the input or output). The magnitude of the a_3 coefficient in equation (3) was selected using the formula [4]:

$$P_{3,output} = \frac{2a_1^3}{3|a_3|} \tag{4}$$

and a target $P_{3,input}$ value that was set to 10 dB above a target $P_{1,input}$ value of -24.5 dBm. The sign of a_3 was chosen to be negative, since this is required for gain suppression rather than gain enhancement at higher input voltages. Using this selection process, the LNA model perfectly provides the target P_3 value. However, it is only fortuitous that the achieved P_1 value of -22.2 dBm is close to the target value of -24.5 dBm. The final coefficient, a_5, was selected to make the output voltage stay as close as possible to "flat" for high input voltage magnitudes.

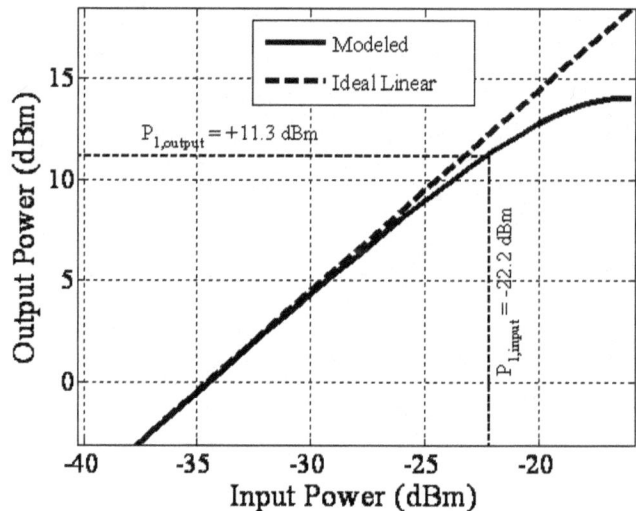

Figure 6-29. Modeled LNA Input-Output Power Characteristics

Response of LNA to LightSquared Emissions

Noting that the input-output characteristics are virtually unchanged for input power levels below -20 dBm by truncating the Taylor series to $N = 3$, here we focus on the simpler LNA input-output voltage model:

$$y = a_1 x + a_3 x^3 \qquad (5)$$

with the input voltage presumed to be well-modeled as a Gaussian, wide sense stationary random process.

The output voltage autocorrelation may be determined as:

$$
\begin{aligned}
R_y(\tau) &\equiv E\left[y(t+\tau)y(t)\right] \\
&= E\left[\left(a_1 x(t+\tau) + a_3 x^3(t+\tau)\right)\left(a_1 x(t) + a_3 x^3(t)\right)\right] \\
&= \left(a_1^2 + 6a_1 a_3 \sigma_x^2 + 9a_3^2 \sigma_x^4\right) R_x(\tau) + 6a_3^2 R_x^3(\tau)
\end{aligned} \qquad (6)
$$

where $R_x(\tau)$ is the input voltage autocorrelation and $\sigma_x^2 = R_x(0)$ is the variance of $x(t)$ (i.e., input power aside from a possible scale factor for a non-unity resistance).

From equation (6), the following expression may be derived to relate the output power spectrum, $S_y(f)$, of the LNA to its input power spectrum, $S_x(f)$:

$$S_y(f) = \left(a_1^2 + 6a_1 a_3 \sigma_x^2 + 9a_3 \sigma_x^4\right) S_x(f) + 6a_3^2 S_x(f) * S_x(f) * S_x(f) \qquad (7)$$

where * is the convolution operator.

Results with No Preselection Filtering

Figure 6-30 through Figure 6-32 show the LNA input and output power spectra for various LightSquared received power levels, presuming no filtering prior to the LNA. Phase 1 emissions are assumed, and these emissions are very simply modeled as perfectly rectangular 5-MHz blocks centered at 1528.8 MHz and 1552.7 MHz with total input power as indicated on each figure. An input noise floor of -201.5 dBW/Hz is also included[3].This truly would not fully present at the LNA input even for a receiver with this effective N_0 value, since some of the effective N_0 is due to the LNA noise figure.

In Figure 6-30, the LightSquared signal at the input of the LNA is at a power level of -45 dBm, which is much greater than the power from the thermal noise floor. This input power level is well below the LNA's 1-dB input compression point, and the LNA is operating very linearly. The output appears to be perfectly identical to the input, with the exception that the output power level is 34.5 dB (the nominal gain value) greater than the input.

In Figure 6-31 and Figure 6-32, the LightSquared input levels are increased to -35 dBm and -25 dBm, respectively. The LNA is being driven closer to its 1-dB compression point, and the output signal is seen to be increasingly distorted with a significant third-order intermodulation product clearly visible centered at $2 \times 1552.7 - 1528.8 = 1576.6$ MHz.

---

[3]This level would not truly be present at the LNA input even presuming that the overall front-end had precisely this effective N_0 value, since a good portion of the effective N_0 arises from the LNA noise figure. Nonetheless, ignoring rigor in this area does not materially affect the results presented here.

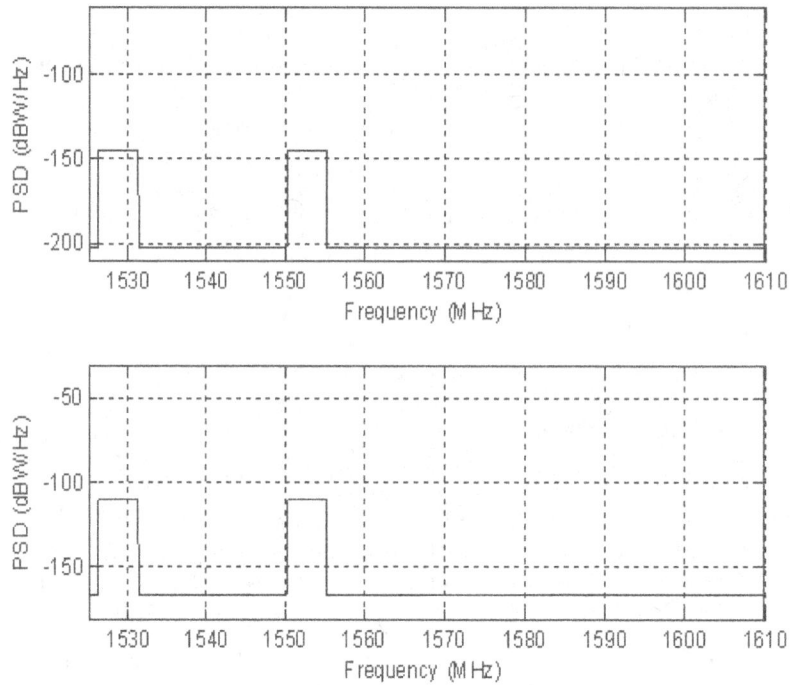

Figure 6-30. Input (top) and Output Power Spectrum of Modeled LNA, for Input Power of -45 dBm (LNA in Linear Region)

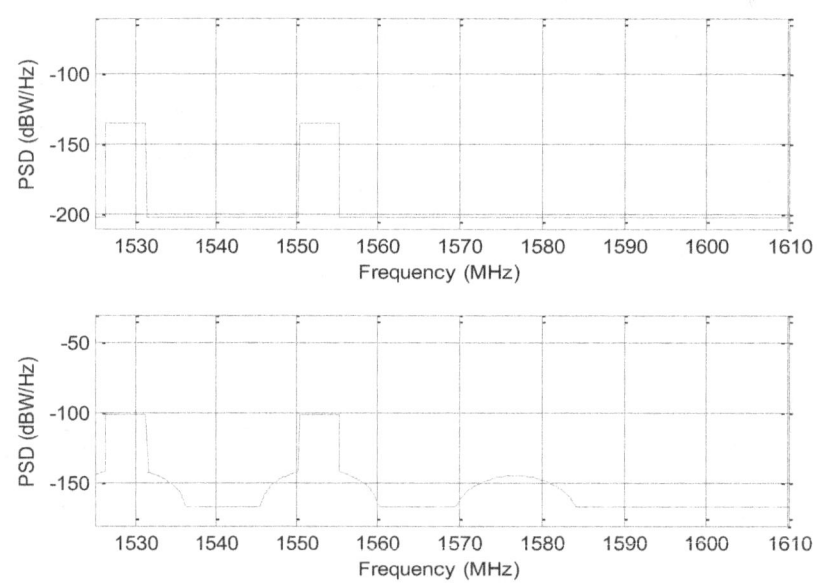

Figure 6-31. Input (top) and Output Power Spectrum of Modeled LNA, for Input Power of -35 dBm (LNA Entering into Compression)

6-36

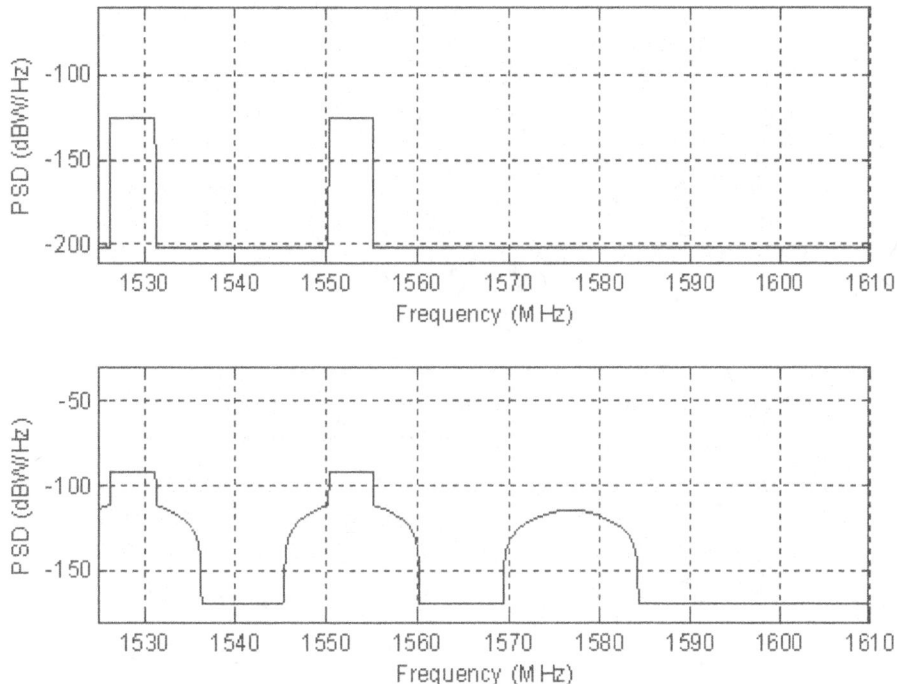

Figure 6-32. Input (top) and Output Power Spectrum of Modeled LNA, for Input Power of -25 dBm (LNA Nearly to 1-dB Compression Point)

Results with Preselection Filtering

Preselection filtering can significantly diminish the strength of the third-order intermodulation product. For example, a representative 3-pole ceramic filter provides the attenuation characteristics shown in Figure 6-33. This particular filter has an insertion loss of 2.2 dB, and for the results to follow an additional 0.5 dB insertion loss for protection circuitry is presumed to be present between the passive antenna output port and LNA input. With this configuration, Figure 6-34 through Figure 6-36 show input-output power spectra for the modeled LNA using the same remaining assumptions as were used for Figure 6-30 through Figure 6-32.

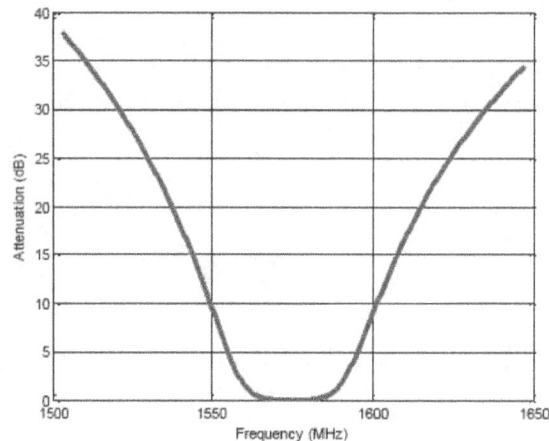

Figure 6-33. 3-Pole Ceramic Preselection Filter Attenuation (24 MHz 1-dB Bandwidth)

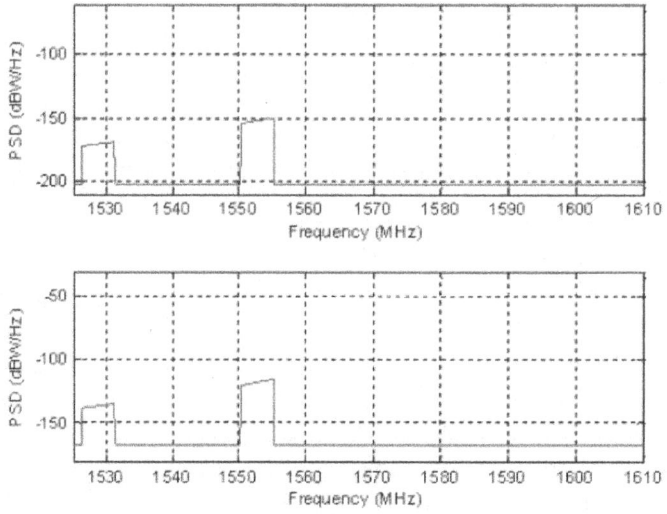

Figure 6-34. Input (top) and Output (bottom) Power Spectrum of Modeled LNA; LightSquared Signal Power at Antenna Output Port is -45 dBm, LNA Input Power is -57.5 dBm (LNA in Linear Region)

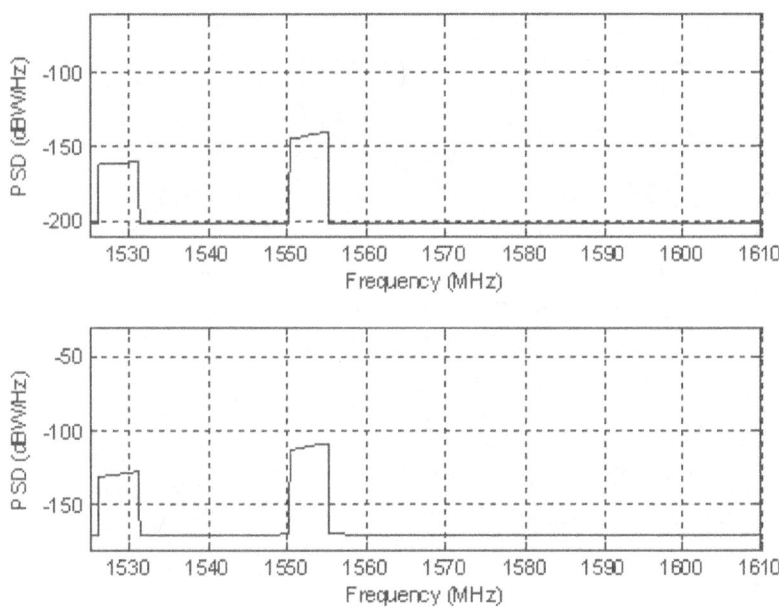

Figure 6-35. Input (top) and Output (bottom) Power Spectrum of Modeled LNA; LightSquared Signal Power at Antenna Output Port is -35 dBm, LNA Input Power is -47.6 dBm (LNA Lightly Entering into Compression)

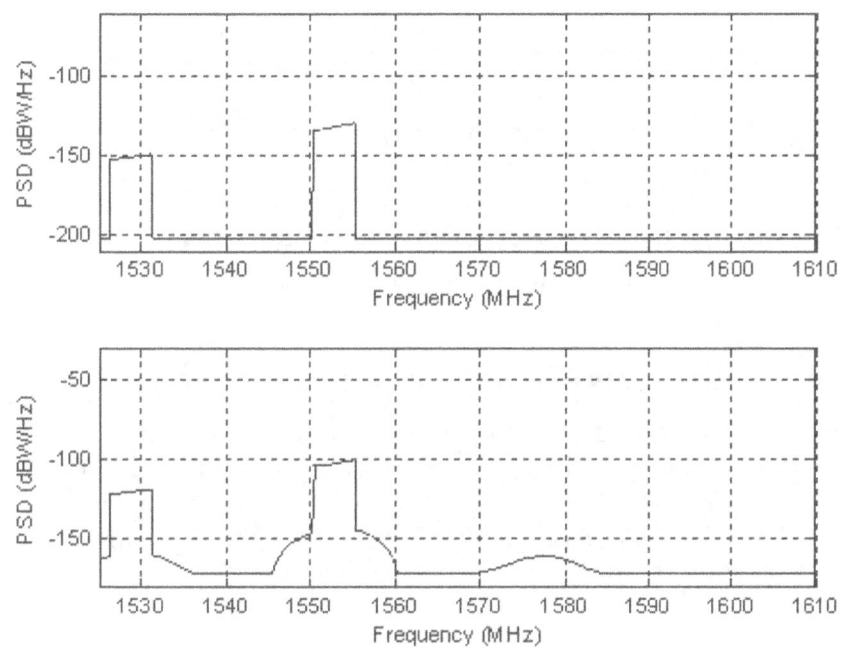

Figure 6-36. Input (top) and Output (bottom) Power Spectrum of Modeled LNA; LightSquared Signal Power at Antenna Output Port is -25 dBm, LNA Input Power is -37.6 dBm (LNA Entering Deeper into Compression)

Figure 6-37 shows the degradation to the effective N_0 for a C/A-code receiver due to the third-order intermodulation product, presuming that the remainder of the receiver front-end is perfectly linear and perfectly bandlimited to 20 MHz[4]. The plot was produced by computing the inner product of the LNA output power spectrum, referred back to the passive antenna port by scaling by the true LNA gain and assumed 2.7 dB insertion loss (for the preselector filter and protection circuitry), against the normalized power spectrum of the C/A-code. The inner product was computed over L1 +/-10 MHz under the presumption that the fundamental LightSquared emissions would be suppressed completely by later filtering within the receiver. A 0.5 dB degradation is seen at a LightSquared received power level of -31.5 dBm.

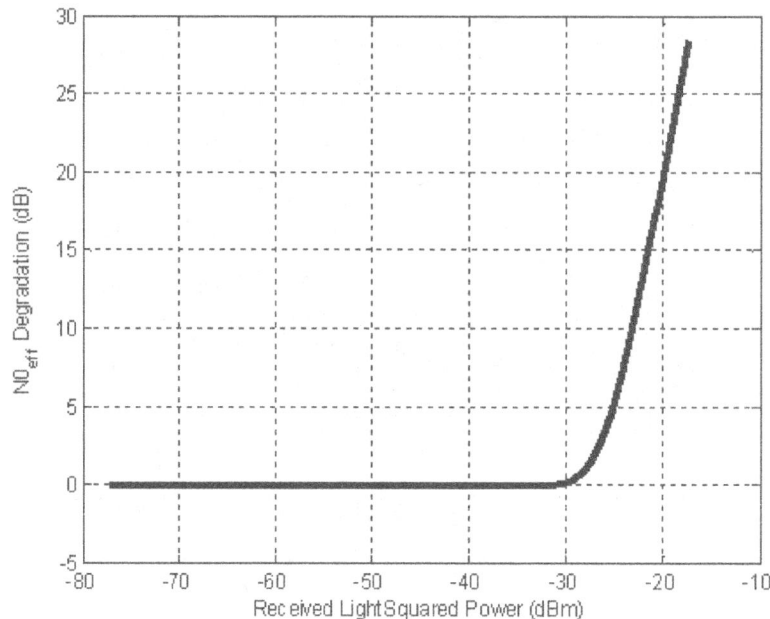

Figure 6-37. Degradation to Receiver Effective Noise Floor due to the Third Order Intermodulation Product

Comparison with Simulations and Measurements

Figure 6-36 looks very similar to a simulation result produced for the same Phase 1 emission scenario, but for a commercially available GPS receiver front-end module, see Figure 6-38 (from [2]). To produce this figure, the author of [2] created a time-domain simulation of the LightSquared Long Term Evolution (LTE) signals and fed these signals through a time-domain model of the front-end module.

---

[4]These are obviously big assumptions that are not likely to be true for most fielded receivers. In fact, it is the authors' view that saturation is far more likely in later receiver components such as LNAs or mixers within the receiver before appreciable attenuation of the fundamental LightSquared emissions is provided by distributed filtering (if at all).

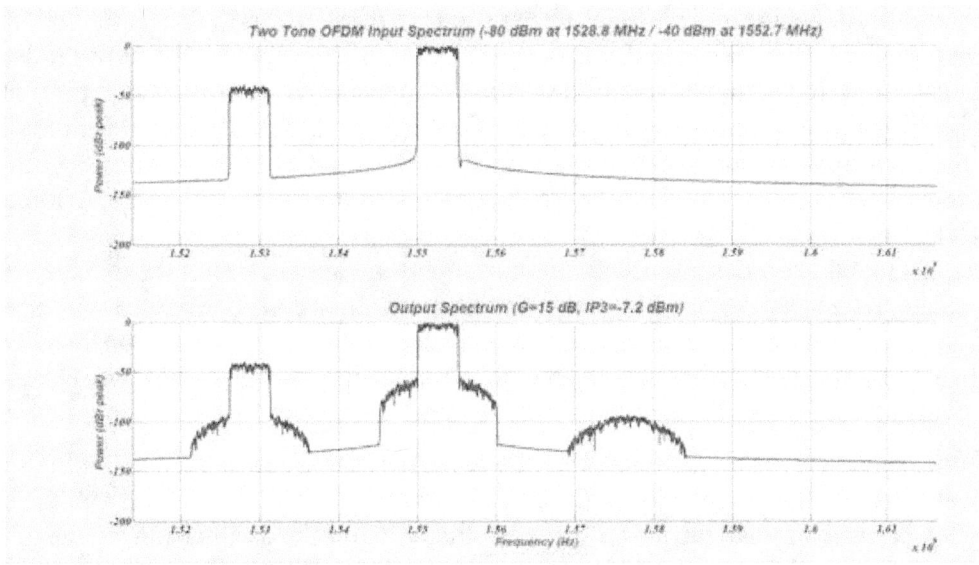

Figure 6-38. .Maxim MAX2741 Input (top) and Output (bottom) Power Spectra based Upon Simulations [2]

The model-predicted power spectra are also similar to those measured at the output of a GPS LNA from a live LightSquared base station. Figure 6-39 shows a measurement that was made by Jet Propulsion Laboratory (JPL) personnel at the Holloman Air Force Base Live Sky test event. A third-order intermodulation product is clearly visible in this spectrum analyzer screen-shot with some similar features as observed in the model results earlier in this note.

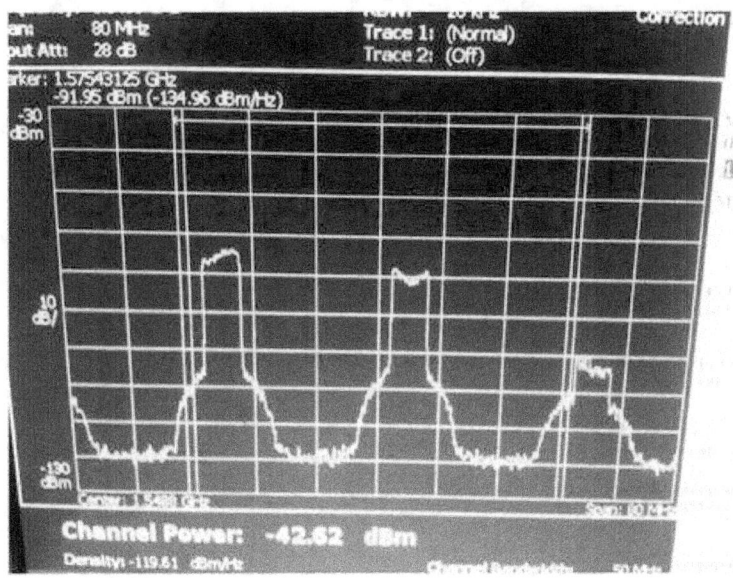

Figure 6-39. Measured Output Power Spectrum of LNA as Measured by JPL at the Holloman Live Sky Test Event

There is, however, one noticeable difference between the measured power spectra and the model results. The spectrum of the measured third-order intermodulation product is not as broad in bandwidth as that predicted by the model described in this note, or as was seen in the simulation results in [2]. This difference cannot be attributed to the fact that the LNA used for the measurement was somehow different than the one that was modeled in this note or within [2]. Note that regardless of the "tuning" of the LNA model described in this note (i.e., choice of particular Taylor series coefficients to match the actual LNA's input-output voltage characteristics), the third-order intermodulation products are always predicted to have a power spectrum shape that looks like one of the two fundamental emissions convolved with itself three times, i.e., a bandwidth that is three times larger than each fundamental emission. The live measurement intermodulation product, on the other hand, appears to have a power spectrum that is only as wide as each of the fundamental emissions near its peak.

One potential, speculative explanation is that the two carriers were produced using the same "dummy" data so that the baseband signal for each carrier was identical, or that there is some inherent characteristic of dual-carrier LTE signals that violates the assumptions made in deriving the model described in this note. This topic will be the subject of further study.

References

[1]   Pozar, David M., *Microwave Engineering*, 3rd Edition, Hoboken, New Jersey: John Wiley & Sons, 2005.

[2]   Scott, Logan, "Comments on LightSquared Ancillary Terrestrial Component (ATC) Interference Potential," GPS World Market Insights Webinar, 21 April 2011.

7. Subtask 7 - Work Plan, Test Planning, and Field Test Activities

Task Statement

Coordinate work plan, test planning, and field activities with the FAA, LightSquared, NTIA, and the EXCOM departments and agencies to measure emissions and determine representative technical and operational GPS receiver effects as a function of distance from a LightSquared terrestrial base station.

Overview

The LightSquared test strategy was designed to investigate possible incompatibilities between LightSquared ATC and GPS User Equipment. The NPEF performed various conductive tests as well as an Anechoic Chamber and Live Sky test to investigate these concerns. In general, the test team modulated the power of the LightSquared signal to replicate varying distances from a single ATC tower.

Conducted emissions tests were performed at Zeta, JPL, SPAWAR and 746th Test Squadron Laboratories. LightSquared was present for all unclassified tests and provided their ATC Emission Mask Filters for these events.

The Army Research Laboratory (ARL) EMVAF, located at WSMR, houses an Anechoic Chamber measuring 110' x 70' x 40'. This chamber was large enough to house the military and commercial user equipment, an antenna platform containing all UE antennas spaced so no antenna shielded any other from the GPS or LightSquared signal. The WSMR EMVAF Anechoic Chamber housed the Advanced Global Navigation Simulator (AGNS), GPS UE and antennas, and the LightSquared ATC Tower signal simulator and hardware. LightSquared was present for this test to comment on the setup and provide technical guidance.

Following anechoic chamber testing, the team transitioned test operations to an open air venue known as the "Balloon Pad" on the western portion of Holloman Air Force Base (HAFB). The 870 ft x 470 ft asphalt surface Pad provided sufficient level area for a test command center tent and even spatial distribution of the participating test organizations, their equipment and mobile diesel generators. This test was performed in close coordination with LightSquared and utilized actual LightSquared ATC equipment.

The approved details of the two tests are contained in the Anechoic Chamber Test Plan and the Live Sky Test Plan. These plans were coordinated with the NPEF, LightSquared, NTIA and FCC.

8. Subtask 8 – Identify & Evaluate Potential Mitigations for GPS Applications

Task Statement

Assess potential mitigation techniques and their expected effectiveness/costs for various representative GPS receivers in each of the selected scenarios. Assessments should include analysis, simulation, and prototype testing (as practical).

Overview

This task report addresses possible mitigation techniques applicable to GPS equipment and the GPS constellation. Four mitigations are considered: the use of additional filtering, adaptive antennas, GPS system changes, and operational solutions. The last section addresses costs associated with each of these mitigation approaches.

Additional Filtering

Fielded GPS receivers were, for the most part, designed with the expectation that the 1525 – 1559 MHz band would continue to be "quiet", as it has been occupied for many years primarily by low-level (as seen by GPS users on or near the Earth's surface) downlink signals for satellite communications. Although all known fielded GPS receivers include some filtering, the amount of attenuation provided by this filtering towards LightSquared emissions in the 1525 – 1559 MHz band is, in many cases, quite limited. This subsection considers the inclusion of additional filtering as a possible mitigation.

Filter Characteristics

Important filter characteristics for GPS applications are described in the following subsections. As will be discussed in the Filter Technologies section below, selecting from available filter technologies often involves making tradeoffs among these characteristics.

Type

Bandpass and low pass filters are most commonly used for GPS applications. As illustrated in Figure 8-1, ideal bandpass and low pass filters allow only a range of frequencies to pass through and completely suppress signals outside of this frequency range. For bandpass filters, the frequency range spans between two positive frequency values. Bandpass filters are used within GPS receivers or active antennas to pass the desired radiofrequency (RF) GPS signals before downconversion (e.g., at L1 ± 15 MHz for a receiver wishing to process all of the L1 signals), and may also be used at an intermediate frequency (IF) after downconversion. Low pass filters are often found after downconversion within receivers that utilize a low or no IF, or at times even with a high IF to suppress harmonics generated within the mixers used for downconversion.

8-1

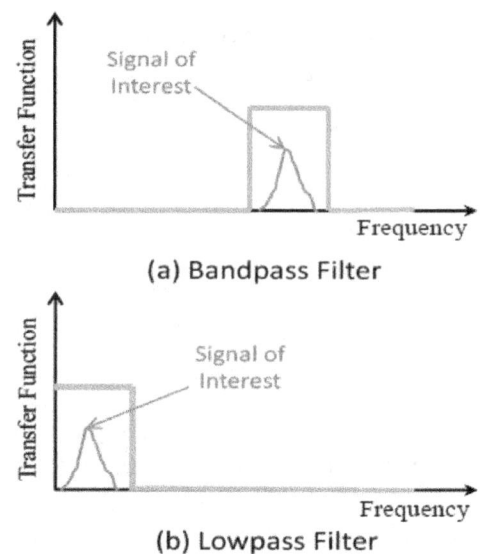

Figure 8-1. Ideal Bandpass and Low Pass Filters

Selectivity

Selectivity is the amount of attenuation that is provided by the filter towards undesired signals (i.e., those that fall outside of the filter passband). Although as illustrated in Figure 8-1 ideal filters completely suppress signals outside of the passband, as will be seen in typical characteristics to be presented throughout this section, realizable filters can only provide a finite amount of attenuation. Achievable attenuation in realizable filters typically is generally small close to the passband, and increases as frequency separation from the passband grows.

The passband is selected based upon the signals that are intended to be processed. Figure 8-2 depicts the current and future GPS L1 signals. Although 90% of the C/A-code power is contained within L1 ± 1 MHz, importantly, the ability of a GPS receiver to precisely range upon the C/A-code or any other GPS signal is enhanced tremendously in the presence of noise and multipath by additionally processing the sidelobes (see, e.g., [8-1]). Modern high-precision receivers generally utilize the full bandwidth of the signals transmitted by the GPS satellites (up to L1 ± 20 MHz for some of the operational satellites) and often use a passband that is even broader than this for reasons related to group delay (see discussion in the Group Delay section) and/or the desire to track signals that are or will be broadcast by other satellite navigation systems in this band (e.g., GLONASS, Galileo, COMPASS, satellite-based augmentation systems [SBAS], QZSS).

Selectivity is generally described using the magnitude of the transfer function, $|H(f)|$, of the filter, which is the ratio of the filter output spectrum to the spectrum of its input. Decibel (dB) units are typically used, with attenuation in dB equal to $20\log_{10}|H(f)|$. For RF filters, vendors often provide scattering matrix parameters (S-parameters) with the S_{21} parameter providing the transfer function.

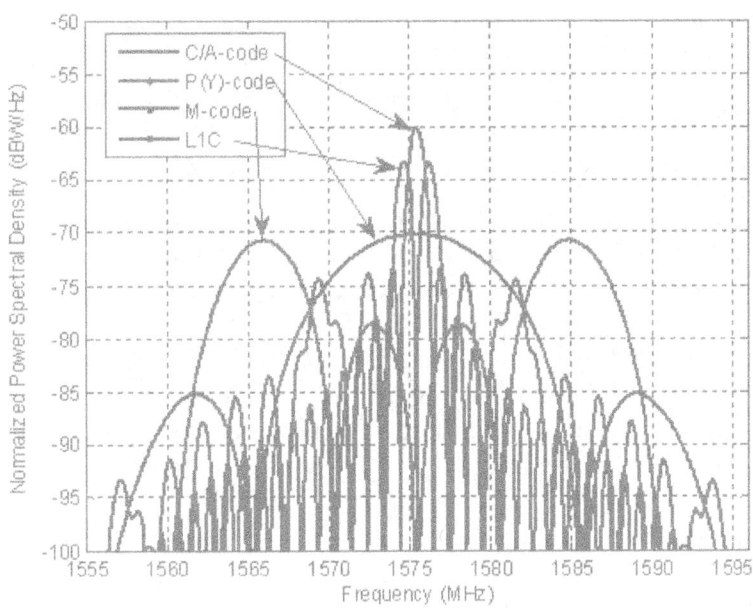

Figure 8-2. Power Spectra of GPS L1 Signals

Insertion Loss

Realizable analog filters will always provide some undesired attenuation of signals in the passband, which is referred to as *insertion loss*. Minimizing insertion loss is important, especially for any filter prior to the first significant gain stage within a GPS receiver's front-end since this filter characteristic impacts the receiver's noise floor. In a benign environment, GPS receivers see a noise floor that is due to:

- Undesired energy received from the antenna

- Undesired energy from sources internal to the receiver/antenna, e.g., due to thermal agitation of electrons within the antenna/receiver components.

Additional filtering will always increase the noise floor, and the extent to which this occurs can be quantified using the expressions:

$$N_0 = kT_{sys} \tag{8-1}$$

$$T_{sys} = T_s + T_0 \left[L_1 - 1 + L_1 \left[NF_1 - 1 + G_1^{-1} \left[L_2 - 1 + ... \right] \right] \right] \tag{8-2}$$

where N_0 is the noise density (in units of W/Hz) referenced to the output port of the passive antenna, $k = 1.38E-23$ J/K is Boltzmann's constant, and T_{sys} is the system temperature (in units of K). T_s is the source or antenna temperature (75 – 100 K for a typical GPS antenna that provides a broad gain pattern, i.e., the upper hemisphere), T_0 is 290 K, and the second term in the right-hand-side of equation 8-2 is the receiver temperature. Of importance to the present discussion,

8-3

the receiver temperature is influenced greatly by the first loss (with loss, in linear units, L_1) suffered between the output port of the passive antenna and the first gain stage (with gain, in linear units, G_1) in the receiver, as well as the noise figure, NF_1, of the first amplifier. Losses and noise figures of components further downstream in the receiver front-end is of lesser importance if the gain, G_1, is sufficiently high. Equation 8-2 is recursive, in that its form repeats for additional losses, gains and noise figures.

For the reasons described above, it is desirable for any filtering prior to the first low noise amplifier (LNA) within a GPS receiver front-end to have extremely low insertion loss. Insertion loss adds to the noise. Typical target design values can range from under 2.2 dB for aviation receivers with a clear view of the sky to less than 0.5 dB for some other applications. Filters with higher insertion losses can often be tolerated later within the RF/IF chain provided that the preceding net gain far outweighs the preceding net loss. So for instance, filters with insertion losses of up to 15 – 20 dB may be found at IF in numerous fielded receivers with little detrimental impact on receiver noise floor.

Group Delay

The phase response of a filter is also of great importance for many applications. Any phase response within the passband that is not linear with frequency will distort the desired signals. The derivative of the phase response with respect to frequency is referred to as the *group delay response* because this function of frequency describes how much time delay is incurred upon each frequency component of the desired signal.

For navigation and positioning applications, the absolute value of the group delay is not consequential since it does not affect position accuracy. For such applications, the group delay differential, which describes how much the group delay varies over the passband, is the critical characteristic. It is desirable to keep the group delay differential as small as possible over the passband to enable better positioning performance. This design goal is especially important for receivers that make measurements from more than one satellite navigation system within a band, see, e.g., [8-2]. Receivers used for time transfer, ionospheric mapping, and other science applications also require the group and phase delays to be stable over variations in temperature.

Group delay differential generally grows with increasing filter selectivity, and the frequencies where maximum group delay differential is typically seen are in the transition region between the passband and stopband. For these reasons, many fielded high-precision receivers use passbands that extend beyond the 1559 – 1610 MHz radionavigation satellite services (RNSS) band. It is also possible for some filter technologies to use specialized designs to provide delay compensation to minimize group delay differential. The use of narrow filters with sharp cutoffs, as well as some implementations of delay compensation, increases the variation of group delay and phase versus temperature.

Size, Weight, and Cost

Size, weight, and cost are of obvious importance to ensure that the filters can fit within the form factor and weight allowance for the receiver and antenna, and are additionally affordable.

Filter Technologies

As described in the following sections, a wide variety of filtering technologies are commonly used for GPS receiver applications. These technologies are described and typical and specified performance characteristics are presented. As a caveat on the typical performance characteristics, it is important to note that components can only be relied upon to meet specifications not "typical" values to allow for manufacturing and temperature variations. The relevance of specifications over typical performance is particularly true for filters with sharp cutoff transitions for which small variations can have very significant effects. The specifications allow for margin to account for such effects.

Dielectric Resonators

Dielectric resonators are a very popular technology for GPS RF and, occasionally, IF filters. These filters use a small disc or cube of low-loss high dielectric constant material as a microwave resonator to provide a low-cost, high-selectivity bandpass response [8-3]. They are also often referred to as *ceramic filters*, since ceramic is a common dielectric material used in their fabrication.

Figure 8-3 shows the selectivity of representative commercially available 3- and 4-pole dielectric resonator filters for GPS L1[5]. Both filters provide a minimum passband of 24 MHz as defined by the range of frequencies between 1-dB attenuation points. The maximum insertion losses of the 3-pole and 4-pole filters are 2.2 dB, and 3.0 dB, respectively. The 3-pole filter size is 0.80 × 0.55 × 0.27 inches, and the 4-pole filter size is 1.04 × 0.55 × 0.27 inches, both in a leadless surface mount package. A smaller form factor is available, with about one-half the volume for each, but at the cost of increased insertion loss (+0.7 dB for each) and poorer selectivity characteristics. Very little attenuation (4 – 6 dB) is provided for the upper LightSquared carrier, which extends to 1555.2 MHz. Greater attenuation (20 – 30 MHz) is provided for the lower LightSquared carrier, which extends to 1536 MHz. To increase the selectivity, more poles can be added (implemented by adding dielectric resonator sections in the filter construction, which increases filter size), but the insertion loss will also increase beyond an acceptable level for use before the first LNA (see the Insertion Loss section).

Importantly, the quality factor (Q) of dielectric resonators is not high enough to support smaller passbands centered at the GPS L1 frequency. Achievable 1-dB fractional bandwidths (ratio of 1-dB passband to carrier frequency) for this technology is typically in the range of 1.5 – 20% (24 MHz and up at L1), so receivers that use dielectric filters that desire smaller passbands will generally accomplish this through additional filtering at IF or baseband. This commonly implemented solution leaves LNAs and mixers utilized in the front-end up until the narrower bandwidth IF or baseband filters vulnerable to saturation from strong out-of-band signals, such as the planned LightSquared emissions.

---

[5] Specifically, these are part numbers 4DR35-1575/U24-1.9 and 3DR35-1575/U24-1.9 from K&L Microwave. Their S-parameters can be obtained by entering the part numbers into K&L Microwave's Filter Wizard at www.klfilterwizard.com.

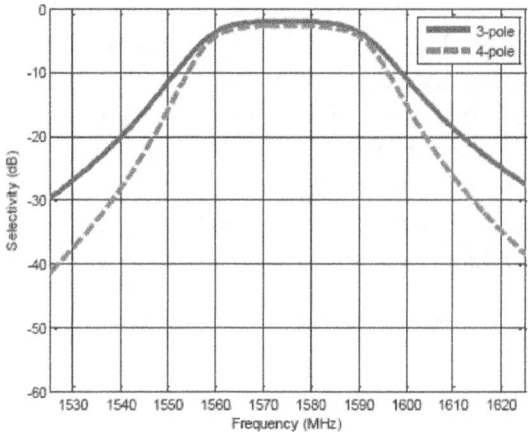

Figure 8-3. Selectivity of Representative 3- and 4-Pole Dielectric Resonator Filters with 24 MHz (1-dB Bandwidth) Passband

Even less selectivity is possible for receivers requiring wider passbands (e.g., for high-precision applications, or military equipment that is processing the wide-bandwidth P(Y)-code or M-code signals). Figure 8-4 shows representative selectivity for 3- and 4-pole dielectric filters with a 40 MHz (1-dB Bandwidth) passband. There is no attenuation provided at the upper LightSquared carrier frequency, and only a modest amount (10 – 20 dB) of attenuation for the lower carrier.

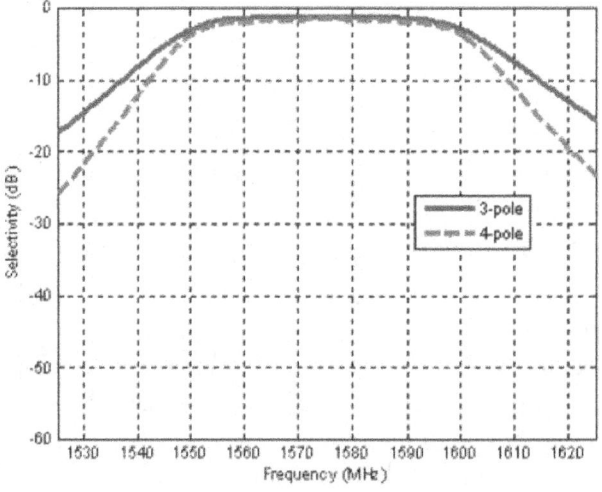

Figure 8-4. Selectivity of Representative 3- and 4-Pole Dielectric Resonator Filters with 40 MHz (1-dB Bandwidth) Passband

The group delay characteristics of the four dielectric resonator filters described in this section are shown in Figure 8-5. Over 24 MHz centered at L1, the differential group delays for the four filters in the order listed in the figure legend are 4.2 ns, 5.7 ns, 1.1 ns, and 1.5 ns. Note that improved differential group delay performance is obtained as the passband bandwidth is widened.

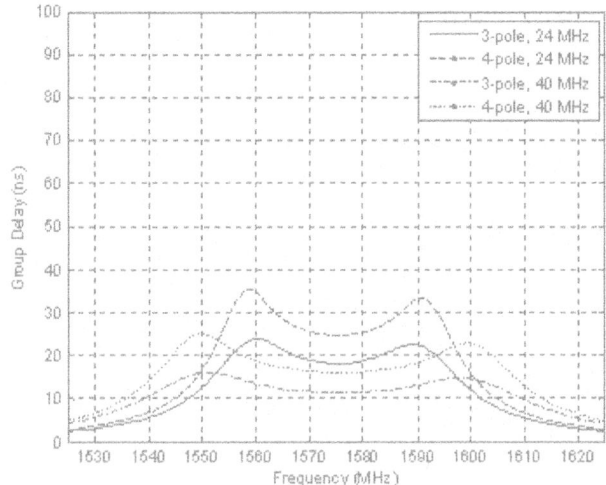

Figure 8-5. Group Delay Characteristics for Representative 3- and 4-Pole Dielectric Resonator Filters

Surface acoustic wave (SAW) filters are available for both RF and IF frequencies for GPS receivers. SAW filters use resonators that operate by converting the input electrical signal into an acoustic wave that propagates along the surface of a piezoelectric substrate [8-4]. They are inexpensive and typically much smaller than dielectric resonators, which makes them an extremely popular choice for applications where size is of utmost importance, such as GPS receivers integrated into cell phones and other mobile devices.

Low insertion loss SAW filters for use at the GPS L1 frequency are offered by many vendors. These filters are primarily marketed for low-bandwidth, low-precision C/A-code applications. They are not readily found with specified bandwidths wide enough for high precision GPS applications or for military receivers that process the wideband P(Y) or M-code signals. For instance, TriQuint Semiconductor offers 10 GPS L1 SAW filter models with advertised bandwidths ranging only from 2 – 2.4 MHz. The selectivities of two representative TriQuint RF SAW filter models are shown in Figure 8-6. Both models are only 1.4 × 1.2 × 0.46 mm in size, and have insertion losses over a passband defined as L1 ±1 MHz of less than 1.4 dB. Note that very little attenuation (< 5 dB) is provided at the upper LightSquared carrier frequency, and greater attenuation at the lower frequency (~20 - 30 dB). Importantly, the selectivity of SAW filters is sensitive to frequency, and the passband upper and lower limits may vary by up to ±5 MHz over the temperature range of -30°C to +85°C (-22°F to 185°F).

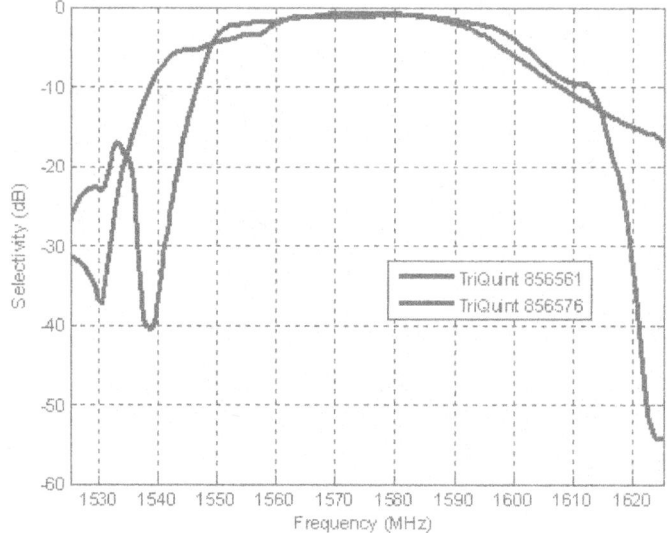

Figure 8-6. Selectivity of Two Representative GPS L1 RF SAW Filter Models

The group delay characteristics for the two representative GPS L1 RF SAW filters are shown in Figure 8-7. Although the differential group delay for these two examples is fairly small over L1 ±12 MHz, group delay performance is highly variable with temperature and manufacturing tolerances and thus generally not even specified for GPS RF SAW filters. For these reasons, in addition to the bandwidth limitation mentioned earlier, RF SAW filters are usually avoided for high-precision GPS applications.

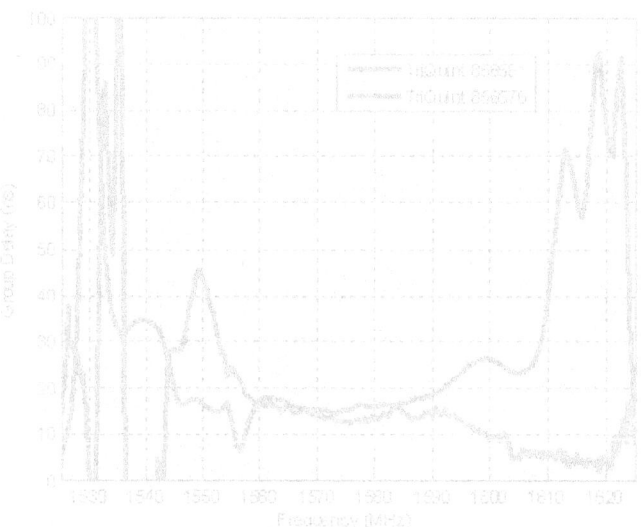

Figure 8-7. Group Delay Characteristics of Two Representative GPS L1 RF SAW Filter Models

SAW filters are also commonly used in GPS receivers at IF. SAW IF filters provide great selectivity, but at the drawback of high insertion loss (~10 – 20 dB). This tradeoff is generally desirable at IF because of the considerations discussed in Section 8.2.1.3. At typical GPS IF frequencies, which range from tens to hundreds of MHz, SAW filters are available in a wide variety of bandwidths ranging from 2 – 40 MHz. Figure 8-8 shows the selectivity characteristics of 3 representative GPS IF SAW filters for an IF frequency of 70 MHz. The filters have minimum specified 3-dB bandwidths of 40 MHz, 20 MHz, and 2 MHz. Their maximum specified insertion losses are 22 dB, 15 dB, and 8.25 dB, respectively, and their maximum specified group delays are 90 ns (over 36 MHz), 90 ns (over 18 MHz), and 340 ns (over 1.4 MHz). The large group delay differentials might preclude even the widest bandwidth IF SAW from use for high-precision applications.

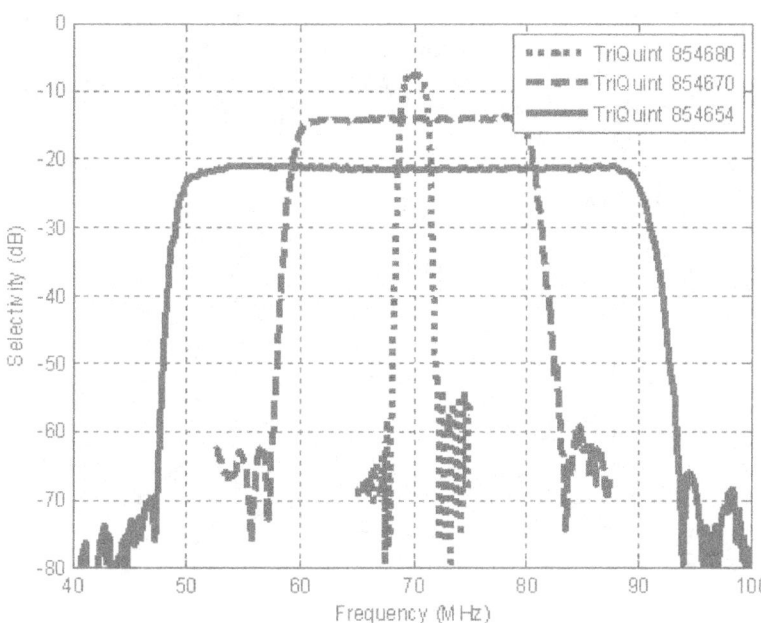

Figure 8-8. Selectivity of Three Representative GPS IF SAW Filters (70 MHz IF)

To achieve an IF frequency of 70 MHz, a GPS receiver must mix the incoming received L1 signal with a local oscillator at either 1505.42 MHz (low-side mix) or 1645.42 MHz (high-side mix). The LightSquared signals would end up, in the low-side mix case, at 20.6 – 30.6 MHz (lower carrier) and 39.8 – 49.8 MHz (upper carrier). All three of the IF SAW filters would suppress the LightSquared lower carrier signal by over 50 dB. The 2 MHz and 20 MHz filters would suppress the upper carrier signal by around this same amount, but the 40 MHz filter would provide very little suppression (relative to the 22 dB insertion loss that is also applied to the desired signal).

Bulk Acoustic Wave (BAW)

Bulk acoustic wave (BAW) filters [8-5] operate in a similar fashion to SAW filters in that they both operate through the use of resonators in which electrical signals are converted to acoustic waves. The difference between BAW and SAW filters is that in BAW filters the acoustic waves propagate through the substrate rather than along the surface before they are converted back into electrical signals. BAW filters have been gaining market share over SAW filters for mass-market RF applications because they can offer lower insertion losses and improved selectivity. BAW filter technologies include free-standing bulk acoustic resonators (FBAR) and solidly mounted resonators (SMR). BAW filters tend to be exhibit less sensitivity to temperature (by about two-fold) than SAW filters. A principle BAW drawback with respect to SAW filters is that they are more difficult to manufacture and thus slightly more costly.

At the present time, BAW filters are only available for use at GPS RF frequencies (and not for typical IF frequencies). GPS BAW filters are available in wider bandwidths at L1 (15 – 30 MHz) than SAW filters, but the wideband BAW filters tend to have slightly higher insertion losses. Figure 8-9 shows the selectivity of two representative RF BAW filters. The first (TriQuint 880273) has a specified minimum 3-dB bandwidth of 30-MHz bandwidth and a specified maximum insertion loss of 4 dB. The second (TriQuint 880085) has a specified minimum 3-dB bandwidth of 15 MHz, and a specified maximum insertion loss of 2.5 dB. The package size for each is $3.26 \times 1.6 \times 0.84$ mm.

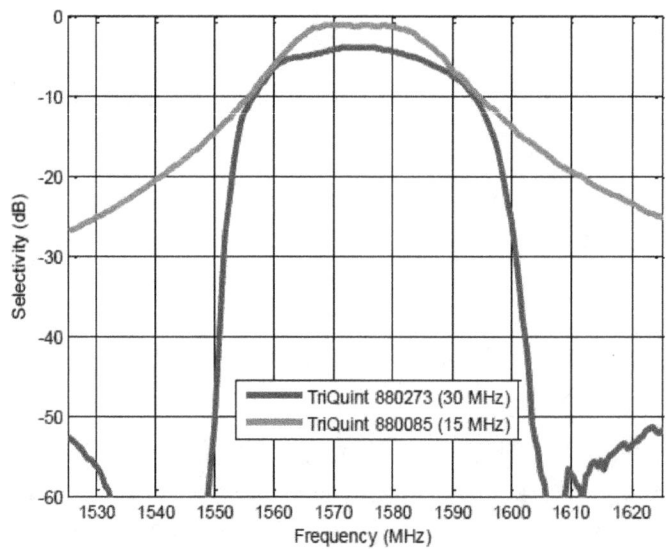

Figure 8-9. Selectivity of Two Representative BAW Filters

The 15-MHz BAW filter provides about 8 dB attenuation for the upper LightSquared carrier, and greater than 20 dB for the lower carrier. The 30-MHz BAW filter provides only around 6 dB attenuation for the upper carrier, but over 50 dB for the lower carrier.

Figure 8-10 shows the group delay responses for these two BAW filters. The differential group delay for the 30-MHz filter is around 24 ns and the group delay for the 15-MHz filter is just under 10 ns, both as measured across the specified minimum 3-dB bandwidth.

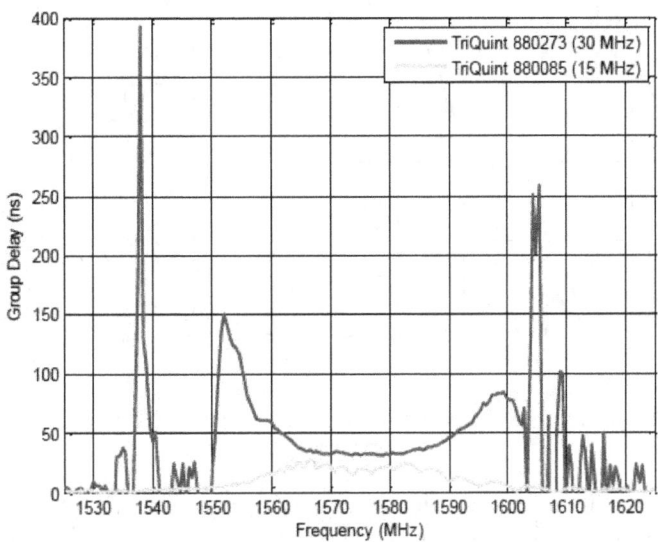

Figure 8-10. Group Delay of Two Representative BAW Filters

Cavity filters

Cavity filters [8-3] offer low-insertion loss and high out-of-band attenuation, with their main drawback being that they are extremely large and heavy. They operate using similar principles as dielectric resonators, except that they utilize an air-filled cavity within a conductor rather than a dielectric block as the microwave resonator.

Figure 8-11 shows the selectivity of one vendor's 20 MHz 1-dB bandwidth cavity filter (K&L Microwave part number 5C40-1575-U20-O/O) centered at 1575 MHz. The filter has an insertion loss of < 1.1 dB and provides ~25 dB of attenuation at 1555 MHz and over 50 dB of attenuation at 1536 MHz. However, this performance comes at the cost of size. This particular filter is 5.88 × 1.24 × 2.58 inches. A closely related model (5C42-1575-U20-O/O) provides even lower insertion loss with, with a maximum specified value of 0.7 dB, and slightly better selectivity and group delay characteristics at the price of growth in size to 9.38 × 1.94 × 2.52 inches. Because of their extremely large size and weight, cavity filters are only sporadically used for GPS equipment, and then only at RF, in niche applications such as very high-performance reference stations.

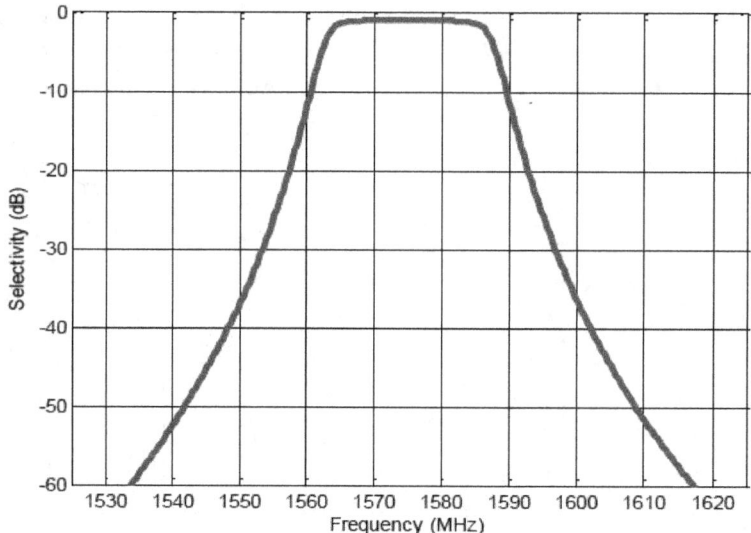

Figure 8-11. Selectivity of a 5-Section Cavity Filter with 20 MHz 1-dB Bandwidth Centered at 1575.42 MHz

The group delay for this particular product is shown in Figure 8-12. The differential group delay over the 20 MHz 1-dB bandwidth passband is approximately 25 ns.

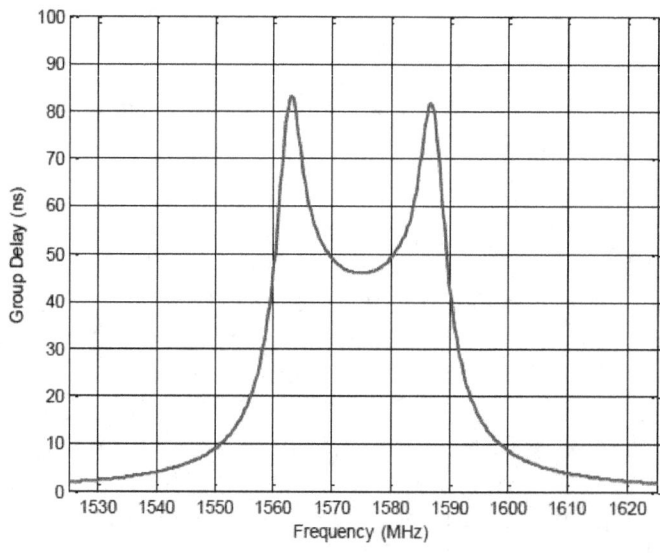

Figure 8-12. Group Delay of 5-Section Cavity Filter with 20 MHz 1-dB Bandwidth Centered at 1575.42 MHz.

Lumped Component Filters

Filters built using inductors, capacitors, and resistors are used at IF or baseband within many fielded GPS receivers. Some lumped component filters that only utilize inductors and capacitors are referred to as *LC filters*, which follows from the common engineering symbols for inductance (L) and capacitance (C). As examples of chipsets that utilize external discrete inductors and capacitors as their only means for IF filtering, see [8-6], [8-7], and [8-8]. The amount of attenuation provided by such filtering at the LightSquared frequencies depends on the design bandwidth of the LC filter and the order of the filter. As one example, [8-7] describes a GPS chipset that relies on a second-order, 15 MHz 3-dB bandwidth Butterworth LC filter centered at an IF frequency of 183 MHz. This filter provides ~10 dB of attenuation to the upper LightSquared carrier and ~40 dB to the lower carrier.

Active resistor-capacitor (RC) filters are also quite common in GPS chipsets. These offer the benefit that they can be implemented internal to the chip, see, e.g., [8-9].

Summary of Filter Technologies

Table 8-1 summarizes the filter technologies identified as being applicable for use for GPS RF applications. The most commonly used technologies – dielectric resonators, SAW, and BAW filters – are not capable of providing a significant amount of attenuation at the frequencies used for the upper LightSquared carrier (1545.2 – 1555.2 MHz). Even the most narrowband filters using these technologies at the GPS L1 frequency only provide an extremely limited typical attenuation of 4 – 8 dB at 1555.2 MHz. The minimum attenuation at this frequency is even less (nearly zero) when temperature variations are considered, especially for SAW and BAW filters. These common technologies, however, are capable of providing a more meaningful (~20 dB) attenuation of the LightSquared lower carrier (1526 – 1536 MHz)

Cavity filters are commercially available and are capable of providing much greater suppression of the LightSquared upper and lower carriers within GPS receiver RF processing. Such filters are rarely used today because they are significantly larger (~500,000 times greater volume than a SAW filter) and much more costly (~1000 times more costly than a SAW or BAW filter) than the other technologies.

Table 8-1. Summary of Commercially Available RF Filter Technologies for GPS L1

Technology	3-dB Bandwidth (MHz)	Insertion Loss (dB)	Attenuation for Upper/ Lower Light Squared Carrier (dB)	Differential Group Delay (ns)	Volume (mm^3)	Unit Cost in Large Quantity ($)
Dielectric resonator	24 MHz	2.2	4/20	4.2	2000	< 5
SAW	30 MHz*	1.4*	4/20	15	0.8	< 1

BAW	15 MHz*	2.5	8/20	10	4	< 1
Narrow-band Cavity	4 MHz	1.9	51/67	45	450000	500 - 1000
Wideband Cavity	30 MHz	0.7	8/50	18	600000	500 - 1000

*Commercially available GPS SAW filters are advertised with bandwidths from 2 – 2.4 MHz, but have much wider nominal 3-dB bandwidths. Their specified insertion loss, however, due to large deviations in their center frequency with temperature is only guaranteed over the much narrower advertised bandwidth.

IF filtering, using various commercially-available technologies is capable of much greater suppression of out-of-band and near-band signals provided that the receiver front-end can be adequately protected against saturation and intermodulation products from the RF filtering.

Feasibility of Adding Filtering to Fielded and New Equipment

Fielded GPS receivers can be divided into two categories:

- External antenna units – receivers designed to operate using separate antenna units that are connected to the receiver via a cable.

- Internal antenna unit or receivers integrated within another electronic device –receivers that utilize a built-in antenna (e.g., a handheld device with the antenna contained within the same case that houses the receiver) or include the GPS receiver within another electronic device (e.g., a GPS receiver engine within a mobile phone, iPad, or similar product).

Incorporating additional filtering to fielded receivers in the first category may be possible in some cases, but it is not likely that adding additional filtering to fielded receivers will be practical from a cost standpoint. Adding additional filtering to new products is more likely to be feasible/practical for both types.

Filtering within a well-designed GPS receiver is accomplished in stages. For example, Figure 8-13 shows an illustrative front-end design for an airborne GPS receiver and associated external antenna. The active antenna unit includes a passive patch element, limiter (to protect the antenna from, e.g., lightning), two dielectric resonator (ceramic) filters, and a LNA. The active antenna unit is connected to the receiver via a length of cable. The receiver unit itself includes a limiter, filtering, and LNA, followed by a mixer to downconvert the received signal down to some convenient intermediate frequency (IF). Following down-conversion, the IF signal is filtered by a surface acoustic wave (SAW) filter, amplified, and subsequently digitized by an analog-to-digital converter (A/D).

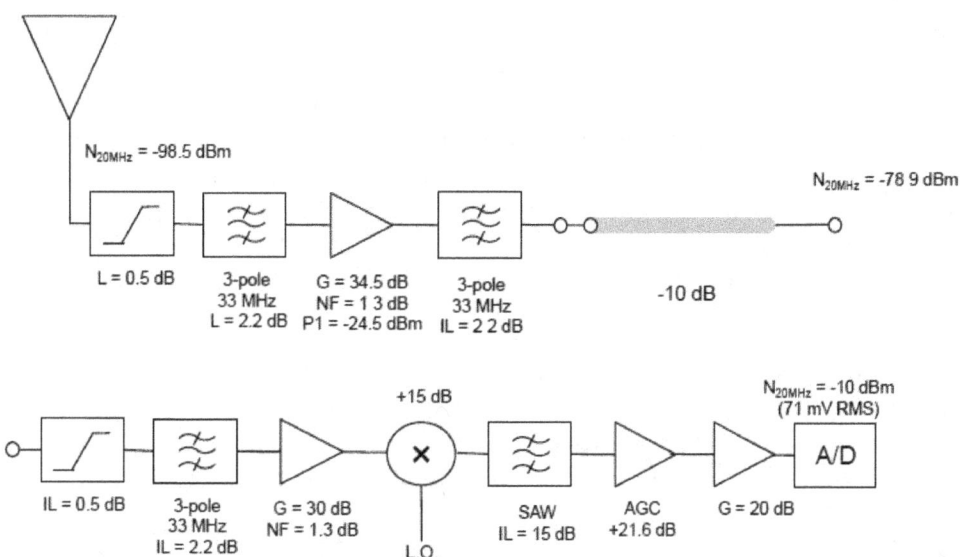

Figure 8-13. Illustrative GPS Receiver Design with an External Antenna Unit

It is important to note that the design in Figure 8-13 is only illustrative. Across the entire set of fielded GPS receivers, even constrained to just those that utilize external antennas, the designs vary greatly. Some configurations use passive antennas (i.e., the external antenna unit only contains the passive antenna element in a protective casing, or *radome*, with a connector). The amount of filtering within active antennas may vary tremendously from one receiver to another and the amount of filtering and filter technologies used within the receiver unit may also vary tremendously. Some receivers may use two or three stages of downconversion vs. the single-stage illustrated, etc. Some receivers sample the RF signal directly, achieving downconversion by intentionally undersampling relative to the Nyquist criteria.

Consider the challenge of adding additional filtering to the illustrative receiver design of Figure 8-13. If additional filtering was desired for installed equipment with this design, there would be few opportunities to add such filtering. As noted earlier, opening up the receiver is not likely to be cost-effective versus buying a new receiver. Thus, the only possible option would be to either replace the antenna with another unit that includes additional filtering or to place a filter in between the antenna and receiver units.

Increasing the selectivity of the active antenna would be extremely challenging since only one of the filter technologies now available for GPS equipment identified in Section 8.2 provides significantly better rejection of the upper LightSquared carrier frequency than the current design. The one filter technology that could improve selectivity is a cavity filter, which would not fit within the antenna unit.

The size constraint of the cavity filter might be accommodated by placing the cavity filter in between the active antenna and the receiver unit. However, the group delay differential characteristics of an ordinary cavity filter (see Figure 8-12) would be too large to meet the applicable performance requirements. A total group delay differential of less than 25 ns is specified for airborne antennas, and this budget is mostly already consumed by the active antenna in Figure 8-13. It might be possible to employ delay compensation within the cavity

8-15

filter design, which is a customization offered by some microwave filter vendors, but whether such a product would meet all of the other applicable requirements remains to be determined. Also, if the additional filter is provided after the active antenna unit, this design modification provides no further protection to the active antenna LNA from saturation. For the particular design shown in Figure 8-13, the LNA will experience a 1-dB gain compression when it sees an input signal at -24.5 dBm. At even lower power levels, the third-order intermodulation products produced when the two LightSquared carriers pass through the LNA, which will act increasing non-linear as it nears saturation, have been observed during tests to cause significant degradation to some receivers.

For a new product, many degrees of freedom are opened. In this case, the entire receiver and antenna design could be optimized to meet an overarching set of requirements that included the need to tolerate high levels of interference at the LightSquared frequencies. In addition to adding filtering, there are other design modifications that may be necessary to facilitate coexistence with the proposed LightSquared network:

- Local oscillator phase noise and spurs – The fact that the receiver local oscillator (LO) does not have its power perfectly confined to the design frequency results in an effect called *reciprocal mixing* [8-10]. For example, if the intended LO frequency is 1505 MHz, this frequency is likely to be generated using a crystal oscillator operating at 10 – 50 MHz and a frequency synthesizer that multiplies the crystal frequency up to 1505 MHz. In a practical frequency synthesizer there will often be *reference spurs*, which means that the overall LO will produce a tone at 1505 MHz, but may have much smaller tones at integer multiples of the crystal frequency away from 1505 MHz as well. The reference spurs are typically at power levels that are 50 – 80 dB below that of the desired frequency output but may still result in significant problems when high-powered out-of-band signals are present at the receiver input. A carefully designed frequency plan and frequency synthesizer can mitigate reciprocal mixing problems. Developing workable frequency plans become much more difficult when powerful signals are anticipated near the GPS frequencies.

- Saturation – Many receiver front-end components, including LNAs, mixers, and analog-to-digital converters (and associated automatic gain control circuitry) can saturate due to strong out-of-band interference. Careful design of the entire receiver front-end chain is required to make sure that layered filtering is sufficient to ensure that all receiver performance requirements are met in the presence of a specified interference environment.

Given the wide variety of operational uses for GPS, however, the design requirements on receiving equipment also varies tremendously and there are some applications for which a practical receiver design will *NOT* be possible with the additional constraint of coexistence with 40,000 high-powered base stations broadcasting signals separated by only 20 MHz from the L1 carrier frequency.

Adaptive Antennas

Adaptive antenna processing is used for some military high-value platforms as a means to suppress interference. This technology requires the use of multi-element antenna arrays with typically 4 – 7 elements spaced an appreciable fraction of a wavelength apart. The physical antenna is thus very large, heavy, and expensive. There are limitations to the number of interference sources that can be simultaneously suppressed, which would likely be surpassed by the LightSquared network where hundreds of base stations could be simultaneously visible. Lastly, such technologies are export-controlled, which combined with the above limitations as a solution to the LightSquared coexistence problem makes this technology impractical.

System Changes

To counter the signal-to-noise degradation due to the presence of LightSquared signals, the GPS and WAAS L1 signals might be broadcast as higher power levels. This solution is not viewed as practical for several reasons. One, as noted earlier within this Report, the presence of LightSquared signals may result in some equipment being driven into a nonlinear mode of operation resulting in unpredictable performance. Increasing the GPS and WAAS signal power would not ameliorate this undesirable condition. Further, as with any space systems, the costs of broadcasting higher power levels are enormous and the timelines for implementation are very long. The GPS Block IIIA satellites have already passed through critical design review (CDR) and any modifications to their design would be extremely costly at this point in time. These satellites will be launched through 2018.

Operational Solutions

Not utilizing GPS L1 equipment in the vicinity of the LightSquared network may be a viable operational solution for a very small number of GPS users that either work only in remote areas in the United States where LightSquared towers will not be nearby, or in areas of the world outside of the United States.

References

[8-1]   Van Dierendonck, A.J., Pat Fenton, and Tom Ford, "Theory and Performance of Narrow Correlator Spacing in a GPS Receiver," *NAVIGATION: Journal of The Institute of Navigation*, Fall 1992.

[8-2]   Hegarty, C., E. Powers, and B. Fonville, "Accounting for Timing Biases Between GPS, Modernized GPS, and Galileo Signals," *Proceedings of the 36th Annual Precise Time and Time Interval (PTTI) Meeting*, Washington, D.C., December 2004. Updated versions also appeared in the *Proceedings of The Institute of Navigation ION GNSS 2005*, Long Beach, California, September 2005, and in *GPS World*, March 2006.

[8-3]   Pozar, David M., *Microwave Engineering*, 3rd Edition, Hoboken, New Jersey: John Wiley & Sons, 2005.

[8-4] Coon, Allan, "Saw Filters and Competitive Technologies - A Comparative View," *Proceedings of the IEEE Ultrasonics Symposium*, 1991.

[8-5] Bi, Frank Z., and Bradley P. Barber, "Bulk Acoustic Wave RF Technology," *IEEE Microwave Magazine*, October 2008.

[8-6] Anon., Specification Sheet for Princeton Technology Corp PT9120, available from http://www.princeton.com.tw.

[8-7] Anon., "Application Note 2242 -- MAX2538 Uses GPS IF LC filter Optimized for 183.6MHz IF," Maxim Integrated Products, available from www.maxim-ic.com.

[8-8] Anon., "STB5610 – GPS RF front-end IC," STMicroelectronics, available at www.st.com.

[8-9] Gramegna, G., et al., "A 56-mW 23-mm^2 Single-Chip 180-nm CMOS GPS Receiver With 27.2-mW 4.1-mm^2 Radio," IEEE Journal of Solid-State Circuits, Vol. 41, No. 3, March 2006.

[8-10] Hayward, Wes, *Introduction to Radio Frequency Design*, Newington, Connecticut: American Radio Relay League, 1996.

9.　　Subtask 9 - Mitigation Measures Applicable to LightSquared

Task Statement

Assess and recommend potential mitigation measures or techniques that are applicable to the LightSquared system based on the representative GPS receivers and the operational scenarios developed above including, for example, potential variations in emitted power, antenna gain pattern, and operating spectrum for the ATC base stations and mobile handsets.

This report addresses possible mitigation measures that could be implemented by LightSquared to reduce potential interference to GPS receivers while still providing a viable 4G service as required by the FCC. Five possible mitigation measures are examined, including increasing the frequency separation of LightSquared's transmitted signal relative to the lower edge of the RNSS allocated band at 1559-1610 MHz; reducing the transmitted power to reduce the magnitude of the interfering signal; modifying the base station antenna (either by narrowing the vertical beamwidth or increasing the antenna tilt so that less area is covered by each transmitting antenna); through the use of exclusion zones to maintain a minimum separation distance where this the installation is fixed; and by relocating the proposed LightSquared network operating frequencies to a more suitable band for high power terrestrial operations.

Frequency separation options in the MSS L-band

Confining LightSquared to the Lower Portion of the MSS L-band

Studies performed in the NPEF and the Industry Technical Working Group (TWG) indicate that for some GPS receivers there may be sufficient receiver selectivity to prevent receiver overload *if* the LightSquared signal is limited to just the lower portion of the MSS allocated band at 1525-1559 MHz. If the LightSquared deployment were to initially start with a broadband signal of 5 MHz (1526.3-1531.3 MHz) and then transition to a 10 MHz broadband signal from 1526-1536 MHz, the upper edge of the LightSquared signal would then be confined to the lower transmit channel alone and would remain approximately 23 MHz below the lower edge of the RNSS band. This increased frequency separation may be sufficient to avoid interference to some GPS receivers. An additional issue that may require further investigation if the LightSquared network is moved down in the MSS allocated band, is whether 4G broadband services that were an integral consideration in the FCC granting the January 26, 2011 waiver to LightSquared are viable if the available bandwidth is constrained to just 5 or 10 MHz versus 20 MHz.

It is unclear whether limiting the LightSquared signal below 1536 MHz would benefit all categories of receivers, particularly those that employ wide front ends or receivers that are designed to use current and future generations of GNSS systems (e.g., Galileo, Compass) which may have signals closer to the RNSS lower band edge than GPS. As an example, chamber testing with the NASA TriG space receiver which has a wide programmable front-end showed that a single LightSquared 5 MHz or 10 MHz signal at the lower end of the band had essentially the same interference impact as one at the high end of the band. For most terrestrial users it is difficult to establish distinct 'categories' because the same receiver may be used to support multiple applications each with a different set of requirements. Therefore, further investigation is

9-1

recommended based on the frequency separation possibilities for LightSquared and the front end characteristics of GPS receivers if this option is considered viable based on other considerations.

Potential Impacts to in-band MSS Systems

Based on agreements with Inmarsat and certain other MSS providers, LightSquared intends to use the majority of MSS L-band spectrum for providing terrestrial broadband. FCC rules require that terrestrial use of the MSS spectrum should not preclude provision of MSS services (see FCC Part 25.149(a)(6)). LightSquared has indicated that it will maintain a dedicated minimum of 6 MHz of MSS spectrum in which to provide MSS. However, it is not clear what portion(s) of the MSS band will be used to provide such dedicated spectrum for space-based service.

In presentations to NTIA by the U.S. GPS Industry Council, two satellite broadcasts are noted that provide differential corrections for use by GPS systems (e.g., Deere's Starfire network and Omnistar). These channels are currently located in the MSS allocated band at 1535 and 1557 MHz and analysis by Deere indicates severe interference to reception of satellite signals from the LightSquared base stations due to the 90 dB differential in signal power between the base station transmit signal and the signal received on the ground from the MSS satellites. In these instances, it is unclear whether moving LightSquared down in the MSS band and away from the RNSS band would reduce the interference potential to applications where a differential correction is necessary, in addition to the basic GPS signals, to meet user requirements. It is noted that Inmarsat, in its comments on the LightSquared waiver request, indicated it will have to develop special filters to mitigate interference effects from the LightSquared base stations and that these filters "may" be able to reduce the interference to acceptable levels. However, there is as yet no technical evidence that this is feasible or viable.

Potential Impacts to Lower Adjacent Band Users

One possible effect of moving the LightSquared transmissions to the lower portion on the MSS allocated band is that it may increase the interference potential to Aeronautical Mobile Telemetry (AMT) flight test operations below 1525 MHz. The MSS ATC rules require that base stations located within radio line of sight of AMT receivers must be coordinated with test range frequency managers. Currently, the Aerospace and Flight Test Radio Coordinating Council (AFTRCC), which is responsible for non-Federal AMT coordination, is in discussions with LightSquared to determine coordination specifics for the LightSquared network. The original coordination agreement between AFTRCC and MSV, predecessor to LightSquared, did not contemplate the extensive terrestrial deployment now reflected in LightSquared's current plan. Any consideration of moving LightSquared farther down in the MSS allocated band should also consider the potential impacts to AMT operation, both in terms of increased potential interference and the additional coordination burden that would be placed on military and other Federal agency frequency managers and Federal test facilities.

Radiated Power limitations

Power Reduction Necessary to Mitigate Interference

The amount of transmitted power reduction necessary to prevent interference to GPS receivers varies as a function of the receiver characteristics, the scenario for which the device is used (e.g., ground-based, aviation, space-based), and the level of interference that degrades receiver performance beyond a certain amount (e.g., degrades C/No by 1 dB) for the specific receiver type in the scenario in which it is used. The specific receivers and their use scenarios are examined elsewhere in the NPEF Report. An important consideration is that what may be acceptable interference for one class of receivers or for one type of GPS application, may be unacceptable for one or more other GPS applications. Moreover, reducing the power per base station could reduce the interference potential to some GPS operations (e.g., ground-based receivers) but, at the same time, the denser network of base stations would increase the aggregate interference level for other applications (e.g. aviation or space-based receivers) as a consequence of having to increase the number of base stations to maintain the same overall coverage area.

Some categories of GPS receivers, such as those used for aviation in safety-of-life applications, have fairly well-defined levels of interference tolerance. For other receiver types or categories, a determination of what constitutes a tolerable level interference[6] is more complex. For example, if the definition of harmful interference[7] as stated in domestic (FCC) or international (ITU) rules were used to establish tolerable levels of interference, non-aviation safety-related applications would need to define at what level these services were "endangered" and other GPS applications would be subject to disruption at harmful interference levels. In addition, many terrestrial applications such as E-911, vehicle navigation for emergency responders, etc, while not formally considered to be 'safety-of-life' they are nevertheless critical for public safety.

In order to establish the levels of tolerable interference for GPS receivers, metrics such as at what interference level accuracy and other baseline functions of the receiver start to degrade, are necessary. These have largely been, or are being, identified during the testing process. From these metrics, and based on other factors such as other known interference source levels, tolerable levels are defined for each receiver class and type of receiver. While recognizing that the different use scenarios and differing GPS receiver characteristics drives different levels of tolerable interference, reducing the radiated power from LightSquared base stations to that which protects the most susceptible GPS operations avoids choosing which GPS operations will be protected and which will be subject to disruption.

The tolerable levels of interference based on the receiver types and applications are listed below. The level by which LightSquared base station power would need to be reduced to protect the most susceptible GPS operations is listed as the necessary level overall.

---

[6] In some cases, such as advanced scientific applications, setting a "tolerable" level could lead to undesired consequences, such as limiting future innovation and development of advanced applications.

[7] *Harmful Interference.* Interference which endangers the functioning of a radionavigation service or of other safety services or seriously degrades, obstructs, or repeatedly interrupts a radiocommunication service operating in accordance with [the ITU] Radio Regulations. (CS)

Effect on Deployment of LightSquared Network:

Any reduction in the transmitted power of the LightSquared base stations will invariably affect the coverage per base station, the performance (capacity and speed) of the LightSquared network, or both. If it is assumed that there are minimum required performance standards that must be achieved to provide 4G LTE service to cover approximately 92% of the U.S. population once the LightSquared network is fully deployed (end of 2015), the number of base stations would need to be increased to make up the reduced coverage area per base station.

If the power reduction needed to mitigate interference to GPS operations is relatively modest, perhaps less than 10 dB, it may be possible to implement such a reduction and still enable LightSquared to provide an economically feasible broadband network. However, if the required reduction in power is significant, the ability to deploy an economically viable broadband terrestrial network may not be feasible.

Impact to Providing 4G Performance

Any reduction in power transmitted by the LightSquared base stations would result in some impact to the network's ability to provide terrestrial broadband services nationwide. All other factors being the same, network capacity and speed are primarily functions of the available signal power and bandwidth. Assuming the LightSquared network as currently planned was optimized to provide 4G broadband service, any reduction in power per base station would, at some point, have a negative impact on the capacity and performance of the network. It is not known how much of a reduction of LightSquared transmit power could be accommodated without negatively impacting network performance as there would normally be some margin planned into the network by design.

Feasibility of Implementing

The feasibility of using power reduction for the LightSquared base stations as a mitigation measure is dependent on the magnitude of the power reduction required to avoid interfering with GPS reception. If the required power reduction is modest, which is not known at this stage, and then this mitigation option may prove to be a viable course of action. If the required power reduction is significant, it may make this option unworkable for several reasons (e.g., cost to add base stations, limitations on network capacity and performance, ability to provide nationwide broadband services as required by FCC in the Harbinger Order).

Antenna Modifications

Modifications to base station antenna patterns (e.g., through use of narrower and otherwise shaped beams) or increasing the downward tilt angle of the antenna from the currently planned 2 degrees to reduce the area affected by LightSquared base stations, would have similar effects on coverage area as reducing the power per base station, albeit without the additional impacts on overall network performance because the assumed transmit power per base station would remain the same. Since the number of base stations needed to provide the same coverage would increase, the impact of this mitigation technique would likely be to increase the overall interference potential rather than decrease it for the majority of GPS applications.

Effectiveness and Applicability

Increasing the downward tilt of antenna reduces the range of the transmitted interfering signal but increases the level of interference within the reduced coverage area. While this technique may have some utility if the objective was to protect a fixed receive site in a particular direction, it would likely increase the potential interference to the vast majority of GPS users because the interference power per area covered would increase and the overall number of base stations would also necessarily increase if the same coverage area were assumed. Similar to the consequences of increasing the number of base stations because of reduced power per base station, the interference potential to GPS operations that are most susceptible to aggregate interference (e.g., aviation and space-based receivers) would also increase.

Likewise, modifying the radiation pattern of the transmit antenna would only be effective if the objective was to reduce the interfering signal power in a particular direction, such as for specific fixed GPS receive sites. For other GPS applications and use scenarios that are not permanently fixed, the technique would not be effective.

Effect on Deployment of LightSquared Network

Any reduction in the coverage area for individual LightSquared base stations, either by increasing the downward tilt of the antenna to limit the range of the interfering signal or through use of narrower or shaped beams to reduce interference in a particular direction, would result in an overall increase in the number of base stations to maintain the same coverage. At some breakpoint, the costs associated with the increased number of base stations will negatively affect the viability of providing a nationwide broadband terrestrial network.

Feasibility of Implementing

The utility of using antenna modifications for the LightSquared base stations as a mitigation measure is marginal and applicable only in cases where it is necessary to reduce the interfering power in one direction. The potential benefits of this mitigation option for widespread use likely would be negated as a practical matter by the increased costs associated with implementing this option. However, for site-specific interference mitigation, it may be feasible and have some utility for avoiding interference to GPS operations.

Exclusion Zones

Effectiveness and Applicability

Use of exclusion or keep-out zones around individual receive sites would have the effect of maintaining a minimum distance between the interference source (LightSquared base station) and the GPS receiver. This mitigation technique is only applicable to fixed receive sites and

9-5

would have minimal utility otherwise. For fixed GPS receive sites, maintaining a minimum distance between interference source and victim receiver is a well-established mitigation technique. Note that the technique would not be of value in mitigating RFI from LightSquared user handsets.

Feasibility of Implementing

The utility and feasibility of using exclusion zones as a mitigation technique must be evaluated on a case-by-case basis. For example, if to avoid interference to a specific receive location required that LightSquared transmitters were prohibited from serving a large metropolitan area; it would likely not be deemed feasible because of the impacts on LightSquared's coverage area and ability to provide service to large segments of the local population. For example, this could impact GPS receivers that are used in applications critical to public safety (E911, navigation of emergency response vehicles, etc.) where loss of GPS service could result in loss of life.

Moving terrestrial broadband to a different frequency band

Because not all of the interference mitigation techniques discussed previously would prevent interference in all GPS use scenarios, it may be desirable to relocate the LightSquared broadband operations to a different frequency band. There are numerous possibilities that could be considered for a terrestrial broadband network, however because LightSquared is basing their broadband network on a hybrid terrestrial-satellite model, discussion in this section is limited to MSS bands where MSS ATC is currently permitted. However, under the President's Broadband Initiative, up to 500 MHz[8] will be made available for wireless broadband applications in the next 5-10 years and some of the bands already identified via the "Fast Track" process[9] may also be suitable for relocation of the LightSquared network and could be examined in addition to the bands discussed below.

Possible Alternative Frequency Bands

Other than the MSS L-band, there are two MSS bands where terrestrial augmentation has been authorized by FCC. These bands are listed below:

Big LEO band

1610-1626.5 MHz (uplink)/2483.5-2495 MHz (downlink): There are two systems operating in the Big LEO band; Iridium and Globalstar. Of these systems, Globalstar uses the typical uplink channel in the 1610-1626.5 MHz band and downlinks in the 2483.5-2495 MHz band (note that the downlink band was reduced some time ago by FCC action to facilitate introduction of terrestrial wireless services). Iridium uses the upper portion of the 1610-1626.5 MHz on a

---

[8] Presidential Memorandum: Unleashing the Wireless Broadband Revolution, dated June 28, 2010
[9] See: FCC DA-11-444. The bands 1695-1710 and 3550-3650 were identified by NTIA as becoming available within the next 5 years and other bands (e.g., 1755-1850 MHz) are being evaluated for possible reallocation.

bidirectional basis by time-duplexing between uplink and downlink signals, with the uplink allocated on a Primary basis and the downlink on a Secondary basis. Iridium has never applied for MSS ATC authorization, presumably because of the way in which they use the MSS band, which could result in self-interference. Globalstar had received authorization to provide MSS ATC in the Big LEO band but was unable to satisfy FCC "gating criteria" within a prescribed time limit and had their authorization cancelled by the Commission. There are currently no MSS ATC providers in the Big LEO band.

2 GHz MSS Band:

2000-2020 MHz (uplink)/2180-2200 MHz (downlink): Two MSS ATC providers have been authorized to provide service in the 2 GHz band; Terrestar and DBSD (formerly ICO, a spin-off on Inmarsat). Neither Terrestar nor DBSD have proven successful in deploying an MSS ATC system and both are currently in significant financial difficulty and have been, or are currently in, bankruptcy. The FCC has recently added new terrestrial service allocations to the 2 GHz MSS band that would facilitate use of this band by systems such as that proposed by LightSquared. In addition, since testing has shown that even one base station could interfere with GPS reception at considerable distances, rationalizing the terrestrial broadband operations by consolidating them in the 2 GHz band could resolve existing interference issues as well. In this case, the MSS L-band allocation would remain as a satellite component of the network and would be accessed via dual-mode (terrestrial/satellite) handsets with terrestrial operations consolidated in the 2 GHz MSS band.

FCC Report and Order on Making Spectrum Available for Terrestrial Broadband

On April 6, 2011, the FCC issued a Report and Order that makes all three of the MSS bands (L-band at 1525-1559 MHz (downlink) and 1626.5-1660.5 MHz (uplink) available for increased use for terrestrial broadband applications. While flexibility was added via spectrum leasing arrangements for the Big LEO band and 2 GHz MSS band, the FCC took additional measures for the 2 GHz band to facilitate use by terrestrial systems, including making new Primary allocations to the terrestrial Fixed and Mobile Services in the band.

Effectiveness in Mitigating the Interference to GPS Receivers

Because both the Big LEO and 2 GHZ MSS band downlinks are significantly removed from the GPS L1 band, the interference effects caused by the LightSquared proposed network at L-band (e.g., GPS receiver front end overload) would not be a concern. Thus relocating LightSquared's proposed network to either of these other MSS bands would be an extremely effective means of ensuring that GPS L1 receivers are not degraded or disrupted. In addition, Federal agencies and civilian GPS interests were successful in negotiating the same out-of-band emission limitation for all FCC authorized MSS ATC systems in both the Big LEO and 2 GHz MSS bands so that emissions limits into the GPS L1 band would be maintained. The FCC has also included, in their April 6, 2011 MSS ATC Order, text that requires that any use of the MSS ATC bands for terrestrial applications via lease arrangements must conform to the existing MSS ATC rules and all conditions imposed on the authorized MSS ATC providers, meaning the emission constraints would carry forward to any new users if DBSD or Terrestar were to lease their spectrum to terrestrial users. Service rules for the new Fixed and Mobile allocations have not yet been developed. It is also worth noting that existing conditions of the MSS ATC authorizations at 2 GHz include provisions to coordinate with Federal agency satellite operations in the adjacent 2200-2290 MHz downlink band so that existing provisions should protect these Federal agency operations. These protections should be included in any new service rules developed for the Fixed and Mobile Services as necessary.

Effects on LightSquared Network Deployment

The primary impacts to LightSquared, at least in terms of its terrestrial-only network, would be cost increases and delays in implementation. A complicating factor for moving the satellite component of the network is the satellites already on orbit only transmit in the L-band; however, design of multi-band handsets that could span the range between the 2 GHz MSS and the L-band is commonplace in the cellular industry and so not an insurmountable obstacle. Because the build-out schedule for the LightSquared broadband network was a condition imposed by FCC during the Harbinger acquisition of SkyTerra (now LightSquared), it is presumed the FCC can grant any relief to that build-out schedule that might be necessary to allow a transition of the terrestrial-only portion of the LightSquared network to a more suitable MSS band such as the 2 GHz or Big LEO bands.

Cost could become a significant consideration for LightSquared in that they were able to secure the SkyTerra spectrum resources for significantly less than it would have cost to bid at an FCC spectrum auction for terrestrial mobile service spectrum as would typically be required for wireless operators. The cost differential to acquire a 2 GHz MSS ATC licensee compared to the acquisition cost that Harbinger paid for SkyTerra is not known. However, based on wireless spectrum demand alone, it seems reasonable to assume the price may be somewhat higher now than a year ago when Harbinger acquired SkyTerra. On the other hand, operating in 2 GHz and avoiding disruption of RNSS systems would ease international deployment and enable a larger addressable market and associated lower costs due to economies of scale.

Feasibility to Implement

The primary differences between using the L-band spectrum for terrestrial broadband and using spectrum at either 2 GHz or the Big LEO band would be cost and schedule concerns associated with transitioning to one of these bands from the current plans at L-band. In addition, if the terrestrial-only portion of the network uses another frequency than that used by the satellite component, dual-frequency receivers would need to be used for hybrid (satellite-terrestrial) network access, which would require modification to the existing hybrid terminals for dual-band operation (as is typical of many cellular phones that operate with global allocations that are in different frequency ranges). All other considerations being equal, the 2 GHz MSS band may be the more attractive option for extensive terrestrial operations such as that proposed by LightSquared, particularly given the new terrestrial allocations made recently by FCC for that band in particular.